THE AGTA PEOPLE

A Photographic Depiction of The Casiguran Agta people of northern Aurora Province, Luzon Island, the Philippines

Cover design: Barbara Alber

Cover photo: Thomas Nickell

Casiguran Agta—Genealogy

THE AGTA PEOPLE
A Photographic Depiction
of
The Casiguran Agta people of
northern Aurora Province,
Luzon Island, the Philippines

Compiled by

Thomas N. Headland, Janet D. Headland and Ray T. Uehara
with a Foreword by P. Bion Griffin

SIL International®
Dallas, Texas

Copies of this and other publications of SIL International® may be obtained from

SIL International Publications
7500 W. Camp Wisdom Road
Dallas, TX 75236-5699

Voice: 972-708-7404
Fax: 972-708-7363
Email: academic_books@sil.org
Internet: http://www.ethnologue.com

Negritos von Casiguran, Provinz Principe, Ost-Luzon.

This is the earliest known photograph taken of an Agta person. It was taken in Casiguran in 1872 by a German anthropologist named Adolf Bernard Meyer. This photo is taken from his book *Album von Philippinen-Typen*, published in Dresden in 1885. This book is archived in the Filipiniana section of the National Library of the Philippines, in Manila. We thank Mr. Narciso Cruz, head of the Filipiniana section for providing us a copy of this photograph with permission to reproduce it here.

Foreword

A casual observer of *The Agta People* may be intrigued that the Headlands produced a "photo album" of the people among whom they have carried out five decades of anthropological research. The book, however, is just the tip of the iceberg that Tom and Janet Headland have published over the years. The casual observer may not be aware of the range of contributions the Headlands have made to both the Agta people, the Philippines, and to the discipline of anthropology. *The Agta People* represents a labor of love to all three; one needs to look to the book's sister publication to appreciate the priority given to the Agta hosts. *The Agta People* is an English translation of an "identical" volume in the Casiguran Agta language: *Letrato Na Agta: Agta a Tolay a Megiyan ta Probinsiya na Aurora*, so that the reader will realize the importance of this book in their own language to the Agta pictured within. All Agta families have now received their copies. And, appropriately, only secondly may the anthropologists now explore these peoples' demography through *The Agta People*.

The iceberg, however, is much deeper. Two major resources make the Agta demography invaluable. Leaving aside Headlands' other rich ethnographic publications, one might begin with *Population Dynamics of a Philippine Rain Forest People*, co-written with demographer John Early. From there the serious scholar would proceed to the complete on-line Agta Demographic Database found on the SIL website. A close examination of the database reveals that the census extends back into the 19th century! Combined, these resources provide unparalleled understanding of an Asian tropics hunter-gatherer society as well as a foundation for comparisons with societies worldwide.

Another lesson we learn from *The Agta People* is that long-term ethnographic fieldwork, undertaken with personal commitment and with language fluency, has tremendous advantages for both the host community and anthropological knowledge. Tom and Janet Headland have, however, through their publications and their care of members of the Agta community—care too great to explore here—achieved much by concentrating their work in one host group for decades. The depth of close personal relationships that have come out of this ethnographic lifestyle is seldom found in our discipline nowadays. The influence of the Headlands and their style of anthropology has influenced my own work. Most recently, for example, one finds inquiry generated by the Headlands' research in Dr. Tessa Minter's *The Agta of the Northern Sierra Madre: Livelihood Strategies and Resilience among Philippine Hunter-Gatherers* (Leiden University 2010). This is anthropology at its best, and a good example of what we should be doing.

The Agta, while billed as foragers by the Headlands and other scholars, are in fact highly variable in life style and demonstrate fashions of adapting to a rapidly changing world, especially in economic pursuits. Agta are still foragers, but today may carry cell phones, work for NGOs, or engage in logging. Agta may be beauty queens in Manila, Bible scholars and translators, local government officials, peasant farmers, and so on. Within this context of change and of cultural continuity, we may apply our questions to the Agta demographic database and its ethnographic foundation as provided by the Headlands. We may do so with assurance that the data are as reliable as possible. After all, some fifty years went into the production of this photo book. The casual observer, with whom we began this foreword, has now either glanced at the photographs with some degree of wonder, or has moved into the deep and rich ethnography produced by many scholars of the Agta, and has applied the publication to the digital database online. Or, perhaps, our observer is no longer casual, but has been inspired to join the ranks of those who come to know the pleasures of living among Agta.

P. Bion Griffin
Emeritus Professor of Anthropology
University of Hawaii
Honolulu, Hawaii

Preface

This English edition of the Agta photograph album was compiled in 2010 by Thomas Headland and Janet Headland with the technical assistance of computer scientist Ray Uehara. For the past half-century Thomas and Janet Headland have studied demographic change among the Agta, a hunter-gatherer population in the Casiguran municipal area of northern Aurora Province, in the Philippines. Working as lay missionaries under the auspices of SIL International (formerly the Summer Institute of Linguistics) and the Philippine Department of Education, the Headlands began collecting demographic data on the Casiguran Agta people in 1962. This continued for 24 years until their move from the Philippines to Dallas, Texas in 1986, and in subsequent fieldtrips back to the Agta area in 1992, 1994, 1995, 1998, 2000, 2002, 2004, 2006, 2008, and 2010. In 1991 the Headlands began working in collaboration with demographic anthropologist John D. Early (Florida Atlantic University). That resulted in their 1998 book, co-authored with Early, titled *Population Dynamics of a Philippine Rain Forest People* (University Press of Florida). (See reviews in Appendix D at the end of this volume.)

Included in this photo album are the names and facial photographs of 1,054 Agta people, along with their sex, birth and death dates, parents' names, and the names of their spouses. The percentage of non-Agta ancestry of each individual is also indicated. Each photo also shows the year it was taken. This album is generated from a much larger database published online in 2009 by SIL International. It is titled ***Agta Demographic Database: Chronicle of a Hunter-Gatherer Community in Transition***, version 1.0, compiled by Thomas Headland and Janet Headland, with the assistance of computer scientist Ray Uehara. An updated version 2.0 is planned for online publication later in 2010. The entire Database may be downloaded free at www.sil.org/silepubs/abstract.asp?id=49227. The Database is copyright by the Headlands and SIL international. It may be used for non-profit purposes if the copyright owner is acknowledged. (See Appendix A.)

The Agta people cooperated enthusiastically with the Headlands over several decades as the Headlands took photos of them and compiled family life histories of them. They have given the Headlands their full and formal permission, in writing, to publish their genealogies both in the *Agta Demographic Database*, and in the present photo album. (See Appendix B.) Soon after the Philippine national government passed the IPRA Law in 1997 (Republic Act 8371 called *The Indigenous Peoples' Rights Act*), the Agta people learned that to gain recognition as legal IPs (indigenous people) they needed to prove to the government that they are indeed *Agta* and that they have lived in their home areas "since time immemorial" (Rep. Act 8371, Chap. VIII, Sec. 52, d). Proof required includes point #7, "Genealogical Surveys," and points 3, 8 and 9 require "pictures."[1]

The Headlands feel that one of the best gifts they can give to the Agta today is to give one copy of this album to each Agta household. With that goal in mind, a near-identical version of the album was published in 2009 in the Agta language. In February and March of 2010 Janet and Tom distributed free copies of that edition to almost every Agta family in northern Aurora, a total of 79 family households. It is for this reason that this album is published in two editions, this one in English, and the earlier Agta edition for Agta families.

Almost all of the 1,054 photographs in this album were taken by Janet or Tom between the years 1962 to 2010. A few of the photos were taken by others, including one photo taken by Dutch scientist Jan Van der Bloeg in 2008, two photos taken about 1927 and published in *National Geographic Magazine* in 1930, and five photos taken by anthropologist John Early during his trip with Tom to the area in 1994. Twenty of the photos were taken in 1936 by Father Morice Vanoverbergh, a Belgium Catholic priest who visited the area that year. The names of these photographers are acknowledged under the photos that they took.

---

[1]For details on the IPRA Law and its implications for Agta land rights, see T. Headland's essay titled "The Indigenous Peoples' Rights Act: A Triumph of Political Will," published in 1999 in SIL Electronic Working Papers 1999-004. Dallas: Summer Institute of Linguistics. Online at www.sil.org/silewp/1999/004/SILEWP1999-004.html.

Acknowledgments

Thomas and Janet Headland received academic research grants from the Pew Charitable Trusts in 1991 and from the LSB Leakey Foundation in 1994. These grants were given to fund the Headlands' demographic research in the Agta field in 1992, 1994, 1995, and 1998. The Summer Institute of Linguistics (now SIL International) funded the Headlands' field trips to the Agta area for the same purpose in 2000, 2004, and 2008.

We are indebted to John D. Early (Florida Atlantic University) for his enthusiastic interest in our Agta population data, for his help in analyzing our data, and for his co-authorship with us of our 1998 book *Population Dynamics of a Philippine Rain Forest People.* We also thank his wife Jacky Early for helping with compiling the data for our 1998 book and for entering it into a Paradox database. Iris Harrison Dalberto and Anne Kueffer Quirk, two missionaries with New Tribes Mission, kept careful records of Agta births and deaths for us from 1980 to 1982.

Our children, Rachel Headland Ulmer, Steve Headland, and Jenny Headland Hoffman, who were born in the Philippines and grew up with the Agta, helped us collect demographic and other data from the Agta, and Rachel typed much of our population data into an early database in the mid-1980s. Steve collected more Agta demographic data for us on his trips to the Agta in the 1990s. (See their photographs in Appendix C.)

After 1998, several SIL specialists in database management helped us revise our data into Microsoft Access. Michael Cochran helped us in 1999 and continues to advise us. Two other SIL computer specialists, Lars Huttar and Ray Uehara, helped Tom publish the present database on the Internet. Ray, our coauthor, developed the database report that produced the 211 pages of Agta photos here. SIL linguist Roger Stone gave us important database help in 2007. We also thank Renee Carlson, Coordinator of the Institutional Review Board at the University of North Dakota, and her staff for guiding us through the process of obtaining their IRB approval to publish this book and the *Agta Demographic Database.* Our former SIL colleague, Thomas L. Nickell, took the photograph of the Agta camp in 1981 that is featured on the front cover of this book and has given us permission to use it here.

Our greatest assistants over the past forty-eight years have been the Agta people themselves. They have wholeheartedly participated in helping us collect data on their family histories since the early 1960s. They wanted their histories publicly recorded, and the Agta today have given us their unreserved permission to publish the present data on the World Wide Web with their photographs, as well as in the present photo album. (See Appendix B.) We could never have accomplished this project without their assistance.

We must especially mention those respected Agta elders who still remembered the names and family histories of those Agta who lived long ago, and who helped us to reconstruct the family histories of many long dead individuals. The photographs of those Agta elders who helped us during the 1960s and 1970s to record the names of those long deceased Agta are pictured in the *Agta Demographic Database* and in this book. We list them here by name with their identification numbers, their years of birth and death, their sex, and the number of their known descendents in 2010 as calculated by the database.

These are: Alonso #14 (1912-1980), male, 55 known descendents; Away #159 (1919-2000), female, 52 known descendents; Ayogyog #40 (1918-1981), male, 6 known descendents; Didog #129 (1922-1988), male, 23 known descendents; Eleden #191 (1931-2002), male, 4 known descendents; Inek #5173 (1906-1971), female, 79 known descendents; Lipanyaw #5227 (1900-1968), female, 411 known descendents; Liyanita #320 (1917-2000), female, 76 known descendents; Malensiyana #337 (1905-1978), female, 83 known descendents; Maming #246 (1920-2002), female, 35 known descendents; Pekto #461 (1902-1978), male, 139 known descendents; Pidela #391 (1912-1985), female, 98 known descendents; Pilisa #5369 (1899-1965), female, 62 known descendents; Pirente #484 (1916-1979), male, 168 known descendents;

Tigo #5467 (1898-1968), male, 74 known descendents; Tikiman #592 (1901-1983), male, 133 known descendents; Tulio #5483 (1897-1965), male, 411 known descendents; and Upila #608 (1899-1977), female, 117 known descendents.

Agta Photos

This compilation of 1,054 Agta facial photos is generated from a formal report in the revised 2.0 version of the *Agta Demographic Database: Chronicle of a Hunter-Gatherer Community In Transition*, compiled by Thomas Headland and Janet Headland, with the assistance of computer scientist Ray Uehara. This version 2.0 was published on-line by SIL International in 2010. The entire Database may be downloaded free at www.sil.org/silepubs/abstract.asp?id=49227. The Database is copyright by the Headlands and SIL international. It may be used for non-profit purposes if the copyright owner is acknowledged.

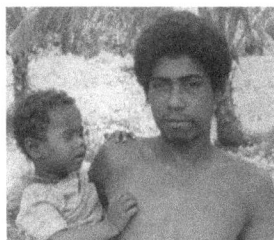

ID: 1	*Sex:* Male

Name: **ABDON**
2nd Name:
Surname: BEKYADEN
Agta Ancestry: 87.5%

Birth Date: 1943 +/-3 years
Death Date: 2009 +/-1 year

Father: BANGHUL
Mother: PILISA

Year: 1976
Abdon-1 with son Medeng-4

1st Spouse: SITENG-2
Last/Current Spouse: PENGPENG-301

ID: 175	*Sex:* Female

Name: **ABENG**
2nd Name: DYOSILIN
Surname: KULIDEG GERERO
Agta Ancestry: 100%

Birth Date: 1976
Death Date:

Father: DYIMI
Mother: EKDET

Year: 2008   2010
Abeng-175   Abeng-175

1st Spouse: WIRNER-1042
Last/Current Spouse: WIRNER-1042

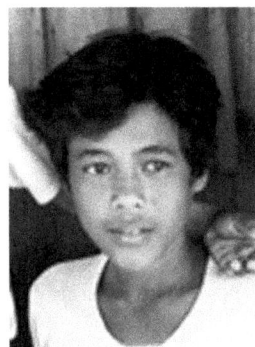

ID: 8350	*Sex:* Male

Name: **ABET**
2nd Name:
Surname:
Agta Ancestry: 25%

Birth Date: 1966 +/-4 years
Death Date:

Father:
Mother: BISELYA

Year: 1978
Abet-8350

1st Spouse:
Last/Current Spouse:

1

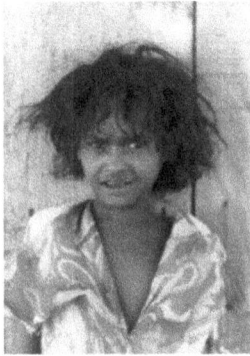

Year: 1976
Abey-383

2008
Abey-383

ID:	383		Sex: Female
Name:	**ABEY**		
2nd Name:	ANALIN		
Surname:	KULIDEG		
Agta Ancestry:	Unknown		
Birth Date:	April 10, 1964		
Death Date:			
Father:	MELANIO		
Mother:	ELI		
1st Spouse:	ATUK-344		
Last/Current Spouse:	UNDUL-79		

Year: 1967
Adiling-6

1978
Adiling-6

ID:	6		Sex: Female
Name:	**ADILING**		
2nd Name:	BINTANA		
Surname:	AGNANAY		
Agta Ancestry:	100%		
Birth Date:	1924 +/-3 years		
Death Date:	July 1978		
Father:	AGNANAY		
Mother:	ABUNDIA		
1st Spouse:	RUMINES-7349		
Last/Current Spouse:	MARTINES-373		

Year: 1978
Adiling-316

ID:	316		Sex: Female
Name:	**ADILING**		
2nd Name:	BIHENG		
Surname:	SADSOY		
Agta Ancestry:	100%		
Birth Date:	1935 +/-1 year		
Death Date:	February 3, 1984		
Father:	SADSOY		
Mother:	DINDAY		
1st Spouse:	LINGKON-5226		
Last/Current Spouse:	LINING-315		

Year: 1972
Adiling-512 phto by Jim
Musgrove

ID:	512		Sex: Female
Name:	**ADILING**		
2nd Name:	HUWANA		
Surname:	ANGIDEW		
Agta Ancestry:	100%		
Birth Date:	1929 +/-3 years		
Death Date:	August 20, 1983		
Father:	ANGIDEW		
Mother:	ASIONA		
1st Spouse:	GAHANG-7076		
Last/Current Spouse:	RONGKEL-511		

ID:	9	*Sex:* Male

Name: **ADING**
2nd Name:
Surname: BITIGAN
Agta Ancestry: 100%

Birth Date: 1952 +/-2 years
Death Date: 2005

Father: BITIGAN
Mother: KANORA
1st Spouse: PINING-73
Last/Current Spouse: PINING-73

Year: 1976
Ading-9

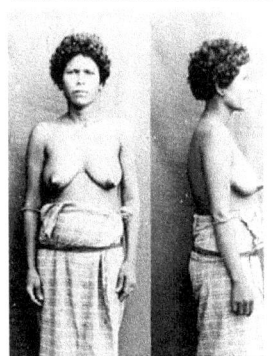

ID: 5007   *Sex:* Female

Name: **AGAPITA**
2nd Name:
Surname:
Agta Ancestry: 75%

Birth Date: 1902 +/-5 years
Death Date: 1958 +/-5 years

Father: BEKYADEN
Mother: DONGGASILAN
1st Spouse: TIKIMAN-592
Last/Current Spouse: TIKIMAN-592

Year: 1936
Agapita-5007
photo by Vanoverbergh

ID: 280   *Sex:* Male

Name: **AGONG**
2nd Name: KARDING, PIYAGONG
Surname: SIMIN
Agta Ancestry: 100%

Birth Date: 1970 +/-1 year
Death Date:

Father: WILSON
Mother: NARSING
1st Spouse:
Last/Current Spouse:

Year: 1977
Agong-280

ID: 10   *Sex:* Male

Name: **AGOS**
2nd Name:
Surname: RAMUS
Agta Ancestry: 100%

Birth Date: 1954 +/-1 year
Death Date: July 1990

Father: BINONG
Mother: LIGAYA
1st Spouse: SINING-11
Last/Current Spouse: KARMIN-2049

Year: 1977
Agos-10

ID: 7003   *Sex:* Female

Name: **AKEP**
2nd Name: MADELLA
Surname:

Agta Ancestry: 100%

Birth Date: 1967 +/-2 years
Death Date: June 26, 1993

Father: DINEGTUNAN
Mother: KARMEN

1st Spouse: TELENG-585
Last/Current Spouse: WILENG-456

Year: 1977
Akep-7003

ID: 3053   *Sex:* Male

Name: **ALBIN**
2nd Name: KULOLYAT, LELAT
Surname:

Agta Ancestry: 81.25%

Birth Date: August 1, 1993
Death Date:

Father: TONILIN
Mother: ANALI

1st Spouse:
Last/Current Spouse:

Year: 2004   2010
Albin-3053   Albin 3053

ID: 617   *Sex:* Male

Name: **ALEHANRO**
2nd Name:
Surname: MABONGA

Agta Ancestry: 50%

Birth Date: 1944
Death Date:

Father: SEBERO
Mother: LAWDAMYA

1st Spouse:
Last/Current Spouse:

Year: 1977   2008
Alehanro-617   Alehanro-617

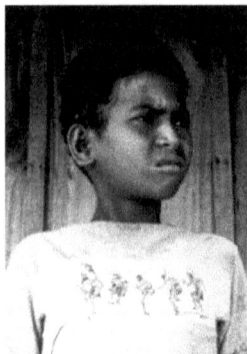

ID: 133   *Sex:* Male

Name: **ALEK**
2nd Name: GELAK
Surname: ADUANAN

Agta Ancestry: 100%

Birth Date: 1968
Death Date: March 3, 2009

Father: DIDOG
Mother: POMPOEK

1st Spouse: LINDA-307
Last/Current Spouse: LINDA-307

Year: 1978   2008
Alek-133   Alek-133

4

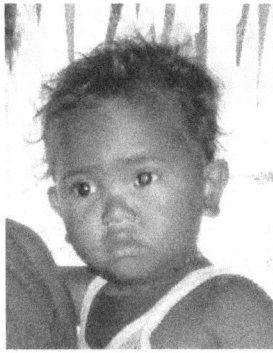

ID:	3625
Sex:	Male
Name:	**ALEKSANDER**
2nd Name:	
Surname:	ADUANAN
Agta Ancestry:	100%
Birth Date:	March 22, 2008
Death Date:	
Father:	ALEK
Mother:	LINDA
1st Spouse:	
Last/Current Spouse:	

Year: 2010
Aleksander-3625

ID:	310
Sex:	Female
Name:	**ALENG**
2nd Name:	
Surname:	
Agta Ancestry:	93.75%
Birth Date:	1964 +/-1 year
Death Date:	
Father:	BESTIAN
Mother:	NIYEBES
1st Spouse:	
Last/Current Spouse:	

Year: 1977
Aleng-310

 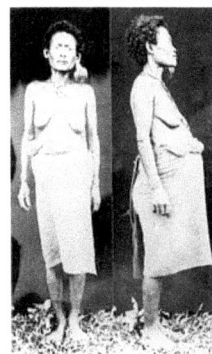

ID:	349
Sex:	Female
Name:	**ALILI**
2nd Name:	
Surname:	PAWISAN
Agta Ancestry:	87.5%
Birth Date:	1969 +/-2 years
Death Date:	
Father:	MANINGTING
Mother:	SARING
1st Spouse:	UDENG-317
Last/Current Spouse:	UDENG-317

Year: 2004
Alili-349 & daughtr Kendi-3445 phto by Iris Dalberto

2010
Alili-349

ID:	5016
Sex:	Female
Name:	**ALIMANIA**
2nd Name:	
Surname:	
Agta Ancestry:	100%
Birth Date:	1908 +/-9 years
Death Date:	1945 +/-9 years
Father:	MAKSEMINO
Mother:	PAYES
1st Spouse:	ABADAN-5001
Last/Current Spouse:	ABADAN-5001

Year: 1936
Alimania-5016
photo by Vanoverbergh

Year: 2008
Alma-7952 holding daughtr
Terimi-3615

ID:	7952	*Sex:* Female

Name: **ALMA**
2nd Name:
Surname:

Agta Ancestry: Unknown

Birth Date: 1989 +/-5 years
Death Date:

Father: TILEN
Mother: NALENGLENG

1st Spouse: DYENDYEN-8288
Last/Current Spouse: DYENDYEN-8288

Year: 2010
Alona-3597

ID:	3597	*Sex:* Female

Name: **ALONA**
2nd Name:
Surname:

Agta Ancestry: 93.75%

Birth Date: April 14, 2007
Death Date:

Father: UDENG
Mother: ALILI

1st Spouse:
Last/Current Spouse:

Year: 1978
Alona-8030

ID:	8030	*Sex:* Female

Name: **ALONA**
2nd Name: ALENA
Surname: TABUHARA

Agta Ancestry: 25%

Birth Date:
Death Date:

Father: JUAN
Mother: PASING

1st Spouse:
Last/Current Spouse:

Year: 1976
Alonso-14

ID:	14	*Sex:* Male

Name: **ALONSO**
2nd Name:
Surname: KUKUAN

Agta Ancestry: 100%

Birth Date: 1912 +/-3 years
Death Date: July 27, 1980

Father: MANWEL
Mother: SINDINA

1st Spouse: TIRAY-15
Last/Current Spouse: TIRAY-15

6

Year: 1977
Alunet-17

ID: 17   *Sex:* Male

Name: **ALUNET**
2nd Name:
Surname: TOMAY, RADA

Agta Ancestry: 100%

Birth Date: 1936 +/-4 years
Death Date: February 1983

Father: RADA
Mother: TINANG
1st Spouse: PERLING-5365
Last/Current Spouse: LUDING-465

Year: 1978
Aluping-25

ID: 25   *Sex:* Male

Name: **ALUPING**
2nd Name:
Surname: SALOD, SALOK

Agta Ancestry: Unknown

Birth Date: 1941 +/-3 years
Death Date:

Father: SELOK
Mother: AHADUD
1st Spouse: KONSITA-7218
Last/Current Spouse: KONSITA-7218

Year: 2004
Ampang-9199 phto by Iris
Dalberto

ID: 9199   *Sex:* Male

Name: **AMPANG**
2nd Name: GASPAR
Surname: MANONG

Agta Ancestry: 0%

Birth Date: 1975 +/-5 years
Death Date:

Father:
Mother:
1st Spouse: EDNALIN-227
Last/Current Spouse: EDNALIN-227

Year: 1978
Anali-190

2008
Anali-190 with her six kids.

ID: 190   *Sex:* Female

Name: **ANALI**
2nd Name: ANALIN
Surname: MANDOSA, TALUDEP

Agta Ancestry: 87.5%

Birth Date: 1972 +/-1 year
Death Date:

Father: ROHEL
Mother: NEMI
1st Spouse: TONILIN-226
Last/Current Spouse: TONILIN-226

Year: 1978
Anali-8028

ID:	8028	*Sex:*	Female

Name: **ANALI**
2nd Name:
Surname: TABUHARA

Agta Ancestry: 25%

Birth Date:
Death Date:

Father: JUAN
Mother: PASING

1st Spouse:
Last/Current Spouse:

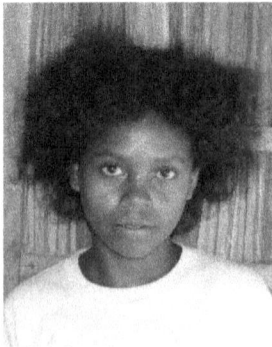

Year: 2010
Anamey-3329

ID:	3329	*Sex:*	Female

Name: **ANAMEY**
2nd Name:
Surname:

Agta Ancestry: 93.75%

Birth Date: April 4, 1997
Death Date:

Father: WIRNER
Mother: ABENG

1st Spouse:
Last/Current Spouse:

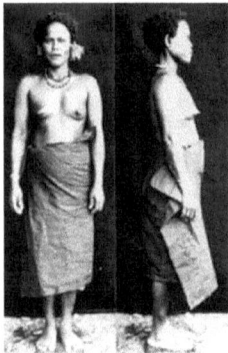

Year: 1936
Anatolia-5025
photo by Vanoverbergh

ID:	5025	*Sex:*	Female

Name: **ANATOLIA**
2nd Name: PATENG
Surname:

Agta Ancestry: 100%

Birth Date: 1910 +/-5 years
Death Date: 1970 +/-5 years

Father:
Mother:

1st Spouse: AMELIO-5023
Last/Current Spouse: AMELIO-5023

Year: 1978
Andres-29

ID:	29	*Sex:*	Male

Name: **ANDRES**
2nd Name: ADIT
Surname: BALENSIA

Agta Ancestry: 100%

Birth Date: 1938 +/-2 years
Death Date: May 17, 1987

Father: NANDET
Mother: LIWAYWAY

1st Spouse: TESI-30
Last/Current Spouse: TESI-30

Year: 2010
Andyelika-3525

ID: 3525   Sex: Female

Name: **ANDYELIKA**
2nd Name:
Surname:

Agta Ancestry: 95.315%

Birth Date: May 25, 2003
Death Date:

Father: SENING
Mother: DALAGA

1st Spouse:
Last/Current Spouse:

Year: 1936
Angelita-5572, by
Vanoverbergh

ID: 5572   Sex: Female

Name: **ANGELITA**
2nd Name:
Surname:

Agta Ancestry: 100%

Birth Date: 1912 +/-5 years
Death Date: 1950 +/-9 years

Father:
Mother:

1st Spouse: ESMUNDO-5744
Last/Current Spouse: MEDSOR-9027

Year: 1973
Anghilita-5030

ID: 5030   Sex: Female

Name: **ANGHILITA**
2nd Name:
Surname:

Agta Ancestry: 100%

Birth Date: 1923 +/-5 years
Death Date: 1973

Father: APERIT
Mother: TILIYENG

1st Spouse: SINABUYAN-543
Last/Current Spouse: DUBENG-162

Year: 1962
Anghilita-5931 with son
Pikson-488

ID: 5931   Sex: Female

Name: **ANGHILITA**
2nd Name:
Surname:

Agta Ancestry: 100%

Birth Date: 1936 +/-4 years
Death Date: February 1966

Father: BASELO
Mother: SISA

1st Spouse: ROSADO-5407
Last/Current Spouse: ROSADO-5407

9

ID: 7009	*Sex:* Male

Name: **ANSETA**
2nd Name:
Surname:

Agta Ancestry: Unknown

Birth Date: 1945 +/-7 years
Death Date: 2000 +/-9 years

Father: BAYDEK
Mother: SABEL
1st Spouse: SINGOL-7184
Last/Current Spouse: SINGOL-7184

Year: 1977
Anseta-7009

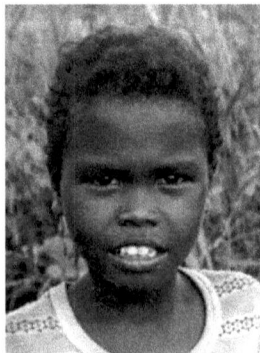

ID: 220	*Sex:* Male

Name: **APANG**
2nd Name: NELSON
Surname: PRADO

Agta Ancestry: 75%

Birth Date: 1966 +/-1 year
Death Date:

Father: HAKOB
Mother: PELI
1st Spouse: ATEK-452
Last/Current Spouse: ATEK-452

Year: 1976
Apang-220

ID: 7279	*Sex:* Female

Name: **APRIKA**
2nd Name:
Surname: DELAPENYA

Agta Ancestry: 100%

Birth Date: 1915 +/-7 years
Death Date: 1987

Father: MATIKO
Mother: ANGHELITA
1st Spouse: DOKDOK-7329
Last/Current Spouse: DESUY-5104

Year: 1978
Aprika-7279

ID: 8257	*Sex:* Male

Name: **ARBING**
2nd Name:
Surname: VARGAS

Agta Ancestry: 35.937%

Birth Date: August 2001
Death Date:

Father: AMBUY
Mother: PANEK
1st Spouse:
Last/Current Spouse:

Year: 2008
Arbing-8257

10

Year: 1984
Arentina-26 1984 &
Headland; phto Bion Griffin

1984
Arentina-26 phto by Bion
Griffin

ID:	26	Sex: Female

Name: **ARENTINA**
2nd Name:
Surname:

Agta Ancestry: Unknown

Birth Date: 1909 +/-7 years
Death Date: 1987 +/-1 year

Father: SIBENG
Mother: MEKYANG

1st Spouse: GAHANG-7076
Last/Current Spouse: DAYMES-7290

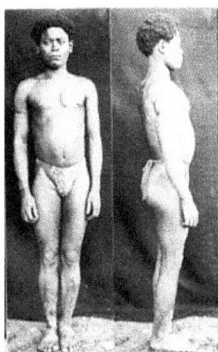

Year: 1936
Ariston-5042
photo by Vanoverbergh

ID:	5042	Sex: Male

Name: **ARISTON**
2nd Name: IRISTON, RISTON
Surname:

Agta Ancestry: 100%

Birth Date: 1914 +/-8 years
Death Date: 1940 +/-5 years

Father: DINSIWEG
Mother: PILISIA

1st Spouse: MAMINA-5263
Last/Current Spouse: MAMINA-5263

Year: 1977
Arman-451

ID:	451	Sex: Male

Name: **ARMAN**
2nd Name:
Surname: MAKSIMINO

Agta Ancestry: 100%

Birth Date: August 22, 1967
Death Date:

Father: PEDONG
Mother: AWILIN

1st Spouse:
Last/Current Spouse:

Year: 1977
Arman-611 held by sistr
Lerling-610

2004
Arman-611 holding son
Mandong-3472 phto by Iris

ID:	611	Sex: Male

Name: **ARMAN**
2nd Name:
Surname: LISIDAY

Agta Ancestry: 50%

Birth Date: 1976
Death Date:

Father: BENI
Mother: UTET

1st Spouse: NORALIN-1109
Last/Current Spouse: NORALIN-1109

Year: 1978
Arnes-33

ID: 33   Sex: Male

Name: **ARNES**
2nd Name: SEGNET
Surname: TOMAY

Agta Ancestry: 100%

Birth Date: 1917 +/-4 years
Death Date: 1982

Father: TOMAY
Mother: LAGEYAN

1st Spouse: EBET-92
Last/Current Spouse: EBET-92

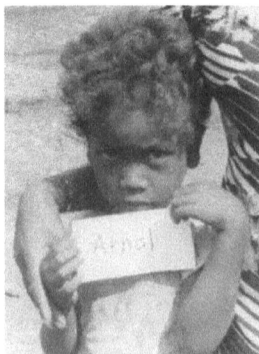

Year: 1977
Arnol-540

ID: 540   Sex: Male

Name: **ARNOL**
2nd Name:
Surname: RAMOS

Agta Ancestry: 100%

Birth Date: 1972 +/-1 year
Death Date: April 1984

Father: SIMEON
Mother: BAGOL

1st Spouse:
Last/Current Spouse:

Year: 2004
Arnol-584 & wife Melani-
3017 phto by Iris Dalberto

2010
Arnol1 Aloy-584

ID: 584   Sex: Male

Name: **ARNOL1 ALOY**
2nd Name: ALOY
Surname: KUKUAN

Agta Ancestry: 93.75%

Birth Date: March 1977
Death Date:

Father: TEKOK
Mother: LITA

1st Spouse: MIKMIK-206
Last/Current Spouse: MELANI-3017

Year: 2002
Arnol2-7535

2002
Arnol2-7535

ID: 7535   Sex: Male

Name: **ARNOL2**
2nd Name: DYOKOY
Surname: KORPUS

Agta Ancestry: 100%

Birth Date: 1976 +/-3 years
Death Date: 2007 +/-2 years

Father: ARNING
Mother: NINYENG

1st Spouse: MIKMIK-206
Last/Current Spouse: MIKMIK-206

ID: 34	*Sex:* Male

Name: **ARSIL**
2nd Name:
Surname: TOMAY
Agta Ancestry: 93.75%

Birth Date: 1949 +/-2 years
Death Date:

Father: TETYOK
Mother: ISTING
1st Spouse: NORMA-7392
Last/Current Spouse: LODI-363

Year: 1978
Arsil-34

ID: 287	*Sex:* Male

Name: **ARTUL**
2nd Name: LAKAY, DYUNYOR
Surname: KABUNOK, PERNANDO
Agta Ancestry: 87.5%

Birth Date: 1959 +/-1 year
Death Date: September 16, 1985

Father: BUDEGDEG
Mother: IDING
1st Spouse: KALINENG-2011
Last/Current Spouse: KALINENG-2011

Year: 1977
Artul-287

ID: 563	*Sex:* Male

Name: **ASENG**
2nd Name: DYESI
Surname: ISTANES
Agta Ancestry: 100%

Birth Date: 1970 +/-2 years
Death Date:

Father: TANES
Mother: PORMING
1st Spouse: MARILIN-473
Last/Current Spouse: MASE-7696

Year: 1978   2010
Aseng-563   Aseng-563

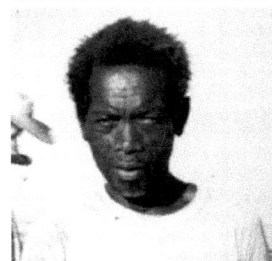

ID: 35	*Sex:* Male

Name: **ASION**
2nd Name:
Surname: TULIO
Agta Ancestry: 100%

Birth Date: 1929 +/-3 years
Death Date: March 1990

Father: TULIO
Mother: LIPANYAW
1st Spouse: SULIDAD-36
Last/Current Spouse: SULIDAD-36

Year: 1976
Asion-35

Year: 1971
Asiona-5574

ID: 5574   Sex: Female

Name: **ASIONA**
2nd Name: SIYONA
Surname:

Agta Ancestry: 100%

Birth Date: 1916 +/-5 years
Death Date: August 1976

Father:
Mother:

1st Spouse: SIMIN-5531
Last/Current Spouse: BANYES-5632

Year: 1984
Atek-452 with father
Pedong-446

ID: 452   Sex: Female

Name: **ATEK**
2nd Name: KARULINA
Surname: MAKSIMINO

Agta Ancestry: 100%

Birth Date: 1970 +/-1 year
Death Date:

Father: PEDONG
Mother: AWILIN

1st Spouse: APANG-220
Last/Current Spouse: APANG-220

Year: 1977
Ateng-248

2010
Ateng-248

ID: 248   Sex: Male

Name: **ATENG**
2nd Name: NATENG, DYUNYOR
Surname: KUKUAN

Agta Ancestry: 100%

Birth Date: 1962 +/-1 year
Death Date:

Father: IPOY
Mother: MAMING

1st Spouse: PEPOT-478
Last/Current Spouse: PEPOT-478

Year: 1963
Ating-5316

ID: 5316   Sex: Female

Name: **ATING**
2nd Name: ATENG
Surname:

Agta Ancestry: 100%

Birth Date: 1922 +/-2 years
Death Date: 1965 +/-4 years

Father: AGNANAY
Mother: ABUNDIA

1st Spouse: BERSOSA-64
Last/Current Spouse: BERSOSA-64

14

Year: 2010
Atorni-7876

ID: 7876   *Sex:* Male

Name: **ATORNI**
2nd Name: BATEG
Surname: DELAPENYA

Agta Ancestry: 100%

Birth Date: 1964 +/-5 years
Death Date:

Father: BITIGAN
Mother: POLIYA
1st Spouse: GLORIA-7875
Last/Current Spouse: GLORIA-7875

Year: 1976
Atuk-344

2010
Atuk-344

ID: 344   *Sex:* Male

Name: **ATUK**
2nd Name: HERSON
Surname: TALODEP

Agta Ancestry: 100%

Birth Date: 1961 +/-1 year
Death Date:

Father: MANDOSA
Mother: KORDING
1st Spouse: ABEY-383
Last/Current Spouse: TELMA-309

Pl. 11. Away, the Negrito belle of Kasagunan.

Year: 1936
Away-159 phto by Morice
Vanoverbergh

1977
Away-159

ID: 159   *Sex:* Female

Name: **AWAY**
2nd Name:
Surname: ADUANAN

Agta Ancestry: 100%

Birth Date: 1919 +/-1 year
Death Date: April 2000

Father: TALIMANGON
Mother: MONIKA
1st Spouse: DOYEG-158
Last/Current Spouse: DOYEG-158

Year: 1978
Awilin-447 holding daughtr
Soksok-453

1984
Awiling-447 holding child
Nora-1127

ID: 447   *Sex:* Female

Name: **AWILIN**
2nd Name: ANALIN, AWALING
Surname: BANYES

Agta Ancestry: 100%

Birth Date: 1941 +/-2 years
Death Date: June 27, 1998

Father: BANYES
Mother: ADELA
1st Spouse: PEDONG-446
Last/Current Spouse: PEDONG-446

15

ID:	3648
Sex:	Male
Name:	**AYBAN**
2nd Name:	LARAUS
Surname:	
Agta Ancestry:	100%
Birth Date:	May 13, 2008
Death Date:	
Father:	TOTOY
Mother:	DINA
1st Spouse:	
Last/Current Spouse:	

Year: 2010
Ayban-3648 & Totoy-1111

ID:	9173
Sex:	Female
Name:	**AYDA**
2nd Name:	ALDA
Surname:	RAMUS
Agta Ancestry:	0%
Birth Date:	1952 +/-8 years
Death Date:	
Father:	
Mother:	
1st Spouse:	SINON-548
Last/Current Spouse:	SINON-548

Year: 1992
Ayta-9173

ID:	3095
Sex:	Female
Name:	**AYLIN**
2nd Name:	
Surname:	
Agta Ancestry:	96.875%
Birth Date:	July 1987
Death Date:	
Father:	ELPI
Mother:	WAYNALIN
1st Spouse:	
Last/Current Spouse:	

Year: 2008
Aylin-3095

ID:	40
Sex:	Male
Name:	**AYOGYOG**
2nd Name:	
Surname:	ADUANAN
Agta Ancestry:	100%
Birth Date:	1918 +/-2 years
Death Date:	July 25, 1981
Father:	MAHEW
Mother:	AKILINA
1st Spouse:	PILISING-5373
Last/Current Spouse:	LIMINIDA-41

Year: 1972
Ayogyog-40 phto by Jim Musgrove

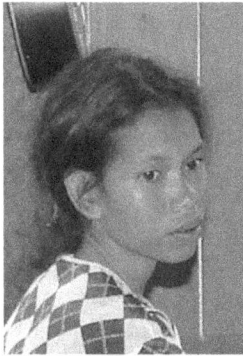

Year: 2008
Ayrin-1108 phto by Iris Dalberto

2008
Ayrin-1108 & husband Hilin-385 + their 5 childrn.

ID: 1108   Sex: Female
Name: **AYRIN**
2nd Name:
Surname: PRADO KULIDEG
Agta Ancestry: 75%

Birth Date: September 1977
Death Date:

Father: NATENG
Mother: TETET

1st Spouse: HILINTOK-385
Last/Current Spouse: HILINTOK-385

Year: 2010
Ayrin-2010

ID: 7906   Sex: Female
Name: **AYRIN**
2nd Name:
Surname: GONSALES
Agta Ancestry: 100%

Birth Date: 1979 +/-9 years
Death Date:

Father:
Mother:

1st Spouse: KITOL-291
Last/Current Spouse: KITOL-291

Year: 1978
Ayrin-8339

ID: 8339   Sex: Female
Name: **AYRIN**
2nd Name:
Surname: DEPABLO
Agta Ancestry: 12.5%

Birth Date: 1967 +/-2 years
Death Date:

Father: PABLING
Mother: ELI

1st Spouse:
Last/Current Spouse:

Year: 2010
Aysa-3033

ID: 3033   Sex: Female
Name: **AYSA**
2nd Name:
Surname:
Agta Ancestry: 100%

Birth Date: 1988
Death Date:

Father: ROHEL
Mother: EMILING

1st Spouse: DYUNDYUN-9218
Last/Current Spouse: DYUNDYUN-9218

17

ID:	3094 *Sex:* Female

Name: **AYSA**
2nd Name:
Surname:
Agta Ancestry: 96.875%

Birth Date: August 1989
Death Date:

Father: ELPI
Mother: WAYNALIN

1st Spouse:
Last/Current Spouse:

Year: 2010
Aysa-3094

ID: 8130 *Sex:* Male

Name: **BADAT**
2nd Name: RIKSON
Surname: BALYEHO, BAYEHO
Agta Ancestry: 50%

Birth Date: June 1985
Death Date:

Father: HERI
Mother: RESI

1st Spouse:
Last/Current Spouse:

Year: 2008
Badat-8130

ID: 8349 *Sex:* Male

Name: **BADOL**
2nd Name:
Surname:
Agta Ancestry: 25%

Birth Date: 1969 +/-2 years
Death Date:

Father:
Mother: BISELYA

1st Spouse:
Last/Current Spouse:

Year: 1978
Badol-8349

ID: 3060 *Sex:* Female

Name: **BAGEL**
2nd Name: LONALIN
Surname: ESTEBES
Agta Ancestry: 71.875%

Birth Date: 1986
Death Date:

Father: LITO
Mother: MAYENG

1st Spouse: DANGGULAN-1064
Last/Current Spouse: DANGGULAN-1064

Year: 2010
Bagel-3060

18

ID: 539   Sex: Female

Name: **BAGOL**
2nd Name: BAGEL
Surname: BITIGAN

Agta Ancestry: 100%

Birth Date: 1942 +/-2 years
Death Date: 1990 +/-2 years

Father: BITIGAN
Mother: KANORA
1st Spouse: SIMEON-7183
Last/Current Spouse: NORPING-422

Year: 1977
Bagol-539

ID: 71   Sex: Female

Name: **BAIT**
2nd Name: INELDA
Surname: ANGLENAN, BEKYADEN

Agta Ancestry: Unknown

Birth Date: 1977
Death Date:

Father: BIDOY
Mother: MAKARIA
1st Spouse: WILI-506
Last/Current Spouse: WILI-506

Year: 2010
Bait-71

ID: 495   Sex: Male

Name: **BAIT**
2nd Name: LONI
Surname: BITIGAN

Agta Ancestry: 100%

Birth Date: 1964 +/-3 years
Death Date:

Father: HUWANING
Mother: SILENG
1st Spouse: NINI-9133
Last/Current Spouse: NINI-9133

Year: 1977
Bait-495

ID: 553   Sex: Male

Name: **BAIT**
2nd Name: EDWIN, UNDING, ONDI
Surname: KUKUAN

Agta Ancestry: Unknown

Birth Date: 1976
Death Date:

Father: SITOK
Mother: LINDA
1st Spouse: SUSAN-8043
Last/Current Spouse: NARISA-78

Year: 2002
Bait-553

19

Year: 1977
Baken-7014

ID: 7014 Sex: Female

Name: **BAKEN**
2nd Name:
Surname:

Agta Ancestry: Unknown

Birth Date: 1964 +/-5 years
Death Date:

Father:
Mother:

1st Spouse:
Last/Current Spouse:

Year: 2006
Baladong-1034

2010
Baladong-1034

ID: 1034 Sex: Male

Name: **BALADONG**
2nd Name: PERDINAN
Surname: LISIDAY

Agta Ancestry: 96.875%

Birth Date: February 4, 1982
Death Date:

Father: BERTING
Mother: NOYME

1st Spouse:
Last/Current Spouse:

Year: 1986
Balentin-3153 with mother
Loyda-347

ID: 3153 Sex: Male

Name: **BALENTIN**
2nd Name: PREDIR, ENTENG
Surname: TULIO

Agta Ancestry: 93.75%

Birth Date: February 14, 1986
Death Date:

Father: NATENG
Mother: LOYDA

1st Spouse:
Last/Current Spouse:

Year: 2010
Balilit-3018

ID: 3018 Sex: Female

Name: **BALILIT**
2nd Name: DYENI
Surname:

Agta Ancestry: 84.38%

Birth Date: August 25, 1991
Death Date:

Father: TEMING
Mother: LOYDA

1st Spouse: ERWIN-3121
Last/Current Spouse: ERWIN-3121

ID: 5059   *Sex:* Male

Name: **BALONSE**
2nd Name:
Surname: GERA
Agta Ancestry: 100%

Birth Date: 1928 +/-3 years
Death Date: October 1976

Father: PEKTO
Mother: BINANSA
1st Spouse: KARNASIYON-42
Last/Current Spouse: KARNASIYON-42

Year: 1976
Balonse-5059

Year: 1977
Banghul-45

ID: 45   *Sex:* Male

Name: **BANGHUL**
2nd Name:
Surname: BEKYADEN
Agta Ancestry: 75%

Birth Date: 1913 +/-5 years
Death Date: 1979

Father: BEKYADEN
Mother: DONGGASILAN
1st Spouse: ANENA-5029
Last/Current Spouse: PILISA-360

Year: 1978
Banyes-48

ID: 48   *Sex:* Male

Name: **BANYES**
2nd Name:
Surname: ENERO
Agta Ancestry: 100%

Birth Date: 1922 +/-4 years
Death Date: 1988 +/-2 years

Father: ENERO
Mother: IDEK
1st Spouse: BEDYONA-7234
Last/Current Spouse: TARALING-5537

Year: 1971
Banyes-5632

ID: 5632   *Sex:* Male

Name: **BANYES**
2nd Name:
Surname: ANGIDEW
Agta Ancestry: 100%

Birth Date: 1918 +/-5 years
Death Date: 1976 +/-1 year

Father: ANGIDEW
Mother: AMELIA
1st Spouse: ADELA-5543
Last/Current Spouse: ASIONA-5574

ID: 225	*Sex:* Male

Name: **BATOTENG**
2nd Name: RIDYEL, TOTENG
Surname: ABUNDIO MIRINDU

Agta Ancestry: 75%

Birth Date: December 1963
Death Date:

Father: HAYME
Mother: NATI

1st Spouse:
Last/Current Spouse:

Year: 2004
Batoteng-225 phto by Iris Dalberto

2010
Batoteng-225

ID: 3408	*Sex:* Male

Name: **BATUTUNG**
2nd Name: DANDI, REDYIBOY
Surname: PRADO

Agta Ancestry: 75%

Birth Date: December 27, 1999
Death Date:

Father: NATENG
Mother: TETET

1st Spouse:
Last/Current Spouse:

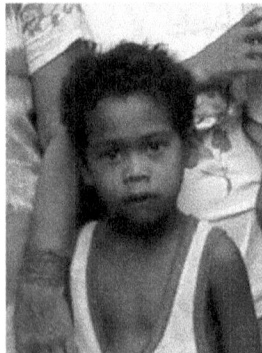

Year: 2006
Batutung-3408

ID: 7820	*Sex:* Male

Name: **BAWE**
2nd Name:
Surname: DUNATO

Agta Ancestry: 100%

Birth Date: 1934 +/-5 years
Death Date:

Father:
Mother:

1st Spouse: LILING-7327
Last/Current Spouse: LILING-7327

Year: 2008
Bawe-7820; photo by Jan van der Ploeg

ID: 49	*Sex:* Male

Name: **BAYANI**
2nd Name:
Surname: KAPINPIN

Agta Ancestry: 50%

Birth Date: 1921 +/-4 years
Death Date: January 1998

Father: HOSE
Mother: HIMENA

1st Spouse: LELYENG-5721
Last/Current Spouse: UDAD-241

Year: 1976
Bayani-49

Year: 2004
Bebi-3014 phto by Iris
Dalberto

ID: 3014   Sex: Female

Name: **BEBI**
2nd Name:
Surname: TANYET KAGAWAD

Agta Ancestry: Unknown

Birth Date: August 1989
Death Date:

Father: NOEL
Mother: RESI

1st Spouse:
Last/Current Spouse:

Year: 2010
Bebimey-3607

ID: 3607   Sex: Female

Name: **BEBIMEY**
2nd Name:
Surname:

Agta Ancestry: 95.315%

Birth Date: May 30, 2007
Death Date:

Father: SENING
Mother: DALAGA

1st Spouse:
Last/Current Spouse:

Year: 1977
Bedbed-52

ID: 52   Sex: Male

Name: **BEDBED**
2nd Name:
Surname: MISAN

Agta Ancestry: 100%

Birth Date: 1936 +/-2 years
Death Date: 1989 +/-2 years

Father: MAGNAY
Mother: SENIKA

1st Spouse: KARNASIYON-53
Last/Current Spouse: KARNASIYON-53

Year: 1964   1970
Beding-5066   Beding-5066 & Kekek-267
                    holding giant python

ID: 5066   Sex: Male

Name: **BEDING**
2nd Name:
Surname:

Agta Ancestry: 100%

Birth Date: 1937 +/-3 years
Death Date: January 1976

Father: PAWISAN
Mother: PILISA

1st Spouse: OPING-7154
Last/Current Spouse: PANSING-7280

Year: 1984
Been-1163 with father Sitok-551

ID: 1163   Sex: Male

Name: **BEEN**
2nd Name: MARIO, LONRI
Surname: KUKUAN

Agta Ancestry: Unknown

Birth Date: March 20, 1978
Death Date:

Father: SITOK
Mother: LINDA

1st Spouse:
Last/Current Spouse:

Year: 1972
Bekneg-260 w mom
Mensiang-257 phto by Jim

1977
Bekneg-260

ID: 260   Sex: Female

Name: **BEKNEG**
2nd Name: NORA, RUSALINDA
Surname: SAGUNED

Agta Ancestry: 100%

Birth Date: 1971 +/-1 year
Death Date: September 25, 1986

Father: KANDEG
Mother: MENSIANG

1st Spouse:
Last/Current Spouse:

Year: 1978
Ben8001

ID: 8001   Sex: Male

Name: **BEN**
2nd Name:
Surname:

Agta Ancestry: 50%

Birth Date: 1956 +/-6 years
Death Date:

Father: KENGKENG
Mother: MOIYO

1st Spouse:
Last/Current Spouse:

Year: 1977
Benduling-7023

ID: 7023   Sex: Female

Name: **BENDULING**
2nd Name: BENDULIN
Surname:

Agta Ancestry: Unknown

Birth Date: 1930 +/-8 years
Death Date: 1990 +/-9 years

Father: IGNASIO
Mother: EBUN

1st Spouse: DESAG-7056
Last/Current Spouse: DESAG-7056

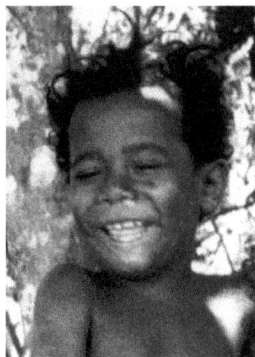

Year: 1978
Bendyi-460

ID: 460   Sex: Male

Name: **BENDYI**
2nd Name: BENGI
Surname: OLIBEROS

Agta Ancestry: 100%

Birth Date: 1974 +/-1 year
Death Date:

Father: PEDRING
Mother: LUNINGNING

1st Spouse:
Last/Current Spouse:

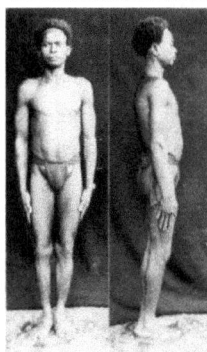

Year: 1936
Benggosa-5073
photo by Vanoverbergh

ID: 5073   Sex: Male

Name: **BENGGOSA**
2nd Name: BINGGOSA
Surname:

Agta Ancestry: 100%

Birth Date: 1909 +/-8 years
Death Date: 1939 +/-5 years

Father: MIYA
Mother: UGAY

1st Spouse: OPISTA-5339
Last/Current Spouse: OPISTA-5339

Year: 2008
Beni-9059

2010
Beni-9059

ID: 9059   Sex: Male

Name: **BENI**
2nd Name:
Surname: DELACRUZ

Agta Ancestry: 0%

Birth Date: 1943 +/-5 years
Death Date:

Father:
Mother:

1st Spouse: UTET-609
Last/Current Spouse: UTET-609

Year: 1977
Berhinya-9129

ID: 9129   Sex: Female

Name: **BERHINYA**
2nd Name:
Surname:

Agta Ancestry: 25%

Birth Date: 1941 +/-5 years
Death Date: 1980 +/-5 years

Father:
Mother:

1st Spouse: unknown-9203
Last/Current Spouse: TETENG-9128

25

ID:	59
Sex:	Male

Name: **BERIONES**
2nd Name: BERYONES
Surname: GEHA, GERA

Agta Ancestry: 100%

Birth Date: 1943 +/-3 years
Death Date: 2000 +/-1 year

Father: PONSENG
Mother: TINANG

1st Spouse: REKREK-60
Last/Current Spouse: MELTING-481

Year: 1978
Beriones-59

ID: 7025   *Sex:* Male

Name: **BERNING**
2nd Name:
Surname:

Agta Ancestry: 93.75%

Birth Date: 1968 +/-4 years
Death Date:

Father: GUBEK
Mother: PENI

1st Spouse: LINDA-242
Last/Current Spouse: LINDA-242

Year: 2010
Berning-7025

ID: 64   *Sex:* Male

Name: **BERSOSA**
2nd Name:
Surname: DUNATO

Agta Ancestry: 100%

Birth Date: 1917 +/-3 years
Death Date: 1986 +/-1 year

Father: ANTON
Mother: BITEK

1st Spouse: ATING-5316
Last/Current Spouse: ILEN-163

Year: 1973
Bersosa-64

ID: 21   *Sex:* Male

Name: **BERTING**
2nd Name:
Surname: LISIDAY

Agta Ancestry: 93.75%

Birth Date: 1959 +/-1 year
Death Date: January 6, 1983

Father: BENDING
Mother: NURING

1st Spouse: NOYME-132
Last/Current Spouse: NOYME-132

Year: 1977
Berting-21

Year: 1976
Bertoso-348

1976
Bertoso-348 with Steve
Headland, on way to

ID: 348	Sex: Male

Name: **BERTOSO**
2nd Name:
Surname: PAWISAN
Agta Ancestry: 87.5%

Birth Date: 1964 +/-1 year
Death Date: February 15, 2003

Father: MANINGTING
Mother: SARING
1st Spouse: KULES-482
Last/Current Spouse: KULES-482

Year: 2010
Bibi-4021

ID: 4021	Sex: Female

Name: **BIBI**
2nd Name:
Surname:
Agta Ancestry: 50%

Birth Date: 1983 +/-6 years
Death Date:

Father: AMBUT
Mother: NORMA
1st Spouse:
Last/Current Spouse:

Year: 1994
Bibian-8266 (?)

2008
Bibian-8266 holding a child

ID: 8266	Sex: Female

Name: **BIBIAN**
2nd Name:
Surname: VARGAS
Agta Ancestry: 25%

Birth Date: January 17, 1983
Death Date:

Father: DOLPING
Mother: LINDA
1st Spouse: RAMEL-1153
Last/Current Spouse: RAMEL-1153

Year: 1976
Biding-115

ID: 115	Sex: Female

Name: **BIDING**
2nd Name:
Surname: TULIO
Agta Ancestry: Unknown

Birth Date: 1931 +/-3 years
Death Date: May 1989

Father: TULIO
Mother: LIPANYAW
1st Spouse: MAWAS-5287
Last/Current Spouse: DANDING-114

27

ID:	65
Sex:	Male

Name: **BIDOY**
2nd Name:
Surname: ANGLENAN, BEKYADEN
Agta Ancestry: 87.5%

Birth Date: 1933 +/-3 years
Death Date: 1995

Father: ANGLENAN
Mother: PILISA
1st Spouse: MAKARIA-2055
Last/Current Spouse: MAKARIA-2055

Year: 1978
Bidoy-65

ID: 8265 *Sex:* Male

Name: **BIK**
2nd Name:
Surname: VARGAS
Agta Ancestry: 25%

Birth Date: October 21, 1980
Death Date:

Father: DOLPING
Mother: LINDA
1st Spouse:
Last/Current Spouse:

Year: 1994
Bik-8265

ID: 9136 *Sex:* Male

Name: **BIK**
2nd Name:
Surname:
Agta Ancestry: Unknown

Birth Date: 1965 +/-3 years
Death Date:

Father: unknown
Mother: BERHINYA
1st Spouse: INGGEL-297
Last/Current Spouse: INGGEL-297

Year: 2010
Bik-9136

ID: 2040 *Sex:* Female

Name: **BIKI**
2nd Name:
Surname: GERA
Agta Ancestry: 100%

Birth Date: 1981
Death Date:

Father: HINGET
Mother: BITA
1st Spouse: DANI-44
Last/Current Spouse: DANI-44

Year: 1984
Biki-2040 with mother Bita-237

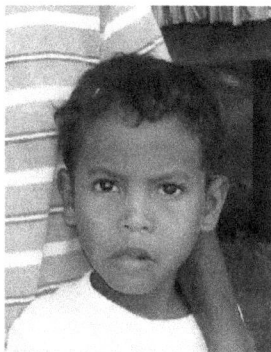

ID:	3504 *Sex:* Male
Name:	**BIKONGEN**
2nd Name:	LUBI
Surname:	
Agta Ancestry:	87.5%
Birth Date:	February 12, 2003
Death Date:	
Father:	TOTOY
Mother:	DINA
1st Spouse:	
Last/Current Spouse:	

Year: 2010
Bikongen-3504

ID:	498 *Sex:* Male
Name:	**BIKTOR**
2nd Name:	KUNDUL, UNDUL, BIK
Surname:	TOPAN
Agta Ancestry:	50%
Birth Date:	1976
Death Date:	November 21, 2007
Father:	LASKO
Mother:	SILENG
1st Spouse:	PANING-9201
Last/Current Spouse:	PANING-9201

Year: 1978
Biktor-498 with mother
Sileng-492

ID:	7381 *Sex:* Female
Name:	**BILIN**
2nd Name:	EBILIN
Surname:	
Agta Ancestry:	100%
Birth Date:	1963 +/-4 years
Death Date:	
Father:	UGKUY
Mother:	PANSING
1st Spouse:	LEDO-7382
Last/Current Spouse:	LEDO-7382

Year: 1972
Bilin-7381

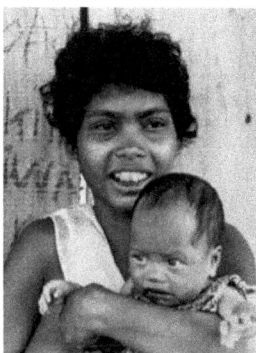

ID:	58 *Sex:* Female
Name:	**BILINDA**
2nd Name:	BELINDA
Surname:	BELYANING, LISIDAY
Agta Ancestry:	50%
Birth Date:	1953 +/-2 years
Death Date:	June 2004
Father:	
Mother:	NATI
1st Spouse:	LOSIO-328
Last/Current Spouse:	RUBEN-9170

Year: 1978
Bilinda-58 holding daughtr
Huana-1016

29

Year: 2008
Bilya-3427 phto by Iris
Dalberto

ID: 3427   Sex: Female

Name: **BILYA**
2nd Name:
Surname:

Agta Ancestry: 93.75%

Birth Date: May 1999
Death Date:

Father: UDENG
Mother: ALILI

1st Spouse:
Last/Current Spouse:

Year: 1976
Bilyanting-72

ID: 72   Sex: Male

Name: **BILYANTING**
2nd Name:
Surname: AGINALDO

Agta Ancestry: 100%

Birth Date: 1940 +/-3 years
Death Date: 1980

Father: AGINALDO
Mother: PASKUALITA

1st Spouse: PINING-73
Last/Current Spouse: PINING-73

Year: 1977
Bilyesa-77 holding son
Undul-79

ID: 77   Sex: Male

Name: **BILYESA**
2nd Name:
Surname: ISTANES, TANES

Agta Ancestry: 100%

Birth Date: 1948 +/-3 years
Death Date: April 5, 1983

Father: TANES
Mother: LIYANING

1st Spouse: NARISA-78
Last/Current Spouse: NARISA-78

Year: 1976   2008
Bilyesa-81   Bilyesa-81

ID: 81   Sex: Male

Name: **BILYESA**
2nd Name: PELOS
Surname: KUKUAN

Agta Ancestry: 100%

Birth Date: 1924 +/-2 years
Death Date:

Father: MANWEL
Mother: SINDINA

1st Spouse: ANDITA-5026
Last/Current Spouse: DENA-9115

30

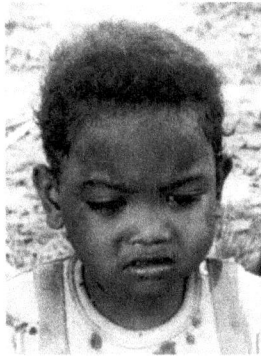

Year: 1977
Bingel-532

1984
Bingel-532

ID:	532
Sex:	Male

Name: **BINGEL**
2nd Name:
Surname: BERNABE
Agta Ancestry: 100%

Birth Date: 1974 +/-1 year
Death Date:

Father: SELTON
Mother: NENENG
1st Spouse: RITENG-420
Last/Current Spouse: RITENG-420

Year: 1977
Binggo-84

ID: 84   *Sex:* Male

Name: **BINGGO**
2nd Name: BINGGO
Surname: PONSENG, TANGKAD
Agta Ancestry: 100%

Birth Date: 1950 +/-2 years
Death Date: 1980

Father: PONSENG
Mother: TINANG
1st Spouse:
Last/Current Spouse:

Year: 1963
Bingoy-5081 with wife
Liminida-41

ID: 5081   *Sex:* Male

Name: **BINGGOY**
2nd Name:
Surname: TOMAY
Agta Ancestry: 100%

Birth Date: 1934 +/-2 years
Death Date: 1964 +/-1 year

Father: INONG
Mother: BEDA
1st Spouse: LIMINIDA-41
Last/Current Spouse: LIMINIDA-41

Year: 1977
Binong-85

ID: 85   *Sex:* Male

Name: **BINONG**
2nd Name: DUPANG, SIBIRINO
Surname: RAMUS
Agta Ancestry: 100%

Birth Date: 1923 +/-4 years
Death Date: July 1990

Father: BETTEY
Mother: ANIKITA
1st Spouse: LIGAYA-156
Last/Current Spouse: LIGAYA-156

31

Year: 1966
Malonduyan-7637 &
husband Binumaun-7607

ID:	7607	Sex:	Male

Name: **BINUMAUN**
2nd Name:
Surname:

Agta Ancestry: Unknown

Birth Date: 1905 +/-9 years
Death Date:

Father: PANGEL
Mother:

1st Spouse: MALONDUYAN-7637
Last/Current Spouse: MALONDUYAN-7637

Year: 1994
Bisal-547

ID:	547	Sex:	Male

Name: **BISAL**
2nd Name:
Surname: SANGBAY

Agta Ancestry: 100%

Birth Date: 1973 +/-2 years
Death Date:

Father: SINABUYAN
Mother: MIDING

1st Spouse: DENING-200
Last/Current Spouse: DENING-200

Year: 1978
Bita-89

ID:	89	Sex:	Female

Name: **BITA**
2nd Name: ABLEG
Surname: BILAS

Agta Ancestry: 100%

Birth Date: 1923 +/-2 years
Death Date:

Father: BILAS
Mother: KENTIN

1st Spouse: RUMING-5875
Last/Current Spouse: RUMING-5805

Year: 1979
Bita-237 holding daughtr
Dina-2039

2006
Bita-237 phto by Iris
Dalberto

ID:	237	Sex:	Female

Name: **BITA**
2nd Name:
Surname: INONG BANAYAD

Agta Ancestry: Unknown

Birth Date: 1960 +/-1 year
Death Date:

Father: BINGGOY
Mother: LIMINIDA

1st Spouse: HINGET-2038
Last/Current Spouse: HINGET-2038

Year: 1978
Bita-2002

ID:	2002	*Sex:* Female

Name: **BITA**
2nd Name:
Surname: RAMOS
Agta Ancestry: 100%

Birth Date: 1952 +/-1 year
Death Date:

Father: DENISA
Mother: AGRAPINA
1st Spouse: ROHELIO-2001
Last/Current Spouse: ROHELIO-2001

Year: 1927
Biya-5085 and husband
Madeng-5250

ID:	5085	*Sex:* Female

Name: **BIYA**
2nd Name:
Surname:
Agta Ancestry: 100%

Birth Date: 1874 +/-7 years
Death Date: 1939 +/-5 years

Father:
Mother:
1st Spouse: MADENG-5250
Last/Current Spouse: MADENG-5250

Year: 1979
Boker-459

ID:	459	*Sex:* Male

Name: **BOKER**
2nd Name:
Surname: OLIBEROS
Agta Ancestry: 100%

Birth Date: 1965
Death Date:

Father: PEDRING
Mother: USING
1st Spouse: NILDA-7836
Last/Current Spouse: NELDA-7735

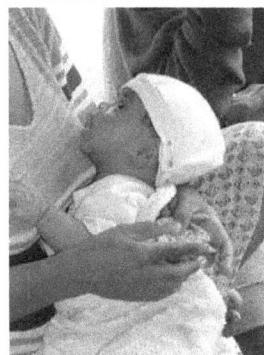
Year: 2004
Bokiyeng-3529

ID:	3529	*Sex:* Female

Name: **BOKIYENG**
2nd Name: RIDYEN
Surname: PRADO
Agta Ancestry: 84.375%

Birth Date: December 10, 2003
Death Date:

Father: RIDYEL
Mother: MERIDYEN
1st Spouse:
Last/Current Spouse:

33

ID: 3373	*Sex:* Male

Name: **BOLDOG**
2nd Name: RITYARD
Surname:

Agta Ancestry: 62.5%

Birth Date: July 1998
Death Date:

Father: UNDI
Mother: HUANA

1st Spouse:
Last/Current Spouse:

Year: 2010
Boldog-3373

ID: 5086	*Sex:* Male

Name: **BONDING**
2nd Name:
Surname:

Agta Ancestry: 87.5%

Birth Date: 1958 +/-2 years
Death Date: January 1972

Father: DIKMIN
Mother: PINYANG

1st Spouse:
Last/Current Spouse:

Year: 1966
Bonding-5086

ID: 93	*Sex:* Male

Name: **BONTOY**
2nd Name: BUROSA
Surname: IMO

Agta Ancestry: 100%

Birth Date: 1919 +/-3 years
Death Date: 1980

Father: DETAG
Mother: UGAY

1st Spouse: ARPENYA-5046
Last/Current Spouse: NENA-94

Year: 1978
Bontoy-93

ID: 5585	*Sex:* Male

Name: **BONTOY**
2nd Name:
Surname:

Agta Ancestry: 100%

Birth Date: 1938 +/-3 years
Death Date: December 14, 1965

Father: BINUMAUN
Mother: MALONDUYAN

1st Spouse: KARNASIYON-6018
Last/Current Spouse: KARNASIYON-6018

Year: 1965
Bontoy-5585

Year: 1978
Borseg-97

2004
Borseg-97

ID: 97   Sex: Male

Name: **BORSEG**
2nd Name:
Surname: LISIDAY
Agta Ancestry: 87.5%

Birth Date: 1944 +/-1 year
Death Date:

Father: LISIDAY
Mother: MAKINAY

1st Spouse: LODI-98
Last/Current Spouse: LODI-98

Year: 2008
Boyboyan-8277

ID: 8277   Sex: Male

Name: **BOYBOYAN**
2nd Name:
Surname: VARGAS
Agta Ancestry: 25%

Birth Date: December 3, 1985
Death Date:

Father: DOLPING
Mother: LINDA

1st Spouse: PANET-3181
Last/Current Spouse: PANET-3181

Year: 1977
Boysang-577

ID: 577   Sex: Male

Name: **BOYSANG**
2nd Name: BERTING
Surname: SIMIN
Agta Ancestry: 100%

Birth Date: 1968 +/-1 year
Death Date:

Father: WILSON
Mother: NARSING

1st Spouse:
Last/Current Spouse:

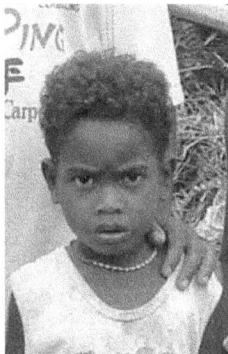

Year: 2004
Brayan-3401

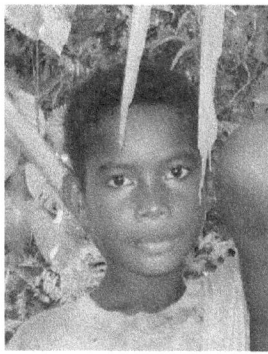

2010
Brayan-3401

ID: 3401   Sex: Male

Name: **BRAYAN**
2nd Name: BATO
Surname:
Agta Ancestry: 81.25%

Birth Date: December 16, 1998
Death Date:

Father: TONILIN
Mother: ANALI

1st Spouse:
Last/Current Spouse:

35

Year: 1966
Bukan-7690

ID:	7690	Sex: Male

Name: **BUKAN**
2nd Name:
Surname:

Agta Ancestry: Unknown

Birth Date:
Death Date:

Father: SERAY
Mother:

1st Spouse: ISTRING-7689
Last/Current Spouse: ISTRING-7689

Year: 1977
Buket-7420

ID:	7420	Sex: Female

Name: **BUKET**
2nd Name:
Surname:

Agta Ancestry: Unknown

Birth Date:
Death Date:

Father:
Mother:

1st Spouse: REMING-7419
Last/Current Spouse: REMING-7419

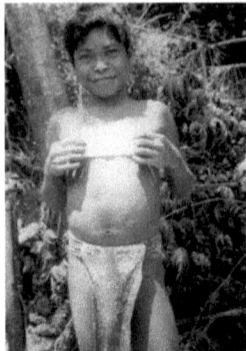

Year: 1977
Buleg-7046

ID:	7046	Sex: Male

Name: **BULEG**
2nd Name:
Surname:

Agta Ancestry: Unknown

Birth Date:
Death Date:

Father:
Mother:

1st Spouse:
Last/Current Spouse:

Year: 1978
Bunaw-102

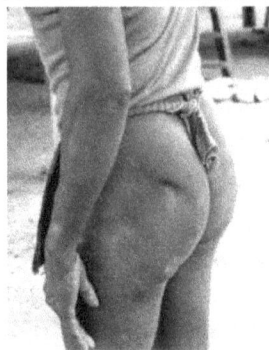

1978
Bunaw-102 showing scar
from bullet on left buttocks.

ID:	102	Sex: Male

Name: **BUNAW**
2nd Name: ALIBUNAW
Surname: DATOG, DEMADES, PREDO

Agta Ancestry: 100%

Birth Date: 1930 +/-2 years
Death Date: 1989 +/-1 year

Father: APREDO
Mother: TETENG

1st Spouse: LODI-103
Last/Current Spouse: LODI-103

36

ID: 2013	*Sex:* Male

Name: **BUTOD**
2nd Name:
Surname: SANSES
Agta Ancestry: 100%

Birth Date: 1929 +/-1 year
Death Date:

Father: AGNASEN
Mother: KADYONG
1st Spouse: MADYEK-106
Last/Current Spouse: MADYEK-106

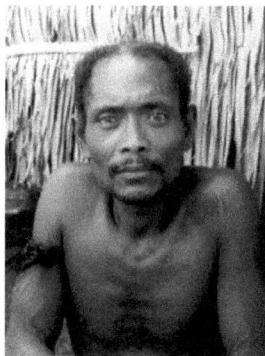

Year: 1978
Butod-2013

2006
Butod-2013

ID: 3141	*Sex:* Female

Name: **DAGA**
2nd Name: DYENILIN
Surname: TANYET KAGAWAD
Agta Ancestry: Unknown

Birth Date: September 1993
Death Date:

Father: NOEL
Mother: RESI
1st Spouse: WINER-4013
Last/Current Spouse: WINER-4013

Year: 2004
Daga-3141 phto by Iris
Dalberto

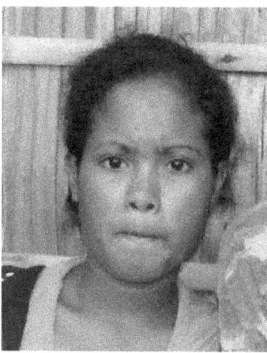

2010
Daga-3141

ID: 142	*Sex:* Female

Name: **DALAGA**
2nd Name:
Surname:
Agta Ancestry: 100%

Birth Date: 1965 +/-1 year
Death Date:

Father: BORDON
Mother: SANING
1st Spouse:
Last/Current Spouse:

Year: 1977
Dalaga-142

ID: 583	*Sex:* Female

Name: **DALAGA**
2nd Name: EBILIN, DYENILIN
Surname: KUKUAN
Agta Ancestry: 93.75%

Birth Date: 1975 +/-1 year
Death Date:

Father: TEKOK
Mother: LITA
1st Spouse: SENING-526
Last/Current Spouse: SENING-526

Year: 2010
Dalaga-583

37

Year: 2010
Dalen-8181

ID: 8181　　　Sex: Female

Name: **DALEN**
2nd Name:
Surname: VARGAS

Agta Ancestry: 25%

Birth Date: 1964 +/-5 years
Death Date:

Father: DOLPING
Mother: LINDA
1st Spouse: NANI-322
Last/Current Spouse: GARDU-9144

Year: 2004
Dalena-3009

ID: 3009　　　Sex: Female

Name: **DALENA**
2nd Name: MAGDALENA
Surname:

Agta Ancestry: 93.75%

Birth Date: January 15, 1992
Death Date:

Father: UDENG
Mother: ALILI
1st Spouse:
Last/Current Spouse:

Year: 2010
Daleng-1048

ID: 1048　　　Sex: Male

Name: **DALENG**
2nd Name: ALAN, GUNDAYA
Surname: DELACRUZ

Agta Ancestry: 50%

Birth Date: March 1978
Death Date:

Father: SIMO
Mother: GURING
1st Spouse: GRES-3069
Last/Current Spouse: GRES-3069

Year: 2004
Dalya-9176 with Katrina-8310

2004
Dalya-9176 phto by Iris Dalberto

ID: 9176　　　Sex: Female

Name: **DALYA**
2nd Name: DESI
Surname: MANYA

Agta Ancestry: 0%

Birth Date: December 11, 1983
Death Date:

Father:
Mother:
1st Spouse: SANIBOY-204
Last/Current Spouse: SANIBOY-204

38

Year: 1970
Damyek-113, phto by Tom
Macleod

ID:	113	*Sex:*	Female

Name: **DAMYEK**
2nd Name:
Surname:

Agta Ancestry: 100%

Birth Date: 1917 +/-5 years
Death Date: 1977 +/-1 year

Father: TAYAMAN
Mother:

1st Spouse: AGAS-7487
Last/Current Spouse: AGAS-7487

Year: 1976
Danding-114

ID:	114	*Sex:*	Male

Name: **DANDING**
2nd Name:
Surname: ADUANAN, TIGO

Agta Ancestry: 100%

Birth Date: 1929 +/-2 years
Death Date: January 3, 1985

Father: TIGO
Mother: KULUMBA

1st Spouse: PILISITA-5375
Last/Current Spouse: BIDING-115

Year: 1979
Dandoy-116

ID:	116	*Sex:*	Male

Name: **DANDOY**
2nd Name: DANDULINO, ABILINO
Surname: ABILINO, BONGKALE

Agta Ancestry: 100%

Birth Date: 1944 +/-3 years
Death Date: January 27, 1998

Father: BUNGKALE
Mother: DITENG

1st Spouse: DINGDINGAN-117
Last/Current Spouse: DINGDINGAN-117

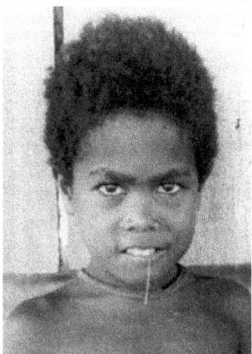

Year: 1977
Dani-44

2002
Dani-44

ID:	44	*Sex:*	Male

Name: **DANI**
2nd Name:
Surname: GERA, PEKTO

Agta Ancestry: 100%

Birth Date: 1971 +/-1 year
Death Date:

Father: BALONSE
Mother: KARNASIYON

1st Spouse: BIKI-2040
Last/Current Spouse: BIKI-2040

39

Year: 2010
Danika-3613

ID: 3613   Sex: Female

Name: **DANIKA**
2nd Name:
Surname:

Agta Ancestry: 62.5%

Birth Date: December 6, 2006
Death Date:

Father: UNDI
Mother: HUANA

1st Spouse:
Last/Current Spouse:

Year: 2008
Danilo-9028

ID: 9028   Sex: Male

Name: **DANILO**
2nd Name: DYUNYOR
Surname: DIYOSINO

Agta Ancestry: 0%

Birth Date: 1945 +/-5 years
Death Date:

Father:
Mother:

1st Spouse: MELI-386
Last/Current Spouse: MELI-386

Year: 2008
Danilo-9177

ID: 9177   Sex: Male

Name: **DANILO**
2nd Name: DANI
Surname: GERERO

Agta Ancestry: 0%

Birth Date:
Death Date:

Father:
Mother:

1st Spouse: TANYA-1039
Last/Current Spouse: TANYA-1039

Year: 1965
Darbing-118

1977
Darbing-118 holding
daughtr Nansi-120

ID: 118   Sex: Male

Name: **DARBING**
2nd Name:
Surname: ISTANES

Agta Ancestry: 100%

Birth Date: 1950 +/-2 years
Death Date: June 1980

Father: TANES
Mother: LIYANING

1st Spouse: NERSI-119
Last/Current Spouse: NERSI-119

40

Year: 2010
Daret-1104 w Danela-3649

ID: 1104   *Sex:* Male

Name: **DARET**
2nd Name: GARI, DARI, HENRI
Surname: LISIDAY

Agta Ancestry: Unknown

Birth Date: November 1981
Death Date:

Father: DOLSING
Mother: MARINENG
1st Spouse: DYEMALIN-7929
Last/Current Spouse: DYEMALIN-7929

Year: 1976
Darning-122

ID: 122   *Sex:* Female

Name: **DARNING**
2nd Name: DARLING
Surname:

Agta Ancestry: 75%

Birth Date: 1932 +/-3 years
Death Date: April 26, 1978

Father: PERNANDO
Mother: PANENENG
1st Spouse: MANINGTING-5275
Last/Current Spouse: TEBAN-9069

Year: 2002
Darwin-3463 w mothr Linda-552

ID: 3463   *Sex:* Male

Name: **DARWIN**
2nd Name:
Surname:

Agta Ancestry: Unknown

Birth Date: February 2, 2000
Death Date:

Father: SITOK
Mother: LINDA
1st Spouse:
Last/Current Spouse:

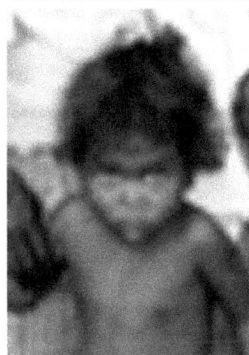

Year: 2002
Dayana-3376

ID: 3376   *Sex:* Female

Name: **DAYANA**
2nd Name:
Surname: BELYANING

Agta Ancestry: 96.88%

Birth Date: July 1998
Death Date: September 25, 2002

Father: TAYUGIT
Mother: KARING
1st Spouse:
Last/Current Spouse:

41

ID:	4015	Sex: Female

Name: **DAYANA**
2nd Name:
Surname:

Agta Ancestry: 0%

Birth Date: 1982 +/-6 years
Death Date:

Father:
Mother:

1st Spouse: ROLI-4014
Last/Current Spouse: ROLI-4014

Year: 2010
Dayana-4015

ID:	502	Sex: Female

Name: **DELI**
2nd Name:
Surname: ASION, TULIO

Agta Ancestry: 100%

Birth Date: 1951 +/-2 years
Death Date: 2004 +/-1 year

Father: ASION
Mother: SULIDAD

1st Spouse: RODI-501
Last/Current Spouse: BITOK-68

Year: 1976
Deli-502

ID:	365	Sex: Male

Name: **DELNING**
2nd Name: DELMING
Surname: TIKIMAN

Agta Ancestry: 93.75%

Birth Date: 1968 +/-1 year
Death Date:

Father: MARIO
Mother: LODI

1st Spouse: MERSI-9134
Last/Current Spouse: MERSI-9134

Year: 1978
Delning-365

ID:	123	Sex: Male

Name: **DELOY**
2nd Name:
Surname: GERA

Agta Ancestry: 100%

Birth Date: 1951 +/-2 years
Death Date:

Father: BALONSE
Mother: KARNASIYON

1st Spouse: PAMING-124
Last/Current Spouse: PAMING-124

Year: 1977
Deloy-123

42

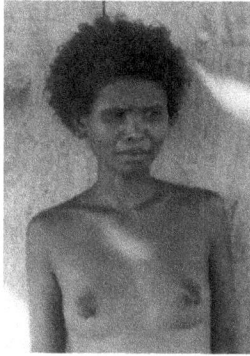

Year: 1976
Dengdeng-2015

ID: 2015   Sex: Female

Name: **DENGDENG**
2nd Name: KIRINENG
Surname:

Agta Ancestry: 100%

Birth Date: 1947 +/-1 year
Death Date: 2007

Father: BUKAN
Mother: ISTRING
1st Spouse: GIBSON-207
Last/Current Spouse: GIBSON-207

Year: 1977
Dening-200 on left with
Edwin-199

1994
Dening-200

ID: 200   Sex: Female

Name: **DENING**
2nd Name: DYENILING
Surname: TULIO

Agta Ancestry: 93.75%

Birth Date: 1974
Death Date:

Father: ENDING
Mother: NUNUK
1st Spouse: BISAL-547
Last/Current Spouse: BISAL-547

Year: 1977
Desag-7056

ID: 7056   Sex: Male

Name: **DESAG**
2nd Name:
Surname:

Agta Ancestry: Unknown

Birth Date: 1930 +/-6 years
Death Date: 1985 +/-9 years

Father: BAYDEK
Mother: SABEL
1st Spouse: BENDULING-7023
Last/Current Spouse: BENDULING-7023

Year: 1966
Desuy-5104

ID: 5104   Sex: Male

Name: **DESUY**
2nd Name:
Surname:

Agta Ancestry: 100%

Birth Date: 1917 +/-4 years
Death Date: 1970 +/-4 years

Father:
Mother:
1st Spouse: SILANG-5437
Last/Current Spouse: LUNING-5245

43

ID:	129
Sex:	Male

Name: **DIDOG**
2nd Name: BENBINIDO
Surname: ADUANAN

Agta Ancestry: 100%

Birth Date: February 27, 1922
Death Date: December 18, 1988

Father: TALIMANGON
Mother: MONIKA

1st Spouse: POMPOEK-130
Last/Current Spouse: POMPOEK-130

Year: 1972
Didog-129 phto by Jim Musgrove

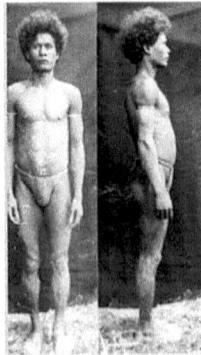

ID: 5107 *Sex:* Male

Name: **DIKMIN**
2nd Name:
Surname:

Agta Ancestry: 75%

Birth Date: 1900 +/-9 years
Death Date: 1940 +/-9 years

Father: BEKYADEN
Mother: DONGGASILAN

1st Spouse: MEDIKAD-5290
Last/Current Spouse: MEDIKAD-5290

Year: 1936
Dikmin-5107
photo by Vanoverbergh

ID: 5108 *Sex:* Male

Name: **DIKMIN**
2nd Name:
Surname: ANGIDEW

Agta Ancestry: 100%

Birth Date: 1912 +/-6 years
Death Date: January 1965

Father: ANGIDEW
Mother: ASIONA

1st Spouse: PINYANG-5376
Last/Current Spouse: PINYANG-5376

Year: 1962
Dikmin-5108

ID: 2018 *Sex:* Male

Name: **DIKONG**
2nd Name:
Surname:

Agta Ancestry: 100%

Birth Date: 1930 +/-3 years
Death Date:

Father: KASAKAP
Mother: MAISANA

1st Spouse:
Last/Current Spouse:

Year: 1984
Dikong-2018

ID: 7061   Sex: Male

Name: **DILISIO**
2nd Name:
Surname:

Agta Ancestry: Unknown

Birth Date:
Death Date:

Father:
Mother:

1st Spouse:
Last/Current Spouse:

Year: 1977
Dilisio-7061

ID: 2039   Sex: Female

Name: **DINA**
2nd Name:
Surname: PRADO

Agta Ancestry: 100%

Birth Date: November 1978
Death Date:

Father: HINGET
Mother: BITA

1st Spouse: TOTOY-1111
Last/Current Spouse: TOTOY-1111

Year: 2002   2010
Dina-2039   Dina-2039

ID: 6064   Sex: Male

Name: **DINEGTUNAN**
2nd Name:
Surname:

Agta Ancestry: 100%

Birth Date: 1927 +/-4 years
Death Date:

Father: DINSIWEG
Mother: PILISIA

1st Spouse: SANING-135
Last/Current Spouse: SANING-135

Year: 1977
Dinegtunan-6064

ID: 117   Sex: Female

Name: **DINGDINGAN**
2nd Name: RODALINDA
Surname: ARISTAN, GERERO

Agta Ancestry: 100%

Birth Date: 1955 +/-2 years
Death Date: 1990 +/-2 years

Father: PIDYONG
Mother: SIDING

1st Spouse: DANDOY-116
Last/Current Spouse: LINING-315

Year: 1979
Dingdingan-117

45

Year: 1976
Diwata-607

ID: 607		*Sex:* Female
Name: **DIWATA**		
2nd Name: DYOSI		
Surname: TOMAY		
Agta Ancestry: 93.75%		
Birth Date: 1975		
Death Date: 1990 +/-1 year		
Father: ULEG		
Mother: HELEN		
1st Spouse: unknown-9169		
Last/Current Spouse: unknown-9169		

Year: 1967
Diyakin-5117

ID: 5117		*Sex:* Male
Name: **DIYAKIN**		
2nd Name: DIAKING		
Surname:		
Agta Ancestry: 100%		
Birth Date: 1925 +/-2 years		
Death Date: 1974		
Father: LENDEK		
Mother: DIWANE		
1st Spouse: LUNING-5245		
Last/Current Spouse: DIYANGKINA-5591		

Year: 1966
Dodeng-5680

ID: 5680		*Sex:* Female
Name: **DODENG**		
2nd Name: LITTAY		
Surname:		
Agta Ancestry: 100%		
Birth Date: 1905 +/-1 year		
Death Date: 1968		
Father: LAYOAN		
Mother: DOMINGA		
1st Spouse: DEGNASAN-5101		
Last/Current Spouse: SANGBAY-5424		

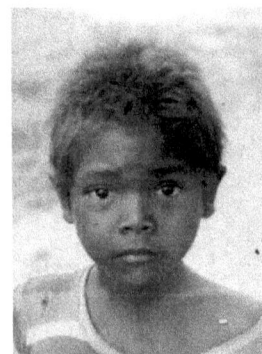

Year: 1978
Dodoy-2014

ID: 2014		*Sex:* Male
Name: **DODOY**		
2nd Name: AGULYANA		
Surname: SANSES		
Agta Ancestry: 87.5%		
Birth Date: 1974		
Death Date:		
Father: BUTOD		
Mother: MADYEK		
1st Spouse:		
Last/Current Spouse:		

Year: 1977
Doling-7065

ID: 7065   Sex: Male
Name: **DOLING**
2nd Name:
Surname: DABID
Agta Ancestry: Unknown
Birth Date: 1950 +/-7 years
Death Date:
Father: BAYDEK
Mother: SABEL
1st Spouse: ETONG-7498
Last/Current Spouse: ETONG-7498

Year: 1977
Dolping-8056

2008
Dolping-8056

ID: 8056   Sex: Male
Name: **DOLPING**
2nd Name:
Surname: VARGAS
Agta Ancestry: 50%
Birth Date: June 10, 1946
Death Date:
Father: BONIFACIO
Mother: TOTO
1st Spouse: LINDA-9010
Last/Current Spouse: LINDA-9010

Year: 1977
Dolsing-19

2010
Dolsing-19

ID: 19   Sex: Male
Name: **DOLSING**
2nd Name:
Surname: LISIDAY
Agta Ancestry: 93.75%
Birth Date: 1956 +/-1 year
Death Date:
Father: BENDING
Mother: NURING
1st Spouse: EMILI-195
Last/Current Spouse: MARINENG-382

Year: 1977
Doming-145

ID: 145   Sex: Male
Name: **DOMING**
2nd Name:
Surname: BALENSIA
Agta Ancestry: 50%
Birth Date: 1937 +/-3 years
Death Date: 1988 +/-1 year
Father: MEDSOR
Mother: LAWTING
1st Spouse: LILYA-146
Last/Current Spouse: LILYA-146

ID:	148	Sex: Male

ID: 148   Sex: Male

Name: **DOMING**
2nd Name:
Surname: KALANGGET
Agta Ancestry: 87.5%

Birth Date: 1943 +/-1 year
Death Date: 1980 +/-1 year

Father: NANEK
Mother: KONSING
1st Spouse: TELENGAN-149
Last/Current Spouse: TELENGAN-149

Year: 1977
Doming-148

ID: 7429   Sex: Male

Name: **DONGDONG**
2nd Name:
Surname:
Agta Ancestry: Unknown

Birth Date:
Death Date:

Father:
Mother:
1st Spouse:
Last/Current Spouse:

Year: 1977
Dongdong-7429

ID: 8005   Sex: Male

Name: **DONGDONG**
2nd Name: DYUNYOR
Surname: DELACRUZ
Agta Ancestry: 43.75%

Birth Date: 1968 +/-1 year
Death Date: January 26, 2009

Father: SIMO
Mother: SALING
1st Spouse: KUNENG-486
Last/Current Spouse: KUNENG-486

Year: 1978
Dongdong-8005

ID: 158   Sex: Male

Name: **DOYEG**
2nd Name:
Surname: BERNABE
Agta Ancestry: 100%

Birth Date: 1919 +/-1 year
Death Date: October 1991

Father: BERNABE
Mother: TOTIYEK
1st Spouse: AWAY-159
Last/Current Spouse: AWAY-159

Year: 1976
Doyeg-158

Year: 1977
Duduyan-168

ID: 168	*Sex:* Male

Name: **DUDUYAN**
2nd Name:
Surname: TOMAY

Agta Ancestry: 100%

Birth Date: 1926 +/-2 years
Death Date: 2003

Father: TOMAY
Mother: LAGEYAN
1st Spouse: GOLBIYENG-169
Last/Current Spouse: GOLBIYENG-169

Year: 2010
Duleng-7502

ID: 7502	*Sex:* Male

Name: **DULENG**
2nd Name: UNDULENG, DOLING
Surname:

Agta Ancestry: Unknown

Birth Date:
Death Date:

Father:
Mother: ETONG
1st Spouse:
Last/Current Spouse:

Year: 2010
Dyak-8224

ID: 8224	*Sex:* Male

Name: **DYAK**
2nd Name:
Surname:

Agta Ancestry: 65.625%

Birth Date: May 27, 1999
Death Date:

Father: DYESI
Mother: ENG-ENG
1st Spouse:
Last/Current Spouse:

Year: 2010
Dyanet-8190

ID: 8190	*Sex:* Female

Name: **DYANET**
2nd Name: ANET
Surname:

Agta Ancestry: 50%

Birth Date: January 2, 1996
Death Date:

Father: BIK
Mother: INGGEL
1st Spouse:
Last/Current Spouse:

49

ID: 3337	*Sex:* Male

Name: **DYEAR**
2nd Name: TOTORIYOT
Surname:

Agta Ancestry: 62.5%

Birth Date: November 4, 1996
Death Date:

Father: UNDI
Mother: HUANA

1st Spouse:
Last/Current Spouse:

Year: 2002
Dyear-3337

ID: 3372	*Sex:* Male

Name: **DYEAR**
2nd Name:
Surname: KUKUAN

Agta Ancestry: 96.88%

Birth Date: May 5, 1998
Death Date: December 2005

Father: ARNOL1 ALOY
Mother: MIKMIK

1st Spouse:
Last/Current Spouse:

Year: 2002
Dyear-3372

ID: 8420	*Sex:* Fetus, still pregna

Name: **DYE-EM**
2nd Name: JM, JOHN MOSES
Surname: INERIA

Agta Ancestry: 18.75%

Birth Date: August 2008
Death Date:

Father: MARBIN
Mother: REHINA

1st Spouse:
Last/Current Spouse:

Year: 2010
Dye-em-8420 & mom
Rehina-8031

ID: 166	*Sex:* Female

Name: **DYEMA**
2nd Name:
Surname: LENDEK

Agta Ancestry: 100%

Birth Date: 1967 +/-2 years
Death Date: 1995 +/-4 years

Father: DUBENG
Mother: ANGHILITA

1st Spouse: NANI-322
Last/Current Spouse: PENANEK-435

Year: 1972
Dyema-166 with Jenny
Headland

1972
Dyema-166 w Janet H phto
by Jim Musgrove

50

ID: 278   Sex: Female

Name: **DYEMA**
2nd Name:
Surname: BEKYADEN
Agta Ancestry: 87.5%

Birth Date: 1968 +/-2 years
Death Date:

Father: RUPINO
Mother: NORMA
1st Spouse: DOMING-9158
Last/Current Spouse: DOMING-9158

Year: 1978
Dyema-278

ID: 8003   Sex: Female

Name: **DYEMA**
2nd Name: NENGNENG
Surname: DELACRUZ
Agta Ancestry: 43.75%

Birth Date: May 3, 1964
Death Date:

Father: SIMO
Mother: SALING
1st Spouse: RIKU-9153
Last/Current Spouse: RIKU-9153

Year: 1978
Dyema-8003

ID: 7929   Sex: Female

Name: **DYEMALIN**
2nd Name:
Surname: LISIDAY
Agta Ancestry: 100%

Birth Date: 1982 +/-9 years
Death Date:

Father:
Mother:

Year: 2008   2010
Dyemalin-7929 w kids   Dyemalin-7929
Matan-7941 and Dyeskia-

1st Spouse: DARET-1104
Last/Current Spouse: DARET-1104

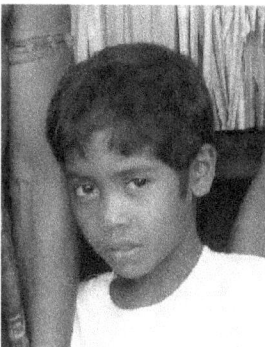

ID: 3437   Sex: Male

Name: **DYEMAR**
2nd Name: TULUK
Surname:
Agta Ancestry: 84.38%

Birth Date: June 2001
Death Date:

Father: TEMING
Mother: LOYDA
1st Spouse:
Last/Current Spouse:

Year: 2010
Dyemar-3437

51

Year: 2006
Dyemari-1125

2010
Dyemari-1125 phto by Anne West

ID:	1125	Sex:	Female

Name: **DYEMARI**
2nd Name:
Surname: ADUANAN
Agta Ancestry: 87.5%

Birth Date: October 26, 1980
Death Date:

Father: SAWE
Mother: KARMEN

1st Spouse:
Last/Current Spouse:

Year: 2010
Dyemari-9299

ID:	9299	Sex:	Female

Name: **DYEMARI**
2nd Name:
Surname:
Agta Ancestry: 50%

Birth Date: 1986 +/-5 years
Death Date:

Father: HUANITO
Mother: MARI

1st Spouse: GLEN-3015
Last/Current Spouse: GLEN-3015

Year: 2008
Dyendyen-8288

ID:	8288	Sex:	Male

Name: **DYENDYEN**
2nd Name: ARDYEN
Surname: VARGAS
Agta Ancestry: 25%

Birth Date: June 5, 1988
Death Date:

Father: DOLPING
Mother: LINDA

1st Spouse: ALMA-7952
Last/Current Spouse: ALMA-7952

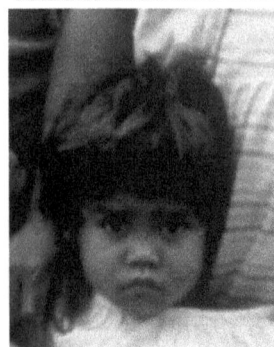

Year: 1994
Dyeni-3209 phto by John Early

ID:	3209	Sex:	Female

Name: **DYENI**
2nd Name:
Surname:
Agta Ancestry: 75%

Birth Date: June 12, 1992
Death Date:

Father: DYERI
Mother: NINI

1st Spouse:
Last/Current Spouse:

52

ID: 3392   *Sex:* Female

Name: **DYENIPER**
2nd Name: BUNSU
Surname: EGMONG

Agta Ancestry: 93.75%

Birth Date: 1992 +/-1 year
Death Date:

Father: MARSILINO
Mother: DYOSIME

1st Spouse:
Last/Current Spouse:

Year: 2002   2008
Dyeniper-3392   Dyeniper-3392

ID: 251   *Sex:* Male

Name: **DYERI**
2nd Name:
Surname: KALANGGET

Agta Ancestry: 93.75%

Birth Date: 1970 +/-1 year
Death Date:

Father: ISON
Mother: NENENG

1st Spouse: SAHINGAN-2069
Last/Current Spouse: SAHINGAN-2069

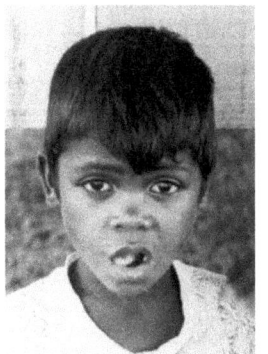

Year: 1978
Dyeri-251

ID: 468   *Sex:* Male

Name: **DYERI**
2nd Name:
Surname: TORIO

Agta Ancestry: 50%

Birth Date: 1969 +/-1 year
Death Date: 2000 +/-1 year

Father: PREDI
Mother: PIRING

1st Spouse: NINI-69
Last/Current Spouse: NARISA-78

Year: 1977
Dyeri-468

ID: 8369   *Sex:* Male

Name: **DYERIKO**
2nd Name:
Surname: KORTES

Agta Ancestry: 37.5%

Birth Date: January 19, 2007
Death Date:

Father: MAYKEL
Mother: PUNENE

1st Spouse:
Last/Current Spouse:

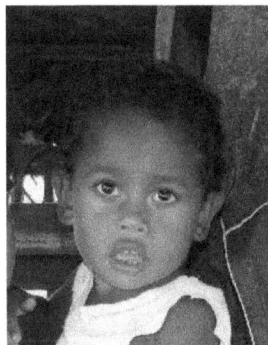

Year: 2010
Dyeriko-8369

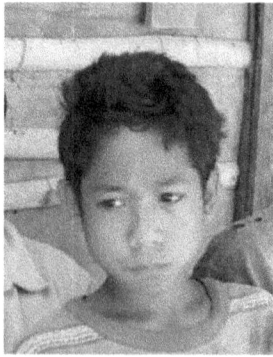

Year: 2008
Dyerom-8290

ID: 8290   Sex: Male

Name: **DYEROM**
2nd Name:
Surname: VARGAS
Agta Ancestry: 25%

Birth Date: January 8, 1995
Death Date:

Father: DOLPING
Mother: LINDA

1st Spouse:
Last/Current Spouse:

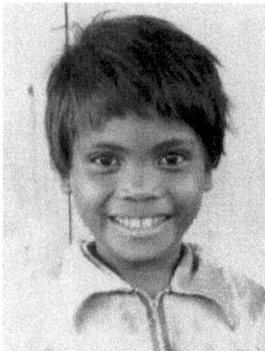

Year: 2002
Dyeron-3144 with mother
Paming-124

ID: 3144   Sex: Male

Name: **DYERON**
2nd Name: ADAW, GUPED
Surname: GERA
Agta Ancestry: 100%

Birth Date: May 1993
Death Date:

Father: DELOY
Mother: PAMING

1st Spouse:
Last/Current Spouse:

Year: 1977
Dyesi-496

2010
Dyesi-496

ID: 496   Sex: Male

Name: **DYESI**
2nd Name:
Surname:
Agta Ancestry: 50%

Birth Date: 1971 +/-1 year
Death Date:

Father: TORIO
Mother: SILENG

1st Spouse: ENG-ENG-292
Last/Current Spouse: ENG-ENG-292

Year: 2008
Dyeskia-7940

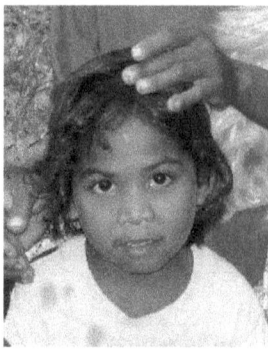

2010
Dyeskia-7940

ID: 7940   Sex: Female

Name: **DYESKIA**
2nd Name:
Surname: LISIDAY
Agta Ancestry: Unknown

Birth Date: December 17, 2002
Death Date:

Father: DARET
Mother: DYEMALIN

1st Spouse:
Last/Current Spouse:

Year: 2006
Dyetli-3563 with Alili 349

ID: 3563   Sex: Male

Name: **DYETLI**
2nd Name:
Surname:

Agta Ancestry: 93.75%

Birth Date: October 20, 2004
Death Date:

Father: UDENG
Mother: ALILI

1st Spouse:
Last/Current Spouse:

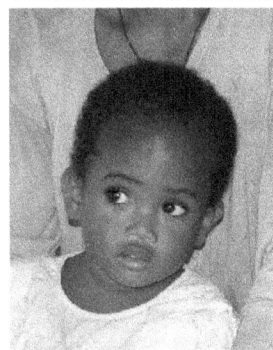

Year: 1976   1977
Dyimi-173   Dyimi-173

ID: 173   Sex: Male

Name: **DYIMI**
2nd Name: DYEMI
Surname: KULIDEG

Agta Ancestry: 100%

Birth Date: 1952 +/-1 year
Death Date: 2007

Father: MANASES
Mother: LUNING

1st Spouse: EKDET-174
Last/Current Spouse: LITA-581

Year: 2008
Dyina-7870 w son Kule-
3626

ID: 7870   Sex: Female

Name: **DYINA**
2nd Name: DAYANA
Surname: RAMUS

Agta Ancestry: Unknown

Birth Date: 1988 +/-4 years
Death Date:

Father: SILONG
Mother: GIWAT

1st Spouse:
Last/Current Spouse:

Year: 2010
Dyinina-3619

ID: 3619   Sex: Female

Name: **DYININA**
2nd Name:
Surname: GERA

Agta Ancestry: 98.44%

Birth Date: February 11, 2008
Death Date:

Father: KATOL
Mother: NANSI

1st Spouse:
Last/Current Spouse:

55

ID:	9198 *Sex:* Male
Name:	**DYOEL**
2nd Name:	NONO
Surname:	LUPAMIYA
Agta Ancestry:	0%
Birth Date:	August 30, 1979
Death Date:	
Father:	
Mother:	
1st Spouse:	HAPEK-1110
Last/Current Spouse:	HAPEK-1110

Year: 2002
Dyoel-9198

2004
Dyoel-9198 w son Dyunel-8249

ID:	8090 *Sex:* Female
Name:	**DYOLIBI**
2nd Name:	OLEN
Surname:	ESTEVES
Agta Ancestry:	25%
Birth Date:	1980 +/-1 year
Death Date:	
Father:	HULYU
Mother:	LEBI
1st Spouse:	MARK-9215
Last/Current Spouse:	MARK-9215

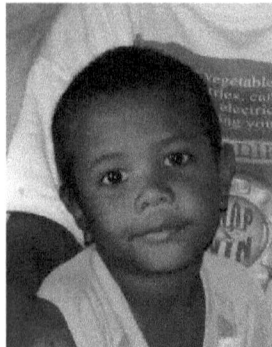

Year: 2008
Dyolibi-8090 & Mark-9215 & 2 kids.

ID:	3593 *Sex:* Male
Name:	**DYONAS**
2nd Name:	
Surname:	
Agta Ancestry:	65.625%
Birth Date:	August 13, 2005
Death Date:	
Father:	DYESI
Mother:	ENG-ENG
1st Spouse:	
Last/Current Spouse:	

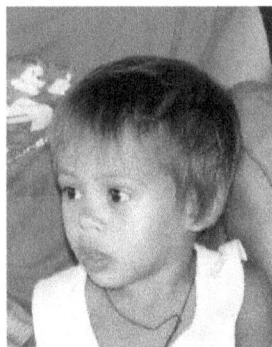

Year: 2010
Dyonas-3593

ID:	8385 *Sex:* Male
Name:	**DYONAS**
2nd Name:	
Surname:	ENERIA
Agta Ancestry:	18.75%
Birth Date:	November 29, 2006
Death Date:	
Father:	MARBIN
Mother:	REHINA
1st Spouse:	
Last/Current Spouse:	

Year: 2010
Dyonas-8385

ID: 176   Sex: Male

Name: **DYONI**
2nd Name: LUISITO, LITO
Surname: LOPES, BUMALUN

Agta Ancestry: 100%

Birth Date: November 7, 1957
Death Date: 2000 +/-1 year

Father: LOPES
Mother: LILYA
1st Spouse: UKES-7856
Last/Current Spouse: UKES-7856

Year: 1978
Dyoni-176

ID: 364   Sex: Female

Name: **DYOSALIN**
2nd Name:
Surname: TIKIMAN

Agta Ancestry: 93.75%

Birth Date: 1966 +/-1 year
Death Date:

Father: MARIO
Mother: LODI
1st Spouse: SIDRO-9014
Last/Current Spouse: SIDRO-9014

Year: 1976
Dyosalin-364

ID: 121   Sex: Female

Name: **DYOSI**
2nd Name: AGNES
Surname: ISTANES, LISIDAY

Agta Ancestry: 96.875%

Birth Date: February 1977
Death Date:

Father: DARBING
Mother: NERSI
1st Spouse: GANI-9241
Last/Current Spouse: GANI-9241

Year: 2008
Dyosi-121

ID: 4026   Sex: Female

Name: **DYOSI**
2nd Name:
Surname:

Agta Ancestry: 100%

Birth Date: 1975 +/-6 years
Death Date:

Father:
Mother:
1st Spouse:
Last/Current Spouse:

Year: 2010
Dyosi-4026

57

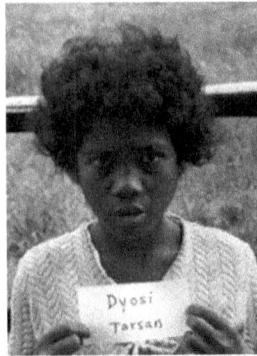

Year: 1978
Dyosime-28

2002
Dyosime-28

ID: 28　　　　Sex: Female

Name: **DYOSIME**
2nd Name:
Surname: AGAM
Agta Ancestry: 100%

Birth Date: 1971 +/-3 years
Death Date: May 2007

Father: GITADEN
Mother: DEBYENG
1st Spouse: MARSILINO-569
Last/Current Spouse: MARSILINO-569

Year: 2008
Dyoyan-8136 holding son
Lideg-8373

ID: 8136　　　　Sex: Female

Name: **DYOYAN**
2nd Name: KOYKOY
Surname: BITIGAN
Agta Ancestry: 50%

Birth Date: 1991
Death Date:

Father: BAIT
Mother: NINI
1st Spouse: RIKI-8032
Last/Current Spouse: RIKI-8032

Year: 1994
Dyundyun-1130 phto by
John Early

ID: 1130　　　　Sex: Male

Name: **DYUNDYUN**
2nd Name: BAHON
Surname: TORIO
Agta Ancestry: 50%

Birth Date: 1980
Death Date:

Father: PREDI
Mother: PIRING
1st Spouse: LANI-7835
Last/Current Spouse: LANI-7835

Year: 2008
Dyundyun-8325

ID: 8325　　　　Sex: Male

Name: **DYUNDYUN**
2nd Name:
Surname: MIRANYA
Agta Ancestry: 50%

Birth Date: June 8, 2004
Death Date:

Father: RENE
Mother: MAYLA
1st Spouse:
Last/Current Spouse:

Year: 1977
Dyunyor-147

2008
Dyunyor-147

ID: 147　　　　　　Sex: Male

Name: **DYUNYOR**
2nd Name:
Surname: BALENSIA
Agta Ancestry: 50%

Birth Date: 1966 +/-1 year
Death Date:

Father: DOMING
Mother: LILYA
1st Spouse: PELUK-2064
Last/Current Spouse: PELUK-2064

Year: 1977
Dyunyor-259

ID: 259　　　　　　Sex: Male

Name: **DYUNYOR**
2nd Name: KALIWETWET
Surname: SAGUNED
Agta Ancestry: 100%

Birth Date: 1965 +/-1 year
Death Date: May 2004

Father: KANDEG
Mother: MENSIANG
1st Spouse: MAAL-606
Last/Current Spouse: ESA-7328

Year: 1978
Ebet-92

ID: 92　　　　　　Sex: Female

Name: **EBET**
2nd Name:
Surname:
Agta Ancestry: 100%

Birth Date: 1917 +/-5 years
Death Date: 1979 +/-1 year

Father: PINTUNGAN
Mother: unknown
1st Spouse: ARNES-33
Last/Current Spouse: ARNES-33

Year: 1998
Eda-178

ID: 178　　　　　　Sex: Male

Name: **EDA**
2nd Name:
Surname: BANTUG
Agta Ancestry: 100%

Birth Date: 1930 +/-3 years
Death Date: 2005 +/-1 year

Father: BANTUG
Mother: KALINGGANG
1st Spouse: TILOKEN-179
Last/Current Spouse: TILOKEN-179

Year: 2010
Edikar-3132

ID: 3132	*Sex:* Male

Name: **EDIKAR**
2nd Name: BATOY
Surname: PRADO

Agta Ancestry: 87.5%

Birth Date: September 14, 1990
Death Date:

Father: HEMPOK
Mother: EDNA

1st Spouse:
Last/Current Spouse:

Year: 2010
Edlin-1017

ID: 1017	*Sex:* Male

Name: **EDLIN**
2nd Name: BAGTAK
Surname: GEHA, GERA

Agta Ancestry: 96.875%

Birth Date: 1982
Death Date:

Father: BERIONES
Mother: MELTING

1st Spouse: MAYLIN-3193
Last/Current Spouse: MAYLIN-3193

Year: 2006
Edna-234

2010
Edna-234

ID: 234	*Sex:* Female

Name: **EDNA**
2nd Name:
Surname: ADUANAN, PRADO

Agta Ancestry: 100%

Birth Date: October 1960
Death Date:

Father: KEKEK
Mother: LUNINGNING

1st Spouse: HEMPOK-233
Last/Current Spouse: HEMPOK-233

Year: 1979
Ednalin-227

2010
Ednalin-227

ID: 227	*Sex:* Female

Name: **EDNALIN**
2nd Name:
Surname: ABUNDIO, AMERINDU

Agta Ancestry: 75%

Birth Date: 1973 +/-2 years
Death Date:

Father: HAYME
Mother: NATI

1st Spouse: AMPANG-9199
Last/Current Spouse: AMPANG-9199

60

Year: 2010
Edwin-388

ID:	388	*Sex:* Male

Name: **EDWIN**
2nd Name: BALINTINO
Surname: DIYOSINO

Agta Ancestry: 46.875%

Birth Date: 1975 +/-1 year
Death Date:

Father: DANILO
Mother: MELI
1st Spouse: SUSAN-3187
Last/Current Spouse: SUSAN-3187

Year: 1979
Edyor-185

ID:	185	*Sex:* Male

Name: **EDYOR**
2nd Name:
Surname: SADYEN

Agta Ancestry: 100%

Birth Date: 1949 +/-3 years
Death Date: June 3, 1984

Father: SADYEN
Mother: LAWTING
1st Spouse: ELPOH-186
Last/Current Spouse: ELPOH-186

Year: 1977
Ekdet-174 holding daughtr
Abeng-175

ID:	174	*Sex:* Female

Name: **EKDET**
2nd Name:
Surname: TIKIMAN

Agta Ancestry: 100%

Birth Date: 1954 +/-2 years
Death Date: June 15, 1985

Father: TIKIMAN
Mother: LAYDING
1st Spouse: DYIMI-173
Last/Current Spouse: DYIMI-173

Year: 1986
Elaw-479

ID:	479	*Sex:* Female

Name: **ELAW**
2nd Name: ALAW
Surname:

Agta Ancestry: 49.5%

Birth Date: 1974 +/-1 year
Death Date:

Father: TARO
Mother: PILISITA
1st Spouse:
Last/Current Spouse:

Year: 1976
Elding-188

ID: 188   Sex: Male

Name: **ELDING**
2nd Name:
Surname: GERERO
Agta Ancestry: 100%

Birth Date: 1950 +/-2 years
Death Date: February 22, 1993

Father: BELYASING
Mother: SAGED

1st Spouse: NEMI-189
Last/Current Spouse: NEMI-189

Year: 1965
Eleden-191 with Rachel
Headland

1972
Eleden-191 phto by Jim
Musgrove

ID: 191   Sex: Male

Name: **ELEDEN**
2nd Name:
Surname: ADUANAN
Agta Ancestry: 100%

Birth Date: 1931 +/-1 year
Death Date: March 30, 2002

Father: BALIWENGWENG
Mother: MONGGEY

1st Spouse: ERMINYA-192
Last/Current Spouse: ERMINYA-192

Year: 1977
Eleng-557

ID: 557   Sex: Male

Name: **ELENG**
2nd Name:
Surname: GERERO
Agta Ancestry: 100%

Birth Date: 1970 +/-1 year
Death Date:

Father: SUWAR
Mother: MILA

1st Spouse: NILDA-7836
Last/Current Spouse: NILDA-7836

Year: 1976
Eli-380 (center) holding
Mayla-384 & son Hilintok-

ID: 380   Sex: Female

Name: **ELI**
2nd Name: NELI
Surname: ANGIDEW
Agta Ancestry: Unknown

Birth Date: 1935 +/-1 year
Death Date: December 1998

Father: DIKMIN
Mother: PINYANG

1st Spouse: MELANIO-379
Last/Current Spouse: MELANIO-379

Year: 1978
Eli-8008

ID: 8008 Sex: Female

Name: **ELI**
2nd Name:
Surname: DEPABLO

Agta Ancestry: 25%

Birth Date: 1948 +/-3 years
Death Date:

Father: PILO
Mother: NENA
1st Spouse: PABLING-9035
Last/Current Spouse: PABLING-9035

Year: 2010
Eliboy-327

ID: 327 Sex: Male

Name: **ELIBOY**
2nd Name: BUTOY, OTOY
Surname:

Agta Ancestry: 46.88%

Birth Date: 1975 +/-1 year
Death Date:

Father: SIDRO
Mother: LOSI
1st Spouse: PUNENE-1013
Last/Current Spouse: OSANG-9223

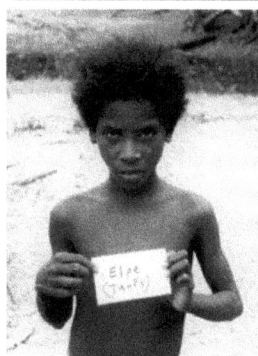

Year: 1978   2008
Elpi-562   Elpi-562

ID: 562 Sex: Male

Name: **ELPI**
2nd Name: ELPE
Surname:

Agta Ancestry: 100%

Birth Date: 1966 +/-3 years
Death Date:

Father: TANES
Mother: PORMING
1st Spouse: WAYNALIN-198
Last/Current Spouse: WAYNALIN-198

Year: 1979
Elpoh-186

ID: 186 Sex: Female

Name: **ELPOH**
2nd Name: MERSING
Surname:

Agta Ancestry: 100%

Birth Date: 1946 +/-3 years
Death Date: July 17, 1985

Father: TANES
Mother: LIYANING
1st Spouse: EDYOR-185
Last/Current Spouse: EDYOR-185

63

Year: 2008
Eman-3516

ID: 3516	Sex: Male

Name: **EMAN**
2nd Name: IMANWEL
Surname: ADUANAN

Agta Ancestry: 100%

Birth Date: February 9, 2004
Death Date:

Father: ALEK
Mother: LINDA

1st Spouse:
Last/Current Spouse:

Year: 1977
Emili-195

ID: 195	Sex: Female

Name: **EMILI**
2nd Name:
Surname: KORITANA

Agta Ancestry: 75%

Birth Date: 1952 +/-2 years
Death Date: 1980

Father: RONGKEL
Mother: PISING

1st Spouse: LALING-299
Last/Current Spouse: NAYDU-567

Year: 1979
Emili-356

ID: 356	Sex: Female

Name: **EMILI**
2nd Name: EMILIN, REMELITA
Surname: ARSENIA

Agta Ancestry: 87.5%

Birth Date: 1960 +/-2 years
Death Date: 1995 +/-4 years

Father: EMPERADOR
Mother: AGEY

1st Spouse: DYIMI-7628
Last/Current Spouse: DYIMI-7628

Year: 1976
Emiling-505

ID: 505	Sex: Female

Name: **EMILING**
2nd Name:
Surname: TULIO

Agta Ancestry: Unknown

Birth Date: 1957 +/-1 year
Death Date:

Father: LAKAY
Mother: KONSITA

1st Spouse: ROHEL-504
Last/Current Spouse: ROHEL-504

Year: 1966
Ending-196

Year: 2008
Ending-196

ID:	196	*Sex:* Male

Name: **ENDING**
2nd Name:
Surname: TULIO
Agta Ancestry: 100%

Birth Date: 1944 +/-1 year
Death Date:

Father: TULIO
Mother: LIPANYAW
1st Spouse: NUNUK-197
Last/Current Spouse: LIMINIDA-41

Year: 1977
Eng-eng-292

Year: 2010
Eng-eng-292

ID:	292	*Sex:* Female

Name: **ENG-ENG**
2nd Name: SEYNAYDA
Surname: MORA
Agta Ancestry: 81.25%

Birth Date: July 15, 1970
Death Date:

Father: GUBEK
Mother: SABILITA
1st Spouse: DYESI-496
Last/Current Spouse: DYESI-496

Year: 1977
Engget-105

ID:	105	*Sex:* Male

Name: **ENGGET**
2nd Name: BENI, DYUNYOR
Surname: DATOG, DEMADES, PREDO
Agta Ancestry: 100%

Birth Date: 1974 +/-1 year
Death Date:

Father: BUNAW
Mother: LODI
1st Spouse:
Last/Current Spouse:

Year: 2010
Eprayan-9306 w mom
Osang-9223

ID:	9306	*Sex:* Male

Name: **EPRAYAN**
2nd Name:
Surname:
Agta Ancestry: 29.69%

Birth Date: February 10, 2009
Death Date:

Father: ELIBOY
Mother: OSANG
1st Spouse:
Last/Current Spouse:

Year: 2010
Epril-8189

ID: 8189   Sex: Female

Name: **EPRIL**
2nd Name:
Surname: DESKARGA
Agta Ancestry: 37.5%

Birth Date: 1990 +/-3 years
Death Date:

Father: BOY
Mother: KUNENG

1st Spouse:
Last/Current Spouse:

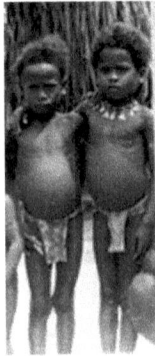

Year: 1973
Erik-545 on left w Dyunyor-259

ID: 545   Sex: Male

Name: **ERIK**
2nd Name: KALIPUNTO
Surname: SANGBAY
Agta Ancestry: 100%

Birth Date: 1965 +/-2 years
Death Date:

Father: SINABUYAN
Mother: MIDING

1st Spouse: AMIKAN-7865
Last/Current Spouse: SAGPO-7866

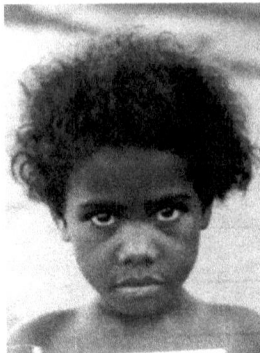

Year: 1978
Erlinda-341

ID: 341   Sex: Female

Name: **ERLINDA**
2nd Name: LINDA, NENENG
Surname: BINGGOSA
Agta Ancestry: 100%

Birth Date: 1972 +/-1 year
Death Date:

Father: MAMORA
Mother: LULITA

1st Spouse: MARIANO-9025
Last/Current Spouse: MARIANO-9025

Year: 1967   1977
Erminya-192   Erminya-192

ID: 192   Sex: Female

Name: **ERMINYA**
2nd Name: NIEK, BIYEK
Surname: PAWISAN
Agta Ancestry: 100%

Birth Date: 1933 +/-1 year
Death Date: March 11, 1995

Father: PAWISAN
Mother: PILISA

1st Spouse: ELEDEN-191
Last/Current Spouse: ELEDEN-191

66

Year: 1978
Erning-201

2008
Erning-201

ID:	201	Sex: Male

Name: **ERNING**
2nd Name: ERNESTO
Surname: MORAL

Agta Ancestry: 50%

Birth Date: 1938 +/-1 year
Death Date:

Father: MORAL
Mother: PIDELA
1st Spouse: ISLING-202
Last/Current Spouse: ISLING-202

Year: 2010
Erwin-3121

ID:	3121	Sex: Male

Name: **ERWIN**
2nd Name: AMBULOY
Surname:

Agta Ancestry: 100%

Birth Date: 1988
Death Date:

Father: SELTON
Mother: NENENG
1st Spouse: BALILIT-3018
Last/Current Spouse: BALILIT-3018

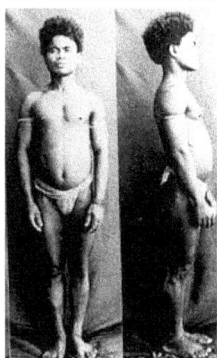

Year: 1936
Esmundo-5744
photo by Vanoverbergh

1963
Esmundo-5744

ID:	5744	Sex: Male

Name: **ESMUNDO**
2nd Name: MOYES
Surname: AMADANG

Agta Ancestry: 100%

Birth Date: 1915 +/-5 years
Death Date: 1973 +/-2 years

Father: AMADANG
Mother:
1st Spouse: ANGELITA-5572
Last/Current Spouse: LELYENG-5217

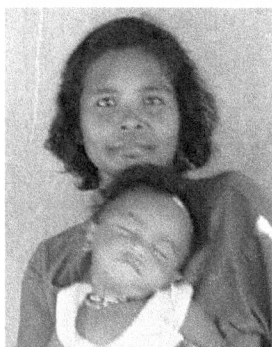

Year: 2008
Eta-7915, holding daughtr
Leya-7947

ID:	7915	Sex: Female

Name: **ETA**
2nd Name:
Surname:

Agta Ancestry: Unknown

Birth Date: 1976 +/-9 years
Death Date:

Father: ELIS
Mother: ESMENYA
1st Spouse: LUSITO-7946
Last/Current Spouse: PALAKOK-1038

67

ID:	7530
Sex:	Female
Name:	**ETEK**
2nd Name:	
Surname:	
Agta Ancestry:	Unknown
Birth Date:	1964 +/-5 years
Death Date:	
Father:	
Mother:	LIYANITA
1st Spouse:	
Last/Current Spouse:	

Year: 1977
Etek-7530

ID:	7498
Sex:	Female
Name:	**ETONG**
2nd Name:	
Surname:	GAMELEN
Agta Ancestry:	Unknown
Birth Date:	1928 +/-9 years
Death Date:	1985 +/-9 years
Father:	AYMAYEN
Mother:	GAMENEN
1st Spouse:	PARIDES-7499
Last/Current Spouse:	DOLING-7065

Year: 1977
Etong-7498

ID:	205
Sex:	Male
Name:	**ETOY**
2nd Name:	
Surname:	LUNA
Agta Ancestry:	100%
Birth Date:	1941 +/-2 years
Death Date:	
Father:	LUNA
Mother:	KUDAY
1st Spouse:	HILING-5157
Last/Current Spouse:	TESI-535

Year: 1977
Etoy-205 holding daughtr
Mikmik-206

ID:	3048
Sex:	Male
Name:	**GABI**
2nd Name:	
Surname:	PAWISAN
Agta Ancestry:	75%
Birth Date:	1987
Death Date:	
Father:	PIKSON
Mother:	HELING
1st Spouse:	LELEMBOT-8188
Last/Current Spouse:	LELEMBOT-8188

Year: 2010
Gabi-3048

Year: 1964
Gahang-7076 holding
Rachel Headland

ID: 7076   Sex: Male

Name: **GAHANG**
2nd Name:
Surname:

Agta Ancestry: 100%

Birth Date: 1901 +/-3 years
Death Date: 1970

Father:
Mother:

1st Spouse: ARENTINA-26
Last/Current Spouse: ADILING-512

Year: 1977
Galampon-55

ID: 55   Sex: Male

Name: **GALAMPONG**
2nd Name: NESTOR
Surname: MISAN

Agta Ancestry: 100%

Birth Date: 1971 +/-1 year
Death Date: February 2001

Father: BEDBED
Mother: KARNASIYON

1st Spouse: MAYLIN-221
Last/Current Spouse: MAYLIN-221

Year: 1977
Galut-431

ID: 431   Sex: Male

Name: **GALUT**
2nd Name:
Surname: BEKYADEN

Agta Ancestry: 93.75%

Birth Date: 1966 +/-2 years
Death Date:

Father: PABLING
Mother: KARMIN

1st Spouse: TENGEDEN-7837
Last/Current Spouse: TENGEDEN-7837

Year: 1966
Ganing-5143 on right with
cousin Lita-581

ID: 5143   Sex: Male

Name: **GANING**
2nd Name:
Surname:

Agta Ancestry: 100%

Birth Date: 1949 +/-2 years
Death Date: 1969 +/-2 years

Father: RUMINES
Mother: ADILING

1st Spouse:
Last/Current Spouse:

69

Year: 2008
Gari-3163

ID: 3163   Sex: Male

Name: **GARI**
2nd Name: BUTAYAW
Surname: KUKUAN
Agta Ancestry: 90.63%

Birth Date: February 7, 1985
Death Date:

Father: LITO
Mother: IMELDA
1st Spouse: MELAGA-3011
Last/Current Spouse: MELAGA-3011

Year: 2008
Gari-8199

ID: 8199   Sex: Male

Name: **GARI**
2nd Name:
Surname:
Agta Ancestry: 46.875%

Birth Date: June 11, 1987
Death Date:

Father: MARIANO
Mother: SELYA
1st Spouse:
Last/Current Spouse:

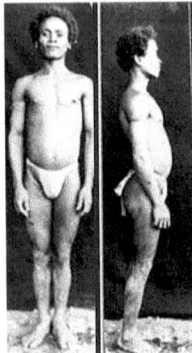

Year: 1936
Gawdensio-5148
photo by Vanoverbergh

ID: 5148   Sex: Male

Name: **GAWDENSIO**
2nd Name:
Surname:
Agta Ancestry: 100%

Birth Date: 1900 +/-7 years
Death Date: 1955 +/-9 years

Father: INGGONA
Mother: OKONG
1st Spouse: PANYANG-5348
Last/Current Spouse: PANYANG-5348

Year: 1978
Getek-612

ID: 612   Sex: Female

Name: **GETEK**
2nd Name:
Surname: TOMAY, TETYOK
Agta Ancestry: 93.75%

Birth Date: 1954 +/-1 year
Death Date:

Father: TETYOK
Mother: ISTING
1st Spouse: WALALO-2075
Last/Current Spouse: WALALO-2075

Year: 2010
Gewel-7511

ID: 7511   *Sex:* Female

Name: **GEWEL**
2nd Name:
Surname:

Agta Ancestry: Unknown

Birth Date:
Death Date:

Father:
Mother:

1st Spouse: LAKAS-9102
Last/Current Spouse: LAKAS-9102

Year: 1966
Gibson-207 & wife
Dengdeng-2015 holding

1967
Gibson-207

ID: 207   *Sex:* Male

Name: **GIBSON**
2nd Name: LAKE
Surname: ADUANAN

Agta Ancestry: 87.5%

Birth Date: 1946 +/-1 year
Death Date: October 12, 1992

Father: DIKMIN
Mother: PINYANG

1st Spouse: DENGDENG-2015
Last/Current Spouse: DENGDENG-2015

Year: 1977
Gidong-7538 holding son
Rodi-7539

ID: 7538   *Sex:* Female

Name: **GIDONG**
2nd Name:
Surname:

Agta Ancestry: Unknown

Birth Date: 1949 +/-5 years
Death Date:

Father: TADIO
Mother: BINING

1st Spouse: ORDONYA-7537
Last/Current Spouse: ORDONYA-7537

Year: 1977
Giwat-333

ID: 333   *Sex:* Female

Name: **GIWAT**
2nd Name: LOSAMINDA
Surname: BERNABE

Agta Ancestry: 100%

Birth Date: 1965 +/-2 years
Death Date:

Father: MADYANING
Mother: KARIDAD

1st Spouse: SILONG-7864
Last/Current Spouse: SILONG-7864

71

Year: 2006
Glaysa-8206

ID:	8206 Sex: Female
Name:	**GLAYSA**
2nd Name:	
Surname:	FRANCISCO
Agta Ancestry:	37.5%
Birth Date:	November 1997
Death Date:	
Father:	IDAG
Mother:	WISAY
1st Spouse:	
Last/Current Spouse:	

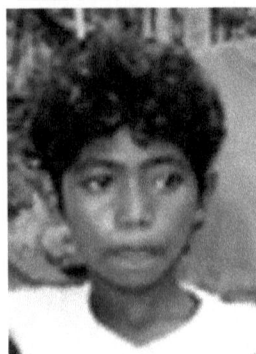

Year: 2002   2010
Glen-3015   Glen-3015

ID:	3015 Sex: Male
Name:	**GLEN**
2nd Name:	
Surname:	
Agta Ancestry:	100%
Birth Date:	March 1987
Death Date:	
Father:	HINGET
Mother:	BITA
1st Spouse:	DYEMARI-9299
Last/Current Spouse:	DYEMARI-9299

Year: 1976
Golbiyeng-169

ID:	169 Sex: Female
Name:	**GOLBIYENG**
2nd Name:	
Surname:	BITIGAN
Agta Ancestry:	100%
Birth Date:	1929 +/-2 years
Death Date:	2003
Father:	BITIGAN
Mother:	KANORA
1st Spouse:	DUDUYAN-168
Last/Current Spouse:	DUDUYAN-168

Year: 1976
Gomel-74 holding sister
Dyeniper-76

ID:	74 Sex: Female
Name:	**GOMEL**
2nd Name:	ROSALINDA
Surname:	AGINALDO
Agta Ancestry:	100%
Birth Date:	1968 +/-1 year
Death Date:	1993 +/-5 years
Father:	BILYANTING
Mother:	PINING
1st Spouse:	DANI-9110
Last/Current Spouse:	DANI-9110

ID: 3069   *Sex:* Female

Name: **GRES**
2nd Name: MARIGRES
Surname: BEKYADEN

Agta Ancestry: 93.75%

Birth Date: March 1985
Death Date:

Father: LENGLENG
Mother: MARILIN
1st Spouse: DALENG-1048
Last/Current Spouse: DALENG-1048

Year: 2010
Gres-3069

ID: 7079   *Sex:* Male

Name: **GUBEK**
2nd Name:
Surname:

Agta Ancestry: 100%

Birth Date: 1935 +/-3 years
Death Date: March 2007

Father: DAWENG
Mother: AWRORA
1st Spouse: PENI-463
Last/Current Spouse: PENI-463

Year: 2006
Gubek-7079

ID: 213   *Sex:* Female

Name: **GURING**
2nd Name:
Surname: MAYNA

Agta Ancestry: 100%

Birth Date: 1943 +/-2 years
Death Date:

Father: MAYNA
Mother: TUKONG
1st Spouse: PELIMON-5361
Last/Current Spouse: SIMO-9041

Year: 1977
Guring-213

ID: 217   *Sex:* Male

Name: **HAKOB**
2nd Name:
Surname: PRADO

Agta Ancestry: 75%

Birth Date: 1944 +/-2 years
Death Date:

Father: PIRENTE
Mother: ISTRING
1st Spouse: PELI-218
Last/Current Spouse: PELI-218

Year: 1976
Hakob-217

73

Year: 2002
Hapek-1110

2004
Hapek-1110 phto by Iris
Dalberto

ID: 1110	*Sex:* Female
Name: **HAPEK**	
2nd Name: PRODILIN	
Surname: PRADO	
Agta Ancestry: 75%	
Birth Date: June 1981	
Death Date:	
Father: NATENG	
Mother: TETET	
1st Spouse: DYOEL-9198	
Last/Current Spouse: DYOEL-9198	

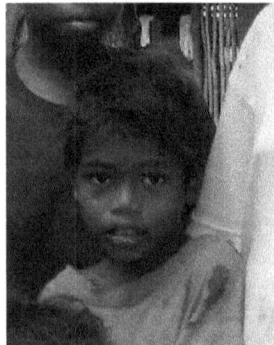

Year: 2010
Harurut-3510

ID: 3510	*Sex:* Male
Name: **HARURUT**	
2nd Name: KRISTUPER, ANDI	
Surname:	
Agta Ancestry: 62.5%	
Birth Date: July 2003	
Death Date:	
Father: UNDI	
Mother: HUANA	
1st Spouse:	
Last/Current Spouse:	

Year: 1977
Hasmen-7081

ID: 7081	*Sex:* Female
Name: **HASMIN**	
2nd Name: DYESI	
Surname:	
Agta Ancestry: Unknown	
Birth Date:	
Death Date:	
Father:	
Mother:	
1st Spouse: SINTON-254	
Last/Current Spouse: SINTON-254	

Year: 1978
Hayme-223

ID: 223	*Sex:* Male
Name: **HAYME**	
2nd Name:	
Surname: ABUNDIO, MIRINDU	
Agta Ancestry: 50%	
Birth Date: 1935 +/-2 years	
Death Date: January 4, 1998	
Father: MILIHINDU	
Mother: PIDELA	
1st Spouse: NATI-2061	
Last/Current Spouse: NATI-2061	

Year: 1976
Hayme-228 holding daughtr
Aylling-231

ID: 228   Sex: Male

Name: **HAYME**
2nd Name:
Surname: MIYA, PASIO
Agta Ancestry: 100%

Birth Date: 1943 +/-2 years
Death Date:

Father: PASIO
Mother: ISTRING
1st Spouse: MIRING-229
Last/Current Spouse: MIRING-229

Year: 2010
Hayme-4025

ID: 4025   Sex: Male

Name: **HAYME**
2nd Name: Kulebung
Surname:
Agta Ancestry: 100%

Birth Date: 1969 +/-7 years
Death Date:

Father: DESAG
Mother: BENDULING
1st Spouse:
Last/Current Spouse:

Year: 1966
Helen-605, holding Steve
Headland

1976
Helen-605

ID: 605   Sex: Female

Name: **HELEN**
2nd Name:
Surname: ANGIDEW
Agta Ancestry: 87.5%

Birth Date: 1952 +/-1 year
Death Date: October 27, 1982

Father: DIKMIN
Mother: PINYANG
1st Spouse: ULEG-604
Last/Current Spouse: ULEG-604

Year: 1978
Heling-489

2010
Heling-489

ID: 489   Sex: Female

Name: **HELING**
2nd Name:
Surname: ADUANAN
Agta Ancestry: 100%

Birth Date: 1955 +/-3 years
Death Date:

Father: MAWAS
Mother: BIDING
1st Spouse: MARIANING-369
Last/Current Spouse: PIKSON-488

Year: 1976
Hempok-233

2010
Hempok-233

ID: 233   Sex: Male

Name: **HEMPOK**
2nd Name: LITO
Surname: PRADO

Agta Ancestry: 75%

Birth Date: 1958 +/-1 year
Death Date:

Father: PIRENTE
Mother: ISTRING
1st Spouse: EDNA-234
Last/Current Spouse: EDNA-234

Year: 1976
Heneroso-193

2008
Heneroso-193

ID: 193   Sex: Male

Name: **HENEROSO**
2nd Name: HENE
Surname: ADUANAN

Agta Ancestry: 100%

Birth Date: August 22, 1961
Death Date:

Father: ELEDEN
Mother: ERMINYA
1st Spouse: LINDA-307
Last/Current Spouse: LINDA-307

Year: 1965
Heranya-7084

ID: 7084   Sex: Female

Name: **HERANYA**
2nd Name:
Surname:

Agta Ancestry: 100%

Birth Date: 1928 +/-4 years
Death Date:

Father: TAYAMAN
Mother: BINITA
1st Spouse: MAKUTEY-7802
Last/Current Spouse: BIDAL-7030

Year: 2004
Hilintok-385 & Ayrin-1108 w
their 5 kids.

ID: 385   Sex: Male

Name: **HILINTOK**
2nd Name: WILYAM
Surname: KULIDEG

Agta Ancestry: Unknown

Birth Date: 1974
Death Date:

Father: MELANIO
Mother: ELI
1st Spouse: AYRIN-1108
Last/Current Spouse: AYRIN-1108

Year: 1984
Hinget-2038 holding
daughter Dina-2039

ID:	2038	*Sex:* Male
Name:	**HINGET**	
2nd Name:	BIKTOR	
Surname:		
Agta Ancestry: 100%		
Birth Date:	1957	
Death Date:	August 21, 2005	
Father:	PANGEL	
Mother:	PINOSA	
1st Spouse:	BITA-237	
Last/Current Spouse:	BITA-237	

Year: 1978
Homer-238

ID:	238	*Sex:* Male
Name:	**HOMER**	
2nd Name:		
Surname:	LUNA	
Agta Ancestry: 100%		
Birth Date:	1946 +/-1 year	
Death Date:		
Father:	LUNA	
Mother:	KUDAY	
1st Spouse:	LIDIA-312	
Last/Current Spouse:	OSA-7428	

Year: 1965
Hosbel-7688 & Hunter-7443

1966
Hosbel-7688

ID:	7688	*Sex:* Male
Name:	**HOSBEL**	
2nd Name:		
Surname:		
Agta Ancestry: 100%		
Birth Date:	1948 +/-1 year	
Death Date:		
Father:	BUKAN	
Mother:	ISTRING	
1st Spouse:	ELI-7709	
Last/Current Spouse:	ELI-7709	

Year: 1998
Hose-8169 & wife Kuluding-
601

2010
Hose-8169

ID:	8169	*Sex:* Male
Name:	**HOSE**	
2nd Name:		
Surname:	MEHARES, ANGARA	
Agta Ancestry: 43.75%		
Birth Date:	1968	
Death Date:		
Father:	ESTONG	
Mother:	MILING	
1st Spouse:	KULUDING-601	
Last/Current Spouse:	MELTING-481	

Year: 1977
Hoseg-483

ID: 483   Sex: Female

Name: **HOSEG**
2nd Name: DYOSI
Surname: SIKATAN
Agta Ancestry: 93.75%

Birth Date: 1969 +/-2 years
Death Date: February 1984

Father: BILYANTING
Mother: ROSITA

1st Spouse:
Last/Current Spouse:

Year: 1977
Huan-67

ID: 67   Sex: Male

Name: **HUAN**
2nd Name: HUWAN
Surname: BEKYADEN
Agta Ancestry: Unknown

Birth Date: 1959 +/-1 year
Death Date:

Father: BIDOY
Mother: MAKARIA

1st Spouse: UKEL-466
Last/Current Spouse: UKEL-466

Year: 2002   2010
Huana-1016 holding Boldog-   Huana-1016
3373

ID: 1016   Sex: Female

Name: **HUANA**
2nd Name:
Surname: ISTANES
Agta Ancestry: 25%

Birth Date: January 1978
Death Date:

Father: JUAN
Mother: BILINDA

1st Spouse: UNDI-319
Last/Current Spouse: UNDI-319

Year: 1978
Huanita-429

ID: 429   Sex: Female

Name: **HUANITA**
2nd Name: WANITA
Surname: BASULEW
Agta Ancestry: 100%

Birth Date: 1955 +/-2 years
Death Date: 1995 +/-3 years

Father: DADUK
Mother: AMPARING

1st Spouse: OSMING-428
Last/Current Spouse: OSMING-428

Year: 1978
Hulyeta-8345

2008
Hulyeta-8345

ID:	8345	Sex: Female

Name: **HULYETA**
2nd Name:
Surname: EPA
Agta Ancestry: 25%

Birth Date: July 4, 1965
Death Date:

Father: MITERIO
Mother: NANITA
1st Spouse: RODYEL-9263
Last/Current Spouse: RODYEL-9263

Year: 1965
Hunter-7443

1966
Hunter-7443

ID:	7443	Sex: Male

Name: **HUNTER**
2nd Name:
Surname:
Agta Ancestry: 100%

Birth Date: 1947 +/-1 year
Death Date:

Father: PAGITULENG
Mother: KENGKENG
1st Spouse: KORDING-7923
Last/Current Spouse: KORDING-7923

Year: 1977
Huwaning-7350

ID:	7350	Sex: Male

Name: **HUWANING**
2nd Name:
Surname: GUSMAN
Agta Ancestry: 100%

Birth Date: 1937 +/-5 years
Death Date:

Father: IGNASIO
Mother: EBUN
1st Spouse: ISING-7093
Last/Current Spouse: ISING-7093

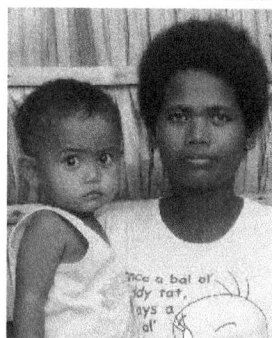

Year: 2010
Ian-Dyo-8400 w mom Dyosi-
121

ID:	8400	Sex: Male

Name: **IAN-DYOSWA**
2nd Name:
Surname: ALKANTARA
Agta Ancestry: 48.437%

Birth Date: October 3, 2008
Death Date:

Father: GANI
Mother: DYOSI
1st Spouse:
Last/Current Spouse:

ID:	2041 *Sex:* Male
Name:	**IBEN**
2nd Name:	
Surname:	PULUMENO DUNATO
Agta Ancestry:	Unknown
Birth Date:	1940 +/-3 years
Death Date:	
Father:	PULUMENO
Mother:	ISAY
1st Spouse:	BERHINYA-7320
Last/Current Spouse:	SITENG-239

Year: 1977
Iben-2041

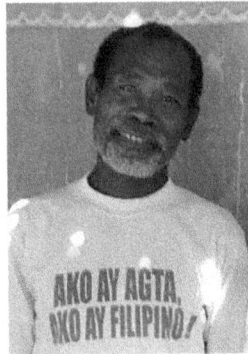

2008
Iben-2041

ID:	9122 *Sex:* Male
Name:	**IDAG**
2nd Name:	ROMOLO
Surname:	FRANCISCO
Agta Ancestry:	0%
Birth Date:	1950 +/-5 years
Death Date:	
Father:	
Mother:	
1st Spouse:	WISAY-203
Last/Current Spouse:	WISAY-203

Year: 2004
Idag-9122 phto by Iris
Dalberto

2004
Idag-9122

ID:	240 *Sex:* Male
Name:	**ILE**
2nd Name:	
Surname:	TALODEP, MAKSIMINO
Agta Ancestry:	100%
Birth Date:	1942 +/-2 years
Death Date:	July 4, 1981
Father:	MANDOSA
Mother:	KORDING
1st Spouse:	MONING-372
Last/Current Spouse:	UDAD-241

Year: 1976
Ile-240

ID:	2042 *Sex:* Male
Name:	**ILEN**
2nd Name:	
Surname:	BASELO
Agta Ancestry:	100%
Birth Date:	1926 +/-1 year
Death Date:	April 1986
Father:	BASELO
Mother:	SISA
1st Spouse:	PANGKUY-243
Last/Current Spouse:	PANGKUY-243

Year: 1977
Ilen-2042

ID: 215   Sex: Female

Name: **ILES**
2nd Name:
Surname: BUSESING
Agta Ancestry: 93.75%

Birth Date: 1969 +/-2 years
Death Date:

Father: PELIMON
Mother: GURING
1st Spouse: KITEK-304
Last/Current Spouse: LATONG-298

Year: 1977
Iles-215

ID: 7829   Sex: Female

Name: **ILIN**
2nd Name: MERILIN
Surname: DUNATO
Agta Ancestry: 100%

Birth Date: 1966 +/-3 years
Death Date:

Father: BAWE
Mother: LILING
1st Spouse: NORNING-7830
Last/Current Spouse: NORNING-7830

Year: 2002
Ilin-7829 son Dyerimaya-7902

ID: 7092   Sex: Male

Name: **ILOK**
2nd Name:
Surname:
Agta Ancestry: Unknown

Birth Date:
Death Date:

Father:
Mother:
1st Spouse:
Last/Current Spouse:

Year: 1977
Ilok-7092

ID: 425   Sex: Female

Name: **IMELDA**
2nd Name: MELDENG
Surname: BEKYADEN
Agta Ancestry: 93.75%

Birth Date: 1975
Death Date:

Father: NORPING
Mother: TALENDUS
1st Spouse: DANTE-9142
Last/Current Spouse: HOSE-9196

Year: 1976
Imelda-425

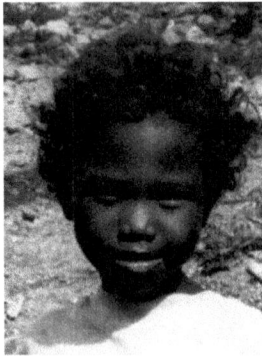

ID:	387
Sex:	Female
Name:	**INDAY**
2nd Name:	SINDAY, POLONG, MELANI
Surname:	DYOSINO
Agta Ancestry:	46.875%
Birth Date:	1972 +/-1 year
Death Date:	September 2006
Father:	DANILO
Mother:	MELI
1st Spouse:	BERTING-9075
Last/Current Spouse:	BERTING-9075

Year: 1978
Inday-387

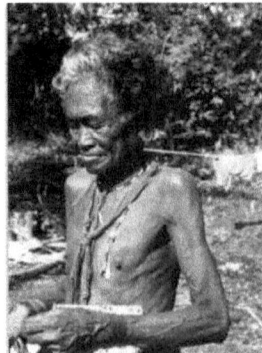

ID:	5173
Sex:	Female
Name:	**INEK**
2nd Name:	
Surname:	
Agta Ancestry:	100%
Birth Date:	1906 +/-6 years
Death Date:	July 29, 1971
Father:	
Mother:	
1st Spouse:	KULIDEG-5206
Last/Current Spouse:	KULIDEG-5206

Year: 1964
Inek-5173

ID:	3325
Sex:	Female
Name:	**INENG**
2nd Name:	NORA, LIONORA
Surname:	PAWISAN
Agta Ancestry:	75%
Birth Date:	1996
Death Date:	
Father:	PIKSON
Mother:	HELING
1st Spouse:	
Last/Current Spouse:	

Year: 2010
Ineng-3325

ID:	219
Sex:	Female
Name:	**INGGEL**
2nd Name:	MERLING, NIDA
Surname:	PRADO
Agta Ancestry:	75%
Birth Date:	1963 +/-1 year
Death Date:	
Father:	HAKOB
Mother:	PELI
1st Spouse:	NALOWADINGAN-404
Last/Current Spouse:	UNGED-7452

Year: 1978
Inggel-219

82

ID: 297   Sex: Female

Name: **INGGEL**
2nd Name: MILINA
Surname: TULIO

Agta Ancestry: Unknown

Birth Date: 1965 +/-1 year
Death Date:

Father: LAKAY
Mother: KONSITA

1st Spouse: BIK-9136
Last/Current Spouse: BIK-9136

Year: 1976
Inggel-297

ID: 244   Sex: Male

Name: **INONG**
2nd Name:
Surname: TOMAY

Agta Ancestry: 100%

Birth Date: 1911 +/-3 years
Death Date: 1985 +/-3 years

Father: TOMAY
Mother: LAGEYAN

1st Spouse: BEDA-5907
Last/Current Spouse: KASTING-265

Year: 1977
Inong-244

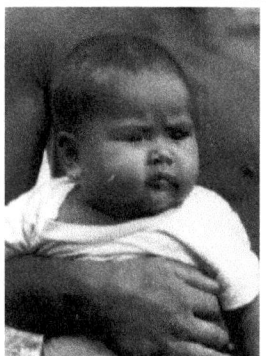

ID: 1137   Sex: Female

Name: **IPEL**
2nd Name: DYNENIPER
Surname: PAWISAN

Agta Ancestry: 75%

Birth Date: December 1977
Death Date: April 1978

Father: PIKSON
Mother: HELING

1st Spouse:
Last/Current Spouse:

Year: 1978
Ipel-1137

ID: 245   Sex: Male

Name: **IPOY**
2nd Name: EPOY
Surname: KUKUAN

Agta Ancestry: 100%

Birth Date: 1918 +/-3 years
Death Date: August 1980

Father: KUKUAN
Mother: SINDINA

1st Spouse: MAMING-246
Last/Current Spouse: MAMING-246

Year: 1978
Ipoy-245

ID:	7022
Sex:	Male
Name:	**ISET**
2nd Name:	RISEL
Surname:	
Agta Ancestry:	100%
Birth Date:	1939 +/-1 year
Death Date:	2004 +/-5 years
Father:	PAGITULENG
Mother:	KENGKENG
1st Spouse:	PANSING-7280
Last/Current Spouse:	PANSING-7280

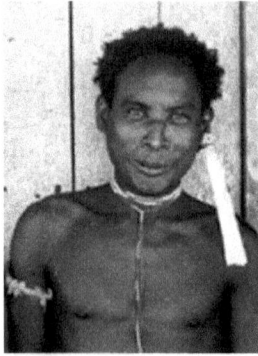

Year: 1978
Iset-7022

ID:	236
Sex:	Female
Name:	**ISID**
2nd Name:	
Surname:	
Agta Ancestry:	100%
Birth Date:	1961 +/-4 years
Death Date:	
Father:	TANES
Mother:	PORMING
1st Spouse:	HINER-235
Last/Current Spouse:	HINER-235

Year: 1978   2010
Isid-236   Isid-236

ID:	7093
Sex:	Female
Name:	**ISING**
2nd Name:	
Surname:	RAMOS
Agta Ancestry:	Unknown
Birth Date:	1942 +/-7 years
Death Date:	
Father:	MILIS
Mother:	DITENG
1st Spouse:	TANDUG-5459
Last/Current Spouse:	HUWANING-7350

Year: 1977
Ising-7093

ID:	202
Sex:	Female
Name:	**ISLING**
2nd Name:	
Surname:	SADSOY
Agta Ancestry:	100%
Birth Date:	1928 +/-2 years
Death Date:	January 5, 2000
Father:	SADSOY
Mother:	DINDAY
1st Spouse:	ERNING-201
Last/Current Spouse:	ERNING-201

Year: 1978   1998
Isling-202   Isling-202

Year: 1978
Ison-249

ID:	249		Sex: Male
Name:	**ISON**		
2nd Name:			
Surname:	KALANGGET		
Agta Ancestry:	87.5%		
Birth Date:	1946 +/-1 year		
Death Date:	May 1989		
Father:	NANEK		
Mother:	KONSING		
1st Spouse:	NENENG-250		
Last/Current Spouse:	NENENG-250		

Year: 1978
Ister-8009

ID:	8009		Sex: Female
Name:	**ISTER**		
2nd Name:	ESTAR		
Surname:			
Agta Ancestry:	50%		
Birth Date:	1952 +/-9 years		
Death Date:			
Father:	KENGKENG		
Mother:	MOIYO		
1st Spouse:	APIGU-9002		
Last/Current Spouse:	GIRIYERMO-9068		

Year: 1978
Isting-591

ID:	591		Sex: Female
Name:	**ISTING**		
2nd Name:			
Surname:			
Agta Ancestry:	87.5%		
Birth Date:	1923 +/-3 years		
Death Date:	August 1998		
Father:	TIKIMAN		
Mother:	AGAPITA		
1st Spouse:	TETYOK-590		
Last/Current Spouse:	TETYOK-590		

Year: 1976
Istring-253

ID:	253		Sex: Female
Name:	**ISTRING**		
2nd Name:			
Surname:	SIKATAN		
Agta Ancestry:	100%		
Birth Date:	1919 +/-3 years		
Death Date:	2001 +/-1 year		
Father:	SIKITAN		
Mother:	LIDONIA		
1st Spouse:	PASIO-5356		
Last/Current Spouse:	KENGKENG-273		

ID: 485   Sex: Female

Name: **ISTRING**
2nd Name:
Surname: TULIO

Agta Ancestry: 100%

Birth Date: 1919 +/-4 years
Death Date: April 25, 1986

Father: TULIO
Mother: LIPANYAW

1st Spouse: PIRENTE-484

Last/Current Spouse: PIRENTE-484

Year: 1976
Istring-485

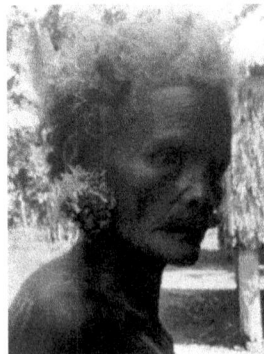

ID: 7689   Sex: Female

Name: **ISTRING**
2nd Name:
Surname:

Agta Ancestry: Unknown

Birth Date:
Death Date:

Father:
Mother:

1st Spouse: BUKAN-7690

Last/Current Spouse: BUKAN-7690

Year: 1966
Istring-7689

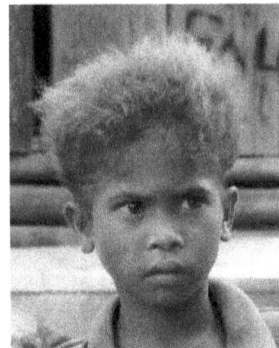

ID: 4022   Sex: Male

Name: **ITOM**
2nd Name:
Surname:

Agta Ancestry: Unknown

Birth Date: 2000 +/-2 years
Death Date:

Father:
Mother:

1st Spouse:

Last/Current Spouse:

Year: 2010
Itom-4022

ID: 7   Sex: Male

Name: **ITUT**
2nd Name:
Surname:

Agta Ancestry: 100%

Birth Date: 1956 +/-1 year
Death Date: August 1989

Father: DIYAKIN
Mother: ADILING

1st Spouse: NELI-7243

Last/Current Spouse: NELI-7243

Year: 1972
Itut-7 phto by Jim Musgrove

Year: 2002
Iyan-3338 and Albin-3053

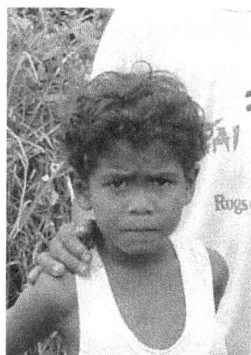

2004
Iyan-3338

ID: 3338   *Sex:* Male

Name: **IYAN**
2nd Name: ANTONI
Surname:
Agta Ancestry: 81.25%

Birth Date: October 13, 1995
Death Date:

Father: TONILIN
Mother: ANALI

1st Spouse:

Last/Current Spouse:

Year: 1977
Kabanting-7095

ID: 7095   *Sex:* Male

Name: **KABANTING**
2nd Name:
Surname: SALBADOR
Agta Ancestry: Unknown

Birth Date: 1942 +/-6 years
Death Date: 2001 +/-9 years

Father: TADIO
Mother: BINING

1st Spouse: LETI-7121

Last/Current Spouse: LETI-7121

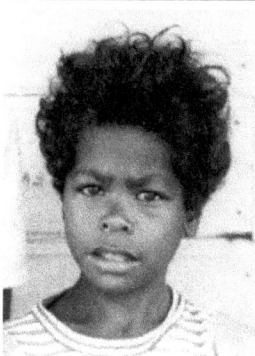

Year: 1977
Kaleng-598

ID: 598   *Sex:* Male

Name: **KALENG**
2nd Name: OSCAR
Surname: ATEG
Agta Ancestry: 100%

Birth Date: 1969 +/-4 years
Death Date:

Father: TONING
Mother: RUSING

1st Spouse: KALINENG-2011

Last/Current Spouse: KALINENG-2011

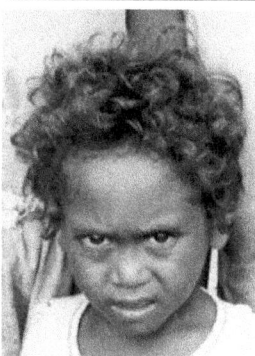

Year: 1977
Kaloy-216

ID: 216   *Sex:* Male

Name: **KALOY**
2nd Name: KARLITO, KARLING, BALDAKAY
Surname: BEKYADEN
Agta Ancestry: 93.75%

Birth Date: 1975 +/-1 year
Death Date:

Father: PELIMON
Mother: GURING

1st Spouse: NENENG-503

Last/Current Spouse: NENENG-503

Year: 1977
Kamlon-141

ID:	141	Sex:	Male

Name: **KAMLON**
2nd Name:
Surname: ALHAMRA
Agta Ancestry: 100%

Birth Date: 1957 +/-1 year
Death Date:

Father: BORDON
Mother: SANING
1st Spouse: KARNASIYON-53
Last/Current Spouse: KARNASIYON-53

Year: 1965
Kandeg-256

1977
Kandeg-256

ID:	256	Sex:	Male

Name: **KANDEG**
2nd Name:
Surname: SAGUNED
Agta Ancestry: 100%

Birth Date: 1927 +/-2 years
Death Date: October 1990

Father: SAGUNED
Mother: DINANSA
1st Spouse: MENSIANG-257
Last/Current Spouse: MENSIANG-257

Year: 1976
Karding-261

2002
Karding-261

ID:	261	Sex:	Male

Name: **KARDING**
2nd Name: BALOK
Surname: MELUS
Agta Ancestry: Unknown

Birth Date: 1950 +/-2 years
Death Date: 2009

Father: MELUS
Mother: NIYEBES
1st Spouse: SIYUNING-262
Last/Current Spouse: SIYUNING-262

Year: 1978
Karin-8022

ID:	8022	Sex:	Female

Name: **KARIN**
2nd Name:
Surname: TABUHARA
Agta Ancestry: 25%

Birth Date: 1960 +/-3 years
Death Date:

Father: JUAN
Mother: PASING
1st Spouse: ABAD-9237
Last/Current Spouse: ABAD-9237

88

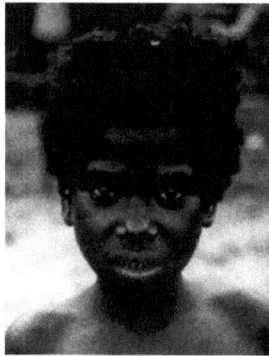

Year: 1978
Karing-536

Year: 2002
Karing with Anghelito 3458

ID:	536	Sex: Female
Name:	**KARING**
2nd Name:	
Surname:	MANDOY
Agta Ancestry:	100%
Birth Date:	1968 +/-2 years
Death Date:	
Father:	SISAR
Mother:	TESI
1st Spouse:	TAYUGIT-570
Last/Current Spouse:	TAYUGIT-570

Year: 2008
Karl-8355 with mom Dyosi-121

ID:	8355	Sex: Male
Name:	**KARL**
2nd Name:	
Surname:	ALKANTARA
Agta Ancestry:	48.437%
Birth Date:	September 20, 2006
Death Date:	
Father:	GANI
Mother:	DYOSI
1st Spouse:	
Last/Current Spouse:	

Year: 1977
Karlos-7101

ID:	7101	Sex: Male
Name:	**KARLOS**
2nd Name:	KALOY
Surname:	DABI
Agta Ancestry:	Unknown
Birth Date:	1952 +/-7 years
Death Date:	
Father:	ANSETA
Mother:	SINGOL
1st Spouse:	
Last/Current Spouse:	

Year: 1979
Karmen-442

ID:	442	Sex: Female
Name:	**KARMEN**
2nd Name:	KARMENSITA
Surname:	
Agta Ancestry:	75%
Birth Date:	1961 +/-1 year
Death Date:	May 1990
Father:	PANSO
Mother:	UPEK
1st Spouse:	SAWE-131
Last/Current Spouse:	SAWE-131

Year: 1977
Karmin-7103

ID: 7103	Sex: Female
Name: **KARMIN**	
2nd Name:	
Surname:	ISPERANSA
Agta Ancestry: Unknown	
Birth Date:	1939 +/-6 years
Death Date:	1995 +/-9 years
Father:	PANAGKEG
Mother:	IPOK
1st Spouse:	WILSON-7211
Last/Current Spouse:	WILSON-7211

Year: 1976
Karnasion-42

ID: 42	Sex: Female
Name: **KARNASIYON**	
2nd Name:	KARNASIO
Surname:	ALAMBRA
Agta Ancestry: 100%	
Birth Date:	1934 +/-2 years
Death Date:	January 1982
Father:	ALAMRA
Mother:	UPILA
1st Spouse:	BALONSE-5059
Last/Current Spouse:	BALONSE-5059

Year: 1977
Karnasiyon-53 with son
Dingkel-57

ID: 53	Sex: Female
Name: **KARNASIYON**	
2nd Name:	KONSING
Surname:	MIYA
Agta Ancestry: 100%	
Birth Date:	1945 +/-2 years
Death Date:	2001 +/-2 years
Father:	PASIO
Mother:	ISTRING
1st Spouse:	BEDBED-52
Last/Current Spouse:	KAMLON-141

Year: 1965
Karnasiyon-6018 &
husband Bontoy-5585

2009
Karnasiyon-6018 phto by
Ingrid Turner

ID: 6018	Sex: Female
Name: **KARNASIYON**	
2nd Name:	KARNA
Surname:	
Agta Ancestry: 100%	
Birth Date:	1940 +/-3 years
Death Date:	
Father:	KELYADEN
Mother:	KURUSINA
1st Spouse:	BONTOY-5585
Last/Current Spouse:	RABIDUNG-7803

90

Year: 1973
Kasting, Jenny Headland, Pompoek, Janet Headland

1977
Kasting-265

ID: 265   *Sex:* Female

Name: **KASTING**
2nd Name:
Surname:

Agta Ancestry: 100%

Birth Date: 1932 +/-3 years
Death Date: December 1993

Father: BULITUG
Mother: ABUNDIA
1st Spouse: MANIBUG-5272
Last/Current Spouse: INONG-244

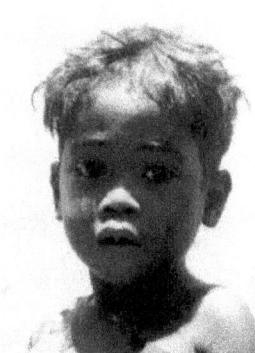

Year: 1977
Katol-125

2010
Katol-125

ID: 125   *Sex:* Male

Name: **KATOL**
2nd Name: DYOEL, PAMPLONA
Surname: GERA

Agta Ancestry: 100%

Birth Date: 1973 +/-1 year
Death Date:

Father: DELOY
Mother: PAMING
1st Spouse: NANSI-120
Last/Current Spouse: NANSI-120

Year: 1978
Kedek-143

ID: 143   *Sex:* Female

Name: **KEDEK**
2nd Name:
Surname: ALAMRA

Agta Ancestry: 100%

Birth Date: 1962 +/-1 year
Death Date:

Father: BORDON
Mother: SANING
1st Spouse: POKES-16
Last/Current Spouse: OLENG-7153

Year: 2006
Kedel-1045

2010
Kedel-1045

ID: 1045   *Sex:* Male

Name: **KEDEL**
2nd Name: WINDEL
Surname: PRADO

Agta Ancestry: 75%

Birth Date: 1983
Death Date:

Father: LORDE
Mother: WISAY
1st Spouse:
Last/Current Spouse:

Year: 1966
Kekek-267

1972
Kekek-267 phto by Jim
Musgrove

ID: 267	*Sex:* Male

Name: **KEKEK**
2nd Name: PELIP
Surname: ADUANAN

Agta Ancestry: 100%

Birth Date: 1936 +/-1 year
Death Date: May 4, 2008

Father: DASEG
Mother: MONGGEY
1st Spouse: LUNINGNING-268
Last/Current Spouse: LUNINGNING-268

Year: 1964
Kelyaden-7801

ID: 7801	*Sex:* Male

Name: **KELYADEN**
2nd Name: BENGEG
Surname:

Agta Ancestry: 100%

Birth Date: 1895 +/-9 years
Death Date: 1966 +/-3 years

Father:
Mother:
1st Spouse: KURUSINA-7800
Last/Current Spouse: KURUSINA-7800

Year: 1977
Kengkeng-273

ID: 273	*Sex:* Male

Name: **KENGKENG**
2nd Name:
Surname: MISAN

Agta Ancestry: 100%

Birth Date: 1917 +/-4 years
Death Date:

Father: MISAN
Mother: NEGAD
1st Spouse: BENDULING-5956
Last/Current Spouse: ELKAG-9092

Year: 2008
Kentin-1050

ID: 1050	*Sex:* Male

Name: **KENTIN**
2nd Name:
Surname: DELACRUZ

Agta Ancestry: 50%

Birth Date: March 1982
Death Date:

Father: SIMO
Mother: GURING
1st Spouse:
Last/Current Spouse:

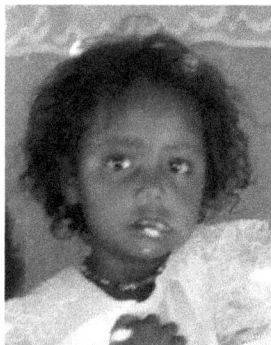

ID:	3562
Sex:	Female
Name:	**KIKAY**
2nd Name:	KRISTINA
Surname:	
Agta Ancestry:	93.75%
Birth Date:	August 7, 2004
Death Date:	
Father:	WIRNER
Mother:	ABENG
1st Spouse:	
Last/Current Spouse:	

Year: 2008
Kikay-3562

ID:	7384
Sex:	Male
Name:	**KILENG**
2nd Name:	MARSILINO
Surname:	DABID
Agta Ancestry:	Unknown
Birth Date:	1954 +/-5 years
Death Date:	2000 +/-9 years
Father:	DESAG
Mother:	BENDULING
1st Spouse:	KOKOK-7383
Last/Current Spouse:	KOKOK-7383

Year: 1977
Kileng-7384

ID:	4018
Sex:	Female
Name:	**KILONG**
2nd Name:	
Surname:	
Agta Ancestry:	100%
Birth Date:	1996 +/-3 years
Death Date:	
Father:	
Mother:	DIWAT
1st Spouse:	
Last/Current Spouse:	

Year: 2010
Kilong-4018

ID:	3358
Sex:	Female
Name:	**KINGKING**
2nd Name:	KATRINA
Surname:	
Agta Ancestry:	65.625%
Birth Date:	August 13, 1997
Death Date:	
Father:	DYESI
Mother:	ENG-ENG
1st Spouse:	
Last/Current Spouse:	

Year: 2010
Kingking-3358

93

ID: 7069   Sex: Male

Name: **KINYOL**
2nd Name: DYUNYOR
Surname: DUNATO

Agta Ancestry: 100%

Birth Date: 1956 +/-4 years
Death Date: May 17, 2009

Father: UGKUY
Mother: PANSING

1st Spouse: TUNING-7851
Last/Current Spouse: TUNING-7851

Year: 2006
Kinyol-7069

ID: 304   Sex: Male

Name: **KITEK**
2nd Name: ROY
Surname: TALODEP

Agta Ancestry: 100%

Birth Date: 1964 +/-1 year
Death Date:

Father: MANDOSA
Mother: KORDING

1st Spouse: ILES-215
Last/Current Spouse: unknown-9042

Year: 1977
Kitek-304

ID: 9261   Sex: Male

Name: **KITI**
2nd Name: EDMAR
Surname: NIPAL

Agta Ancestry: 0%

Birth Date: 1990 +/-1 year
Death Date:

Father:
Mother:

1st Spouse: MERIGRES-1024
Last/Current Spouse: MERIGRES-1024

Year: 2008
Kiti-9261

ID: 291   Sex: Male

Name: **KITOL**
2nd Name: KATOL
Surname: KUKUAN

Agta Ancestry: 81.25%

Birth Date: 1971 +/-1 year
Death Date:

Father: GUBEK
Mother: SABILITA

1st Spouse: AYRIN-7906
Last/Current Spouse: AYRIN-7906

Year: 1976
Kitol-291

Year: 1977
Konsita-295

2010
Konsita-295

ID: 295   Sex: Female

Name: **KONSITA**
2nd Name:
Surname: BITIGAN

Agta Ancestry: 100%

Birth Date: 1939 +/-2 years
Death Date:

Father: BITIGAN
Mother: KANORA

1st Spouse: LAKAY-294

Last/Current Spouse: LAKAY-294

Year: 1978
Konsita-7218 w daughtr
Ribika-7337

ID: 7218   Sex: Female

Name: **KONSITA**
2nd Name:
Surname:

Agta Ancestry: Unknown

Birth Date: 1948 +/-5 years
Death Date:

Father: DEBAK
Mother: LEDTENGAN

1st Spouse: ALUPING-25

Last/Current Spouse: ALUPING-25

Year: 1978
Konsita-8062

ID: 8062   Sex: Female

Name: **KONSITA**
2nd Name:
Surname:

Agta Ancestry: 37.5%

Birth Date: March 13, 1960
Death Date:

Father: TEBAN
Mother: DARNING

1st Spouse: BOY-9096

Last/Current Spouse: BOY-9096

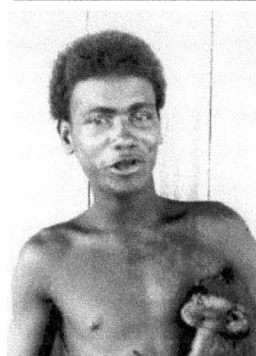

Year: 1977
Kortal-274

ID: 274   Sex: Male

Name: **KORTAL**
2nd Name:
Surname: PORENGGES

Agta Ancestry: 100%

Birth Date: 1952 +/-2 years
Death Date: 1990 +/-2 years

Father: PORENGGES
Mother: NINGNING

1st Spouse:

Last/Current Spouse:

95

Year: 2008
Kris-3003

2010
Kris-3003

ID:	3003	Sex: Male

Name: KRIS
2nd Name:
Surname: MORAL
Agta Ancestry: 84.375%

Birth Date: April 4, 1985
Death Date:

Father: TEMING
Mother: LOYDA
1st Spouse: KRISA-8173
Last/Current Spouse: KRISA-8173

Year: 2010
Krisa-8173 w Krisanto-3659

ID:	8173	Sex: Female

Name: KRISA
2nd Name:
Surname: MORAL
Agta Ancestry: 46.88%

Birth Date: August 12, 1990
Death Date:

Father: ANDRING
Mother: NERSI
1st Spouse: KRIS-3003
Last/Current Spouse: KRIS-3003

Year: 2010
Kristyan-3455

ID:	3455	Sex: Male

Name: KRISTYAN
2nd Name:
Surname:
Agta Ancestry: 62.5%

Birth Date: December 25, 2000
Death Date:

Father: UNDI
Mother: HUANA
1st Spouse:
Last/Current Spouse:

Year: 2008
Kule-3626 w mother Dyina-7870

ID:	3626	Sex: Male

Name: KULE
2nd Name:
Surname:
Agta Ancestry: Unknown

Birth Date: 2006 +/-1 year
Death Date:

Father:
Mother: DYINA
1st Spouse:
Last/Current Spouse:

Year: 1977
Kules-482

ID: 482   Sex: Female

Name: **KULES**
2nd Name: BILMA
Surname: SIKATAN

Agta Ancestry: 93.75%

Birth Date: 1965 +/-2 years
Death Date:

Father: BILYANTING
Mother: ROSITA
1st Spouse: BERTOSO-348
Last/Current Spouse: POLOK-3

Year: 2008
Kulokoy-3010

ID: 3010   Sex: Male

Name: **KULOKOY**
2nd Name: DYOY
Surname: PRADO

Agta Ancestry: 75%

Birth Date: October 7, 1987
Death Date:

Father: NATENG
Mother: TETET
1st Spouse:
Last/Current Spouse:

Year: 2002
Kulokoy-3097

2010
Kulokoy-3097

ID: 3097   Sex: Male

Name: **KULOKOY**
2nd Name:
Surname: ABUNDIO, AMERINDU

Agta Ancestry: 75%

Birth Date: December 1985
Death Date:

Father: HAYME
Mother: NATI
1st Spouse: EBA-1028
Last/Current Spouse: EBA-1028

Year: 1998
Kuluding-601

ID: 601   Sex: Female

Name: **KULUDING**
2nd Name:
Surname: BEKYADEN

Agta Ancestry: 87.5%

Birth Date: 1933 +/-1 year
Death Date: February 23, 2005

Father: BANGHUL
Mother: ANENA
1st Spouse: TOTENG-600
Last/Current Spouse: HOSE-8169

ID:	247 *Sex:* Male
Name:	**KULUT**
2nd Name:	
Surname:	KUKUAN
Agta Ancestry:	100%
Birth Date:	1957 +/-1 year
Death Date:	
Father:	IPOY
Mother:	MAMING
1st Spouse:	SIPOK-450
Last/Current Spouse:	SIPOK-450

Year: 1978   1998
Kulut-247   Kulut-247

ID:	276 *Sex:* Male
Name:	**KULUT**
2nd Name:	
Surname:	BEKYADEN
Agta Ancestry:	87.5%
Birth Date:	1950 +/-2 years
Death Date:	
Father:	BANGHUL
Mother:	PILISA
1st Spouse:	LOLONG-324
Last/Current Spouse:	DEMEK-272

Year: 1977
Kulut-276

ID:	472 *Sex:* Female
Name:	**KULUT**
2nd Name:	
Surname:	ARISTAN
Agta Ancestry:	100%
Birth Date:	1961 +/-3 years
Death Date:	
Father:	PIDYONG
Mother:	SIDING
1st Spouse:	ERNING-519
Last/Current Spouse:	UYA-9093

Year: 1977
Kulut-472

ID:	8080 *Sex:* Female
Name:	**KULUT**
2nd Name:	GEGEK, MARISEL
Surname:	DELAKRUS
Agta Ancestry:	46.88%
Birth Date:	January 1993
Death Date:	
Father:	RENI
Mother:	NENENG
1st Spouse:	BORDIGUL-1021
Last/Current Spouse:	BORDIGUL-1021

Year: 1998   2008
Kulut-8080 (L) & Marites-   Kulut-8080
8102

Year: 2010
Kuneng-486

ID: 486   *Sex:* Female

Name: **KUNENG**
2nd Name: LUING
Surname: PRADO

Agta Ancestry: 75%

Birth Date: 1961
Death Date:

Father: PIRENTE
Mother: ISTRING
1st Spouse: BOY-9033
Last/Current Spouse: DONGDONG-8005

Year: 2000
Kurap-8228 with aunt
Siteng-239

2010
Kurap-8228

ID: 8228   *Sex:* Male

Name: **KURAP**
2nd Name: KRISTIAN
Surname: NIKULAS

Agta Ancestry: 37.5%

Birth Date: September 1999
Death Date:

Father: RAPI
Mother: EDNALIN
1st Spouse:
Last/Current Spouse:

Year: 1964
Kurusina-7800

ID: 7800   *Sex:* Female

Name: **KURUSINA**
2nd Name:
Surname:

Agta Ancestry: 100%

Birth Date: 1900 +/-9 years
Death Date: 1967 +/-4 years

Father:
Mother:
1st Spouse: KELYADEN-7801
Last/Current Spouse: KELYADEN-7801

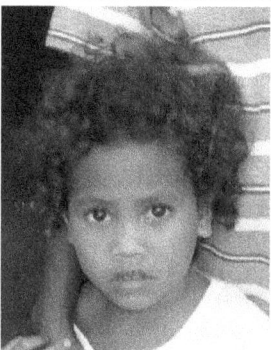
Year: 2010
Lablin-3570

ID: 3570   *Sex:* Female

Name: **LABLIN**
2nd Name: LAGINDIN
Surname:

Agta Ancestry: 87.5%

Birth Date: March 7, 2005
Death Date:

Father: TOTOY
Mother: DINA
1st Spouse:
Last/Current Spouse:

99

Year: 2010
Lagt-8398

ID:	8398 Sex: Female

Name: **LAGA**
2nd Name: DAGA
Surname:

Agta Ancestry: 73.44%

Birth Date: June 2008
Death Date:

Father: SAKLANGEN
Mother: MARITES

1st Spouse:
Last/Current Spouse:

Year: 1977
Lakay-288

ID:	288 Sex: Male

Name: **LAKAY**
2nd Name:
Surname: ALEDIG

Agta Ancestry: 100%

Birth Date: 1948 +/-2 years
Death Date: December 2000

Father: ALEDIG
Mother: LUNING

1st Spouse: OSA-7428
Last/Current Spouse: SABILITA-289

Year: 1977
Lakay-294

2010
Lakay-294

ID:	294 Sex: Male

Name: **LAKAY**
2nd Name:
Surname: TULIO

Agta Ancestry: 100%

Birth Date: 1938 +/-3 years
Death Date:

Father: TULIO
Mother: LIPANYAW

1st Spouse: KONSITA-295
Last/Current Spouse: KONSITA-295

Year: 1976
Lakson-181

ID:	181 Sex: Male

Name: **LAKSON**
2nd Name:
Surname: BANTUG

Agta Ancestry: 100%

Birth Date: 1965 +/-2 years
Death Date: 1996 +/-1 year

Father: EDA
Mother: TILOKEN

1st Spouse:
Last/Current Spouse:

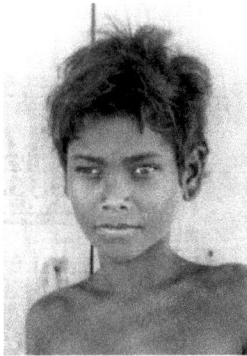

Year: 1978
Lakson-7116

2010
Lakson-7116

ID: 7116　　　　Sex: Male

Name: **LAKSON**
2nd Name:
Surname:　　　　SANSES
Agta Ancestry: 87.5%

Birth Date:　　　1966 +/-2 years
Death Date:

Father:　　　　　BUTOD
Mother:　　　　　MADYEK

1st Spouse:
Last/Current Spouse:

Year: 1977
Laleng-306

ID: 306　　　　Sex: Male

Name: **LALENG**
2nd Name:　　　TONI
Surname:　　　　SADSOY

Agta Ancestry: 100%

Birth Date:　　　1962 +/-2 years
Death Date:

Father:　　　　　TIKIMAN
Mother:　　　　　LAYDING

1st Spouse:　　　NAYLING-161
Last/Current Spouse:　NAYLING-161

Year: 2010
Laleng-4024

ID: 4024　　　　Sex: Male

Name: **LALENG**
2nd Name:
Surname:

Agta Ancestry: 100%

Birth Date:　　　1984 +/-6 years
Death Date:

Father:
Mother:

1st Spouse:
Last/Current Spouse:

Year: 1977
Lalong-300 & son Odi-302

ID: 300　　　　Sex: Male

Name: **LALONG**
2nd Name:
Surname:　　　　BANTUG, RAMUS

Agta Ancestry: 100%

Birth Date:　　　1951 +/-2 years
Death Date:　　　January 15, 1988

Father:　　　　　EDA
Mother:　　　　　LIGAYA

1st Spouse:　　　PENGPENG-301
Last/Current Spouse:　PENGPENG-301

101

Year: 1978
Landu-8011

ID: 8011　　　　Sex: Male

Name: **LANDU**
2nd Name: RULANDU
Surname: AGILAR

Agta Ancestry: 25%

Birth Date: 1954
Death Date:

Father: PILO
Mother: NENA
1st Spouse: LOLONG-324
Last/Current Spouse: LOLONG-324

Year: 2000
Lanea1057

ID: 1057　　　　Sex: Female

Name: **LANEA**
2nd Name:
Surname: ABUNDIO, AMERINDU

Agta Ancestry: 75%

Birth Date: February 24, 1982
Death Date:

Father: HAYME
Mother: NATI
1st Spouse: Ilocano man-9302
Last/Current Spouse: Ilocano man-9302

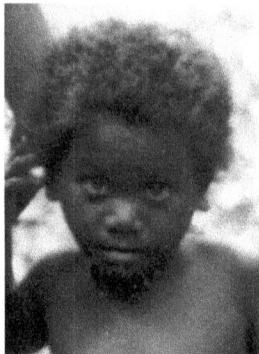

Year: 1977
Lari-1035

ID: 1035　　　　Sex: Male

Name: **LARI**
2nd Name:
Surname: BALENSIA

Agta Ancestry: 50%

Birth Date: 1977 +/-3 years
Death Date:

Father: DOMING
Mother: LILYA
1st Spouse: MEDENG-4
Last/Current Spouse: MEDENG-4

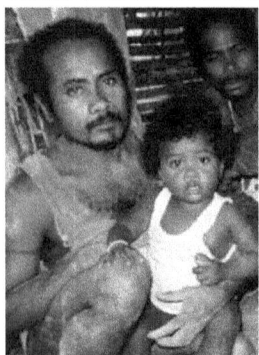

Year: 2002
Lari-3429 with father
Tengteng-43

ID: 3429　　　　Sex: Male

Name: **LARI**
2nd Name: MONSOR
Surname:

Agta Ancestry: 100%

Birth Date: January 2000
Death Date:

Father: TENGTENG
Mother: ILISING
1st Spouse:
Last/Current Spouse:

102

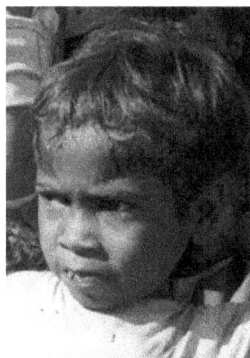

Year: 1976
Latong-298

ID: 298   Sex: Male

Name: **LATONG**
2nd Name: LIBIRITO
Surname: TULIO

Agta Ancestry: Unknown

Birth Date: 1970 +/-1 year
Death Date:

Father: LAKAY
Mother: KONSITA

1st Spouse: ILES-215

Last/Current Spouse: ILES-215

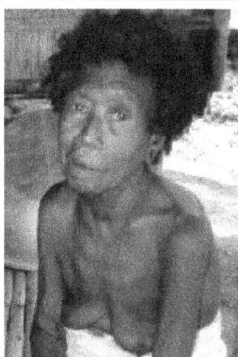

Year: 1977   1998
Layding-305   Layding-305

ID: 305   Sex: Female

Name: **LAYDING**
2nd Name:
Surname:

Agta Ancestry: 100%

Birth Date: 1925 +/-4 years
Death Date: October 14, 2008

Father: SADSOY
Mother: DINDAY

1st Spouse: TIKIMAN-5468

Last/Current Spouse: TIKIMAN-5468

Year: 1978
Layning-282

ID: 282   Sex: Female

Name: **LAYNING**
2nd Name:
Surname: MISAN

Agta Ancestry: 100%

Birth Date: 1944 +/-3 years
Death Date:

Father: DOSE
Mother: TENGTAY

1st Spouse: LAKAY-281

Last/Current Spouse: PIPING-7236

Year: 1977   2008
Lebi-8077   Lebi-8077

ID: 8077   Sex: Female

Name: **LEBI**
2nd Name: LEVY
Surname: ESTEVES

Agta Ancestry: 50%

Birth Date: June 15, 1942
Death Date:

Father: ISKO
Mother: MEDIKAD

1st Spouse: HULYU-9106

Last/Current Spouse: HULYU-9106

Year: 2010
Lelembot-8188

ID:	8188	Sex:	Female

Name: **LELEMBOT**
2nd Name: ANALIN
Surname:

Agta Ancestry: 37.5%

Birth Date: 1994 +/-5 years
Death Date:

Father: BOY
Mother: KUNENG
1st Spouse: GABI-3048
Last/Current Spouse: GABI-3048

Year: 1978
Leleng-7119

ID:	7119	Sex:	Male

Name: **LELENG**
2nd Name:
Surname:

Agta Ancestry: Unknown

Birth Date:
Death Date:

Father:
Mother:
1st Spouse: NENI-7586
Last/Current Spouse: NENI-7586

Year: 1977
Leni-308

2008
Leni-308

ID:	308	Sex:	Female

Name: **LENI**
2nd Name:
Surname: GERERO

Agta Ancestry: 43.75%

Birth Date: 1954 +/-1 year
Death Date:

Father: PRANSISKO
Mother: NIYEBES
1st Spouse: KONDRADO-9061
Last/Current Spouse: KONDRADO-9061

Year: 1972
Leni-370 phto by Jim
Musgove

1976
Leni-370

ID:	370	Sex:	Female

Name: **LENI**
2nd Name: NORMA
Surname: INONG

Agta Ancestry: Unknown

Birth Date: 1956 +/-2 years
Death Date:

Father: BINGGOY
Mother: LIMINIDA
1st Spouse: MARIANING-369
Last/Current Spouse: DOMING-9151

104

Year: 1978
Leni-508

2010
Leni-508

ID: 508   Sex: Female

Name: **LENI**
2nd Name:
Surname: TULIO
Agta Ancestry: 100%

Birth Date: 1954 +/-2 years
Death Date:

Father: ASION
Mother: SULIDAD
1st Spouse: RUMING-507
Last/Current Spouse: RUMING-507

Year: 2002
Lenlen-3202

ID: 3202   Sex: Female

Name: **LENLEN**
2nd Name: DYENDYEN
Surname:
Agta Ancestry: Unknown

Birth Date: September 1993
Death Date:

Father: UNDUL
Mother: ABEY
1st Spouse:
Last/Current Spouse:

Year: 2008
Leovelita-8364 between
parents

ID: 8364   Sex: Female

Name: **LEOVELITA**
2nd Name:
Surname: BASILIO
Agta Ancestry: 12.5%

Birth Date: June 19, 2003
Death Date:

Father: MARK
Mother: DYOLIBI
1st Spouse:
Last/Current Spouse:

Year: 1977
Lerling-610

2010
Lerling-610

ID: 610   Sex: Female

Name: **LERLING**
2nd Name:
Surname: LISIDAY
Agta Ancestry: Unknown

Birth Date: 1968 +/-1 year
Death Date:

Father: NARSISO
Mother: UTET
1st Spouse: TORI-9138
Last/Current Spouse: TORI-9138

Year: 1998
Leya-7740 & father Sawe-131

Year: 2002
Rodel-7890 & Leya-7740

ID: 7740   *Sex:* Female

Name: **LEYA**
2nd Name:
Surname: ADUANAN
Agta Ancestry: 100%

Birth Date: June 27, 1997
Death Date:

Father: SAWE
Mother: MARIYETA

1st Spouse:
Last/Current Spouse:

Year: 1978
Lidia-312

ID: 312   *Sex:* Female

Name: **LIDIA**
2nd Name:
Surname:
Agta Ancestry: 100%

Birth Date: 1955 +/-1 year
Death Date: 2007

Father: TANES
Mother: LIYANING

1st Spouse: HOMER-238
Last/Current Spouse: TAYUGIT-570

Year: 1970
Lidina-314

Year: 1972
Lidina-314 phto by Jim Musgrove

ID: 314   *Sex:* Female

Name: **LIDINA**
2nd Name:
Surname: SAGUNED
Agta Ancestry: 100%

Birth Date: 1955 +/-1 year
Death Date: April 2000

Father: KANDEG
Mother: MENSIANG

1st Spouse: RUHEL-9060
Last/Current Spouse: RUHEL-9060

Year: 1977
Lidya-214

ID: 214   *Sex:* Female

Name: **LIDYA**
2nd Name:
Surname:
Agta Ancestry: 93.75%

Birth Date: 1966 +/-1 year
Death Date:

Father: PELIMON
Mother: GURING

1st Spouse: LUSING-104
Last/Current Spouse: LUSING-104

106

ID:	156
Sex:	Female

Name: **LIGAYA**
2nd Name:
Surname: GASIYENG
Agta Ancestry: 100%

Birth Date: 1927 +/-3 years
Death Date: 1978

Father: GASIYENG
Mother: DONGKES
1st Spouse: BINONG-85
Last/Current Spouse: BINONG-85

Year: 1977
Ligaya-156

ID: 7889   *Sex:* Male

Name: **LILET**
2nd Name:
Surname: DELAPENYA
Agta Ancestry: 100%

Birth Date: 1975 +/-9 years
Death Date:

Father:
Mother:
1st Spouse: PURING-24
Last/Current Spouse: PURING-24

Year: 2010
Lilet-7889

ID: 7327   *Sex:* Female

Name: **LILING**
2nd Name:
Surname:
Agta Ancestry: Unknown

Birth Date: 1946 +/-5 years
Death Date: December 2009

Father: PULUMENO
Mother: ISAY
1st Spouse: BAWE-7820
Last/Current Spouse: BAWE-7820

Year: 2008
Liling-7327; photo by Jan
van der Ploeg

ID: 146   *Sex:* Female

Name: **LILYA**
2nd Name: LILIYA
Surname:
Agta Ancestry: 50%

Birth Date: 1943 +/-3 years
Death Date:

Father: KOSTODIO
Mother: SAGED
1st Spouse: DOMING-145
Last/Current Spouse: DOMING-145

Year: 1977
Lilya-146

107

Year: 1967
Liminida-41

2010
Liminida-41

ID: 41	Sex: Female

Name: **LIMINIDA**
2nd Name:
Surname: BITIGAN DIGASPE
Agta Ancestry: Unknown

Birth Date: 1935 +/-2 years
Death Date:

Father: DIGASPE
Mother: TIYENG
1st Spouse: BINGGOY-5081
Last/Current Spouse: ENDING-196

Year: 1977
Linda-242

2010
Linda-242

ID: 242	Sex: Female

Name: **LINDA**
2nd Name:
Surname: DELAPENYA
Agta Ancestry: 100%

Birth Date: 1961
Death Date:

Father: PANSO
Mother: UDAD
1st Spouse: BERNING-7025
Last/Current Spouse: BERNING-7025

Year: 2008
Linda-307

2010
Linda-307

ID: 307	Sex: Female

Name: **LINDA**
2nd Name: MIMEL
Surname: SADSOY
Agta Ancestry: 100%

Birth Date: 1965 +/-1 year
Death Date:

Father: TIKIMAN
Mother: LAYDING
1st Spouse: HENEROSO-193
Last/Current Spouse: ALEK-133

Year: 1978
Linda-552

ID: 552	Sex: Female

Name: **LINDA**
2nd Name:
Surname: SALAYAN
Agta Ancestry: Unknown

Birth Date: 1956 +/-2 years
Death Date:

Father: SALAYAN
Mother: BALANGAW
1st Spouse: SITOK-551
Last/Current Spouse: SITOK-551

108

ID:	9010
Sex:	Female
Name:	**LINDA**
2nd Name:	
Surname:	
Agta Ancestry:	0%
Birth Date:	1950 +/-5 years
Death Date:	
Father:	
Mother:	
1st Spouse:	DOLPING-8056
Last/Current Spouse:	DOLPING-8056

Year: 1994
Linda-9010 phto by John Early

2008
Linda-9010

ID:	75
Sex:	Female
Name:	**LINGUS**
2nd Name:	LILI, INGOS
Surname:	AGINALDO
Agta Ancestry:	100%
Birth Date:	1972 +/-1 year
Death Date:	
Father:	BILYANTING
Mother:	PINING
1st Spouse:	
Last/Current Spouse:	

Year: 1976
Lingus75

ID:	315
Sex:	Male
Name:	**LINING**
2nd Name:	
Surname:	ISTANES
Agta Ancestry:	100%
Birth Date:	1953 +/-2 years
Death Date:	December 1994
Father:	TANES
Mother:	LIYANING
1st Spouse:	ADILING-316
Last/Current Spouse:	DINGDINGAN-117

Year: 1978
Lining-315

ID:	5227
Sex:	Female
Name:	**LIPANYAW**
2nd Name:	
Surname:	ANGIDEW
Agta Ancestry:	100%
Birth Date:	1900 +/-3 years
Death Date:	1968 +/-3 years
Father:	ANGIDEW
Mother:	ONTIANG
1st Spouse:	TULIO-5483
Last/Current Spouse:	TULIO-5483

Year: 1966
Lipanyaw-5227

Year: 1977
Lisia-7473

ID: 7473   Sex: Female
Name: **LISIA**
2nd Name:
Surname:
Agta Ancestry: Unknown

Birth Date:
Death Date:

Father:
Mother:

1st Spouse:
Last/Current Spouse:

Year: 1977
Lita-38

ID: 38   Sex: Female
Name: **LITA**
2nd Name:
Surname: TULIO
Agta Ancestry: 100%

Birth Date: 1960 +/-2 years
Death Date:

Father: ASION
Mother: SULIDAD

1st Spouse: BEN-9112
Last/Current Spouse: DANI-9174

Year: 1972
Lita-581

1974
Lita-581 holding son Arnol-584

ID: 581   Sex: Female
Name: **LITA**
2nd Name:
Surname: SAGUNED
Agta Ancestry: 100%

Birth Date: 1951 +/-1 year
Death Date: October 28, 2007

Father: KANDEG
Mother: MENSIANG

1st Spouse: TEKOK-580
Last/Current Spouse: DYIMI-173

Year: 1977
Lita-7652

ID: 7652   Sex: Female
Name: **LITA**
2nd Name:
Surname:
Agta Ancestry: Unknown

Birth Date: 1961 +/-9 years
Death Date:

Father:
Mother:

1st Spouse:
Last/Current Spouse:

110

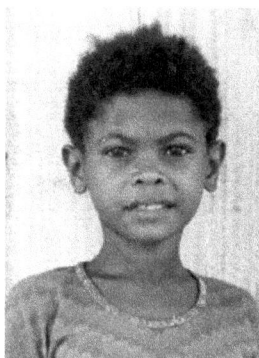

Year: 1976
Lito-290

ID: 290   Sex: Male

Name: **LITO**
2nd Name:
Surname: KUKUAN

Agta Ancestry: 81.25%

Birth Date: 1967 +/-1 year
Death Date:

Father: GUBEK
Mother: SABILITA

1st Spouse: IMELDA-269
Last/Current Spouse: IMELDA-269

Year: 1978
Lito-318

ID: 318   Sex: Male

Name: **LITO**
2nd Name:
Surname: ESTEBES

Agta Ancestry: 50%

Birth Date: 1965 +/-2 years
Death Date:

Father: NABARO
Mother: ADILING

1st Spouse: MAYENG-402
Last/Current Spouse: MAYENG-402

Year: 1977
Lito-493

ID: 493   Sex: Male

Name: **LITO**
2nd Name:
Surname:

Agta Ancestry: 100%

Birth Date: 1960 +/-1 year
Death Date: December 19, 1992

Father: HUWANING
Mother: SILENG

1st Spouse: AME-9113
Last/Current Spouse: AME-9113

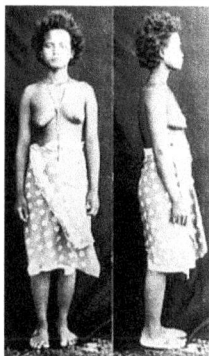

Year: 1936
Liyanita-320
photo by Vanoverbergh

1976
Liyanita-320

ID: 320   Sex: Female

Name: **LIYANITA**
2nd Name:
Surname: KUKUAN

Agta Ancestry: 50%

Birth Date: 1917 +/-2 years
Death Date: January 9, 2000

Father: LUNGUY
Mother: SEMASEM

1st Spouse: BIDEK-5492
Last/Current Spouse: MANULING-5617

111

Year: 1977
Liyanita-389

ID: 389   Sex: Female

Name: **LIYANITA**
2nd Name:
Surname: BESULELEW
Agta Ancestry: 100%

Birth Date: 1932 +/-3 years
Death Date: 1998 +/-7 years

Father: BASOLELEW
Mother: SABUYAT
1st Spouse: MEMETTENG-7529
Last/Current Spouse: MEMETTENG-7529

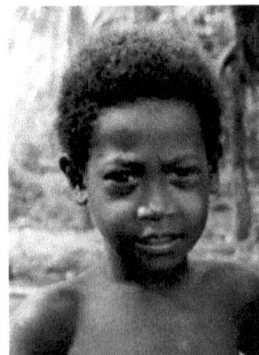

Year: 1977
Liyong-432

ID: 432   Sex: Male

Name: **LIYONG**
2nd Name: LIYON
Surname: BEKYADEN
Agta Ancestry: 93.75%

Birth Date: 1970 +/-1 year
Death Date:

Father: PABLING
Mother: KARMIN
1st Spouse: MARILU-7546
Last/Current Spouse: MARILU-7546

Year: 1976
Liyonida-323

ID: 323   Sex: Female

Name: **LIYONIDA**
2nd Name:
Surname: KAPINPIN
Agta Ancestry: 100%

Birth Date: 1918 +/-4 years
Death Date: June 29, 1978

Father: KAPINPIN
Mother: HIMENA
1st Spouse: BUROSA-9008
Last/Current Spouse: ISIYUNG-9015

Year: 2008   2010
Lodi-98   Lodi-98 & husband Borseg-
                        97

ID: 98   Sex: Female

Name: **LODI**
2nd Name: UGEYED BATANGGAS
Surname: ADUANAN
Agta Ancestry: 100%

Birth Date: 1939 +/-2 years
Death Date:

Father: DASEG
Mother: MONGGEY
1st Spouse: BORSEG-97
Last/Current Spouse: BORSEG-97

Year: 1977	1992
Lodi-103	Lodi-103

ID: 103   *Sex:* Female

Name: **LODI**
2nd Name:
Surname: MARTINES

Agta Ancestry: 100%

Birth Date: 1933 +/-2 years
Death Date: May 18, 1992

Father: MARTINES
Mother: OPISTA
1st Spouse: BUNAW-102
Last/Current Spouse: PIDYONG-470

Year: 1978
Lodi-363

ID: 363   *Sex:* Female

Name: **LODI**
2nd Name: ROSLIN, ROSALI
Surname: DESUY

Agta Ancestry: 100%

Birth Date: 1947 +/-2 years
Death Date:

Father: DESUY
Mother: SILANG
1st Spouse: MARIO-362
Last/Current Spouse: ARSIL-34

Year: 1976
Lolong-324

ID: 324   *Sex:* Female

Name: **LOLONG**
2nd Name:
Surname: AGILAR

Agta Ancestry: 100%

Birth Date: 1954 +/-2 years
Death Date:

Father: SAWILENG
Mother: ARPENYA
1st Spouse: KULUT-276
Last/Current Spouse: LANDU-8011

Year: 1977
Longhino-63

ID: 63   *Sex:* Male

Name: **LONGHINO**
2nd Name:
Surname: GEHA, GERA

Agta Ancestry: 100%

Birth Date: 1968 +/-1 year
Death Date:

Father: BERIONES
Mother: REKREK
1st Spouse: NENGNENGAN-401
Last/Current Spouse: NENGNENGAN-401

113

ID: 5240   Sex: Male

Name: **LOPES**
2nd Name: KUBA
Surname: BUMALON, BUMALOL

Agta Ancestry: 100%

Birth Date: 1934 +/-2 years
Death Date: 1974 +/-1 year

Father: BUMALOL
Mother: PENYADEN

1st Spouse: LILYA-5616
Last/Current Spouse: LILYA-5616

Year: 1973
Lopes-5240

ID: 1120   Sex: Male

Name: **LOPOG**
2nd Name: DYONATAN
Surname: MAKSIMINO

Agta Ancestry: 100%

Birth Date: 1981 +/-1 year
Death Date:

Father: OSMING
Mother: HUANITA

1st Spouse: NANSI-1132
Last/Current Spouse: NANSI-1132

Year: 2010
Lopog-1120

ID: 487   Sex: Male

Name: **LORDE**
2nd Name:
Surname: PRADO

Agta Ancestry: 75%

Birth Date: 1964 +/-1 year
Death Date: July 2, 1986

Father: PIRENTE
Mother: ISTRING

1st Spouse: WISAY-203
Last/Current Spouse: WISAY-203

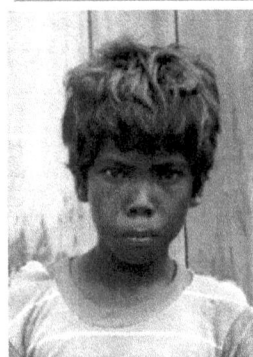

Year: 1976
Lorde-487

ID: 330   Sex: Female

Name: **LOSI**
2nd Name: IDAY
Surname: TANYET

Agta Ancestry: 87.5%

Birth Date: 1952 +/-2 years
Death Date: 1985

Father: MARTINES
Mother: OLIBIA

1st Spouse: MADENG-329
Last/Current Spouse: MADENG-329

Year: 1967
Losi-330

1977
Losi-330 & daughtr Beti-331

114

Year: 1976
Loyda-347

2010
Loyda-347

ID: 347	*Sex:* Female
Name: **LOYDA**	
2nd Name:	
Surname:	PAWISAN
Agta Ancestry: 87.5%	
Birth Date:	1959 +/-1 year
Death Date:	
Father:	MANINGTING
Mother:	SARING
1st Spouse:	NATENG-37
Last/Current Spouse:	NATENG-37

Year: 1977
Loyda-602

2010
Loyda-602

ID: 602	*Sex:* Female
Name: **LOYDA**	
2nd Name:	
Surname:	PULUKIN
Agta Ancestry: 93.75%	
Birth Date:	1961 +/-1 year
Death Date:	
Father:	TOTENG
Mother:	KULUDING
1st Spouse:	TEMING-589
Last/Current Spouse:	TEMING-589

Year: 1977
Lubis-7132

2010
Lubis-7132

ID: 7132	*Sex:* Female
Name: **LUBIS**	
2nd Name:	HUANITA, SINGOT
Surname:	
Agta Ancestry: Unknown	
Birth Date:	1948 +/-5 years
Death Date:	
Father:	
Mother:	LOKINOS
1st Spouse:	NARSING-7953
Last/Current Spouse:	NARSING-7953

Year: 1978
Luding-465

ID: 465	*Sex:* Female
Name: **LUDING**	
2nd Name:	LUDI
Surname:	LISIDAY, TIKIMAN
Agta Ancestry: 87.5%	
Birth Date:	1928 +/-3 years
Death Date:	1982
Father:	TIKIMAN
Mother:	AGAPITA
1st Spouse:	PEPE-464
Last/Current Spouse:	ALUNET-17

ID: 270   *Sex:* Female

Name: **LUDORA**
2nd Name: RODORA
Surname: ADUANAN

Agta Ancestry: 100%

Birth Date: 1974 +/-1 year
Death Date:

Father: KEKEK
Mother: LUNINGNING
1st Spouse: BOYET-525
Last/Current Spouse: BOYET-525

Year: 1998
Ludora-270

ID: 339   *Sex:* Female

Name: **LULITA**
2nd Name: ANGHELITA, LOLITA
Surname: DISONG, MAGING

Agta Ancestry: Unknown

Birth Date: 1944 +/-2 years
Death Date: January 1979

Father: MAGING
Mother: LOLING
1st Spouse: MAMORA-338
Last/Current Spouse: MAMORA-338

Year: 1978
Lulita-339

ID: 268   *Sex:* Female

Name: **LUNINGNING**
2nd Name:
Surname: SARILO

Agta Ancestry: 100%

Birth Date: 1942 +/-1 year
Death Date:

Father: BULITUG
Mother: ABUNDIA
1st Spouse: KEKEK-267
Last/Current Spouse: KEKEK-267

Year: 1972   2010
Luningning-268 phto by Jim   Luningning-268
Musgrove

ID: 455   *Sex:* Female

Name: **LUNINGNING**
2nd Name: LUNINGNI
Surname: ABADAN

Agta Ancestry: 100%

Birth Date: 1932 +/-2 years
Death Date: 1989

Father: ABADAN
Mother: ALIMANIA
1st Spouse: BARBOSA-5062
Last/Current Spouse: PEDRING-454

Year: 1978
Luningning-455

116

Year: 1976
Lusing-104

ID: 104   Sex: Male

Name: **LUSING**
2nd Name:
Surname: DATOB, DEMADES, PREDO
Agta Ancestry: 100%

Birth Date: 1960 +/-1 year
Death Date:

Father: BUNAW
Mother: LODI
1st Spouse: LIDYA-214
Last/Current Spouse: LIDYA-214

Year: 1977   2010
Maal-606   Maal-606

ID: 606   Sex: Female

Name: **MAAL**
2nd Name: DALAGA
Surname: TOMAY
Agta Ancestry: 93.75%

Birth Date: June 16, 1971
Death Date:

Father: ULEG
Mother: HELEN
1st Spouse: DYUNYOR-259
Last/Current Spouse: ORLI-410

Year: 1977
Madeng-329

ID: 329   Sex: Male

Name: **MADENG**
2nd Name:
Surname: PASIO, MIYA
Agta Ancestry: 100%

Birth Date: 1949 +/-2 years
Death Date: 2007 +/-1 year

Father: PASIO
Mother: ISTRING
1st Spouse: LOSI-330
Last/Current Spouse: NENENG-82

Year: 1927
Madeng-5250 and wife Biya-5085

ID: 5250   Sex: Male

Name: **MADENG**
2nd Name:
Surname:
Agta Ancestry: 100%

Birth Date: 1872 +/-8 years
Death Date: 1939 +/-9 years

Father:
Mother:
1st Spouse: BIYA-5085
Last/Current Spouse: BIYA-5085

117

ID: 332   *Sex:* Male

Name: **MADYANING**
2nd Name:
Surname: BERNABE

Agta Ancestry: 100%

Birth Date: 1921 +/-2 years
Death Date: February 14, 1985

Father: BERNABE
Mother: TOTIYEK
1st Spouse: KARIDAD-5187
Last/Current Spouse: NORING-5332

Year: 1976
Madyaning-332

ID: 106   *Sex:* Female

Name: **MADYEK**
2nd Name:
Surname: PRADO

Agta Ancestry: 75%

Birth Date: 1936 +/-3 years
Death Date: November 5, 1982

Father: PIRENTE
Mother: ISTRING
1st Spouse: BUTOD-2013
Last/Current Spouse: BUTOD-2013

Year: 1978
Madyek-106

ID: 112   *Sex:* Male

Name: **MAGNU**
2nd Name: MAGNO
Surname: DISONG

Agta Ancestry: 100%

Birth Date: 1915 +/-4 years
Death Date: July 2, 1983

Father: HUWANITO
Mother: ALEHA
1st Spouse: UGAGEY-5253
Last/Current Spouse: MANTI-335

Year: 1978
Magno-112

ID: 3324   *Sex:* Female

Name: **MAHALYA**
2nd Name:
Surname: PAWISAN

Agta Ancestry: 75%

Birth Date: January 28, 1997
Death Date:

Father: PIKSON
Mother: HELING
1st Spouse:
Last/Current Spouse:

Year: 2010
Mahalya-3324

Year: 1978
Makaria-2055

ID: 2055   Sex: Female

Name: **MAKARIA**
2nd Name:
Surname:

Agta Ancestry: Unknown

Birth Date: 1937 +/-3 years
Death Date: July 1998

Father:
Mother:

1st Spouse: BIDOY-65
Last/Current Spouse: BIDOY-65

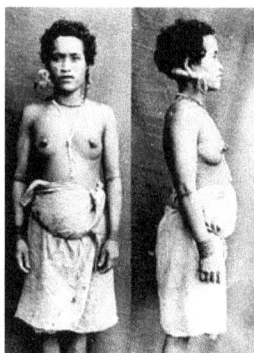

Year: 1936
Makinay-5256
photo by Vanoverbergh

ID: 5256   Sex: Female

Name: **MAKINAY**
2nd Name:
Surname:

Agta Ancestry: 75%

Birth Date: 1908 +/-5 years
Death Date: 1945 +/-1 year

Father: PERNANDO
Mother: PANENENG

1st Spouse: LISIDAY-5229
Last/Current Spouse: LISIDAY-5229

Year: 1965
Makinay-7697

ID: 7697   Sex: Female

Name: **MAKINAY**
2nd Name: TINAY
Surname:

Agta Ancestry: 100%

Birth Date: 1927 +/-5 years
Death Date: 1988 +/-6 years

Father: BALENO
Mother: ANATOLIA

1st Spouse: BERSOSA-64
Last/Current Spouse: GELNOT-7633

Year: 1977
Malensiyana-337

ID: 337   Sex: Female

Name: **MALENSIYANA**
2nd Name: MALENSIA
Surname:

Agta Ancestry: 100%

Birth Date: 1906 +/-8 years
Death Date: 1978

Father: HINUG
Mother: ROSERA

1st Spouse: TANASIYO-5702
Last/Current Spouse: TANASIYO-5702

Year: 1966
Malonduyan-7637 &
husband Binumaun-7607

ID:	7637	Sex: Female

Name: **MALONDUYAN**
2nd Name:
Surname:

Agta Ancestry: Unknown

Birth Date: 1907 +/-9 years
Death Date:

Father:
Mother:

1st Spouse: BINUMAUN-7607
Last/Current Spouse: BINUMAUN-7607

Year: 1977
Maming-246

1998
Maming-246

ID:	246	Sex: Female

Name: **MAMING**
2nd Name:
Surname: ALAMBRA

Agta Ancestry: 100%

Birth Date: 1920 +/-4 years
Death Date: 2002

Father: ALAMRA
Mother: UPILA

1st Spouse: IPOY-245
Last/Current Spouse: IPOY-245

Year: 1978
Mamora-338

ID:	338	Sex: Male

Name: **MAMORA**
2nd Name:
Surname: BINGGOSA

Agta Ancestry: 100%

Birth Date: 1938 +/-2 years
Death Date: November 20, 1979

Father: BENGGOSA
Mother: OPISTA

1st Spouse: LULITA-339
Last/Current Spouse: LULITA-339

Year: 1977
Mandosa-343

ID:	343	Sex: Male

Name: **MANDOSA**
2nd Name:
Surname: TALODEP

Agta Ancestry: 100%

Birth Date: 1918 +/-3 years
Death Date: 1982

Father: TALODEP
Mother: MALINAY

1st Spouse: KORDING-5201
Last/Current Spouse: KORDING-5201

ID: 345	*Sex:* Male

Name: **MANINGTING**
2nd Name: MANINTIN
Surname: PAWISAN

Agta Ancestry: 100%

Birth Date: 1929 +/-3 years
Death Date: December 1979

Father: PAWISAN
Mother: PILISA

1st Spouse: SARING-346
Last/Current Spouse: SARING-346

Year: 1976
Maningting-345

ID: 3148	*Sex:* Female

Name: **MANOK**
2nd Name: SANDRA
Surname: PASIO, MIYA

Agta Ancestry: 100%

Birth Date: September 12, 1992
Death Date:

Father: MADENG
Mother: NENENG

1st Spouse:
Last/Current Spouse:

Year: 2008
Manok-3148

ID: 8176	*Sex:* Male

Name: **MANWEL**
2nd Name:
Surname:

Agta Ancestry: 50%

Birth Date: May 25, 1992
Death Date:

Father: OLIBER
Mother: NARING

1st Spouse:
Last/Current Spouse:

Year: 2010
Manwel-8176

ID: 4012	*Sex:* Male

Name: **MARBIN**
2nd Name:
Surname:

Agta Ancestry: 0%

Birth Date: 1974 +/-7 years
Death Date:

Father: NARSING
Mother: LUBIS

1st Spouse:
Last/Current Spouse:

Year: 2010
Marbin-4012

121

ID: 9244   Sex: Male

Name: **MARBIN**
2nd Name:
Surname: ENERIA

Agta Ancestry: 0%

Birth Date: August 23, 1979
Death Date:

Father:
Mother:

Year: 2010   1st Spouse: REHINA-8031
Marbin-9244   Last/Current Spouse: REHINA-8031

ID: 448   Sex: Female

Name: **MARI**
2nd Name: MARILU
Surname: MAKSIMINO

Agta Ancestry: 100%

Birth Date: 1967 +/-3 years
Death Date: 2000 +/-2 years

Father: PEDONG
Mother: AWILIN

Year: 1977   1st Spouse: HUANITO-9164
Mari-448   Last/Current Spouse: HUANITO-9164

ID: 4019   Sex: Female

Name: **MARI**
2nd Name:
Surname:

Agta Ancestry: 100%

Birth Date: 1993 +/-4 years
Death Date:

Father:
Mother: DIWAT

Year: 2010   1st Spouse:
Mari-4019   Last/Current Spouse:

ID: 3465   Sex: Female

Name: **MARIKAR**
2nd Name:
Surname:

Agta Ancestry: 65.625%

Birth Date: August 12, 2001
Death Date:

Father: DYESI
Mother: ENG-ENG

Year: 2010   1st Spouse:
Marikar-3465   Last/Current Spouse:

Year: 1986
Marilin-473 with Gres 3069

1994
Marilin-473

ID: 473   *Sex:* Female

Name: **MARILIN**
2nd Name: DIMENGKOG, MENGKOG
Surname: ARISTAN

Agta Ancestry: 100%

Birth Date: 1966 +/-3 years
Death Date:

Father: PIDYONG
Mother: SIDING

1st Spouse: LENGLENG-47
Last/Current Spouse: OKEG-353

Year: 1978
Marilin-8346

ID: 8346   *Sex:* Female

Name: **MARILIN**
2nd Name:
Surname: BILYAR

Agta Ancestry: 25%

Birth Date: 1961 +/-3 years
Death Date:

Father: DYUNYOR
Mother: BINELDA

1st Spouse:
Last/Current Spouse:

Year: 1977
Marilu-7546

ID: 7546   *Sex:* Female

Name: **MARILU**
2nd Name:
Surname:

Agta Ancestry: Unknown

Birth Date: 1970 +/-3 years
Death Date:

Father: PANGEL
Mother: BAGEY

1st Spouse: LIYONG-432
Last/Current Spouse: LIYONG-432

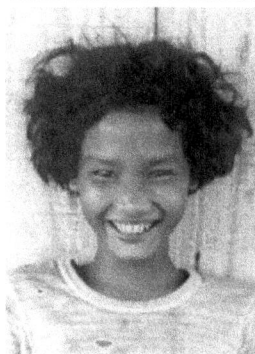

Year: 1976
Marineng-382

1998
Marineng-382 w Dolmeg-3415

ID: 382   *Sex:* Female

Name: **MARINENG**
2nd Name: MARINA, MARIANING
Surname: KULIDEG

Agta Ancestry: Unknown

Birth Date: March 1962
Death Date: January 19, 2001

Father: MELANIO
Mother: ELI

1st Spouse: DOLSING-19
Last/Current Spouse: DOLSING-19

123

ID: 7281	*Sex:* Female

Name: **MARING**
2nd Name:
Surname:

Agta Ancestry: 100%

Birth Date: 1925 +/-5 years
Death Date:

Father: GATENG
Mother: BILANGEG
1st Spouse: SAWILENG-5430
Last/Current Spouse: SIBERO-7182

Year: 1971
Maring-7281

ID: 362	*Sex:* Male

Name: **MARIO**
2nd Name:
Surname: TIKIMAN

Agta Ancestry: 87.5%

Birth Date: 1943 +/-2 years
Death Date: November 14, 1986

Father: TIKIMAN
Mother: AGAPITA
1st Spouse: LODI-363
Last/Current Spouse: LODI-363

Year: 1978
Mario-362

ID: 7407	*Sex:* Female

Name: **MARIRING**
2nd Name: MARLING, MERLIN
Surname:

Agta Ancestry: Unknown

Birth Date: 1975 +/-7 years
Death Date:

Father:
Mother:

1st Spouse: KILENG-7106
Last/Current Spouse: KILENG-7106

Year: 2010
Mariring-7407

ID: 8200	*Sex:* Female

Name: **MARISA**
2nd Name:
Surname:

Agta Ancestry: 46.875%

Birth Date: October 25, 1991
Death Date:

Father: MARIANO
Mother: SELYA
1st Spouse:
Last/Current Spouse:

Year: 2008
Marisa-8200

ID:	3062
Sex:	Female
Name:	**MARISEL**
2nd Name:	
Surname:	GERERO
Agta Ancestry:	87.5%
Birth Date:	April 1986
Death Date:	March 2001
Father:	ELDING
Mother:	NEMI
1st Spouse:	ORLAN-1150
Last/Current Spouse:	ORLAN-1150

Year: 1998
Marisel-3062

1998
Marisel-3062 w husband Orlan on right.

ID:	321
Sex:	Female
Name:	**MARITA**
2nd Name:	
Surname:	KUKUAN
Agta Ancestry:	75%
Birth Date:	1960 +/-1 year
Death Date:	
Father:	MANULING
Mother:	LIYANITA
1st Spouse:	ILOCANO-9165
Last/Current Spouse:	ISAAK-9194

Year: 1977
Marita-321

ID:	8102
Sex:	Female
Name:	**MARITES**
2nd Name:	NAGEK
Surname:	DELAKRUS
Agta Ancestry:	46.88%
Birth Date:	December 1990
Death Date:	
Father:	RENI
Mother:	NENENG
1st Spouse:	SAKLANGEN-3369
Last/Current Spouse:	SAKLANGEN-3369

Year: 2008
Marites-8102

2010
Marites-8102

ID:	7019
Sex:	Female
Name:	**MARIYETA**
2nd Name:	ETENG
Surname:	ALBARES
Agta Ancestry:	100%
Birth Date:	1976 +/-4 years
Death Date:	
Father:	DAGAW
Mother:	ASTING
1st Spouse:	SAWE-131
Last/Current Spouse:	SAWE-131

Year: 1998
Mariyeta-7019

1998
Mariyeta-7019

Year: 2008
Mark-9215 w family

ID: 9215	Sex: Male
Name: **MARK**	
2nd Name:	
Surname: BASILIO	
Agta Ancestry: 0%	
Birth Date: 1969 +/-6 years	
Death Date:	
Father:	
Mother:	
1st Spouse: DYOLIBI-8090	
Last/Current Spouse: DYOLIBI-8090	

Year: 2008
Mark-R- 8261 on left w parents

ID: 8261	Sex: Male
Name: **MARK-ROGER**	
2nd Name: MAKMAK	
Surname: BASILIO	
Agta Ancestry: 12.5%	
Birth Date: November 14, 1998	
Death Date:	
Father: MARK	
Mother: DYOLIBI	
1st Spouse:	
Last/Current Spouse:	

Year: 1977
Marning-371

ID: 371	Sex: Male
Name: **MARNING**	
2nd Name:	
Surname: BUNAW, SALON	
Agta Ancestry: 100%	
Birth Date: 1950 +/-2 years	
Death Date: December 26, 1993	
Father: BUNAW	
Mother: LODI	
1st Spouse: MONING-372	
Last/Current Spouse: BAGEY-7543	

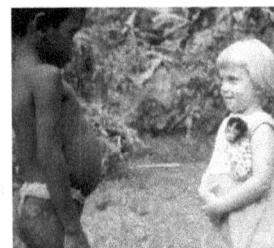

Year: 1967   1978
Marning-381 & Rachel   Marning-381
Headland

ID: 381	Sex: Male
Name: **MARNING**	
2nd Name:	
Surname: KULIDEG	
Agta Ancestry: Unknown	
Birth Date: 1959	
Death Date: May 18, 1989	
Father: MELANIO	
Mother: ELI	
1st Spouse: NENENG-82	
Last/Current Spouse: NENENG-82	

126

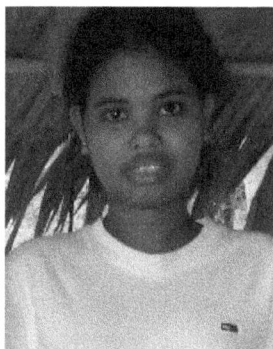

ID:	3026
Sex:	Female
Name:	**MAROS**
2nd Name:	MERILOS
Surname:	
Agta Ancestry:	65.625%
Birth Date:	December 21, 1994
Death Date:	
Father:	DYESI
Mother:	ENG-ENG
1st Spouse:	
Last/Current Spouse:	

Year: 2010
Maros-3026

Year: 1978
Marsilino-569

2002
Marsilino-569

ID: 569   *Sex:* Male
Name: **MARSILINO**
2nd Name:
Surname: EGMONG
Agta Ancestry: 87.5%
Birth Date: 1970 +/-1 year
Death Date:
Father: TARSAN
Mother: SIDING
1st Spouse: DYOSIME-28
Last/Current Spouse: NORA-3500

Year: 1976
Martines-374

ID: 374   *Sex:* Male
Name: **MARTINES**
2nd Name:
Surname: TANYET
Agta Ancestry: 75%
Birth Date: 1921 +/-3 years
Death Date: 1986 +/-2 years
Father: TANYET
Mother: INGGEK
1st Spouse: OLIBIA-375
Last/Current Spouse: OLIBIA-375

Year: 2004
Mase-7696

ID: 7696   *Sex:* Female
Name: **MASE**
2nd Name:
Surname:
Agta Ancestry: 100%
Birth Date: 1950 +/-5 years
Death Date:
Father:
Mother:
1st Spouse: ABO-6005
Last/Current Spouse: ASENG-563

127

Year: 2008
Matan-7941

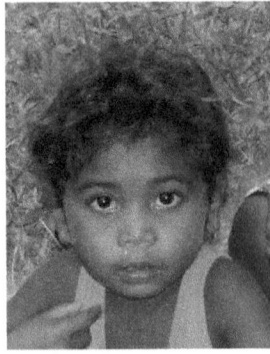

2010
Matan-7941

ID: 7941   Sex: Male

Name: **MATAN**
2nd Name:
Surname: LISIDAY
Agta Ancestry: Unknown

Birth Date: May 7, 2005
Death Date:

Father: DARET
Mother: DYEMALIN

1st Spouse:
Last/Current Spouse:

Year: 1978
Matong-61

ID: 61   Sex: Male

Name: **MATONG**
2nd Name: ROHELIO
Surname: GEHA, GERA

Agta Ancestry: 100%

Birth Date: 1964 +/-1 year
Death Date:

Father: BERIONES
Mother: REKREK

1st Spouse:
Last/Current Spouse:

Year: 1978
Mayeng-402

ID: 402   Sex: Female

Name: **MAYENG**
2nd Name: MERLING
Surname: LISIDAY

Agta Ancestry: 93.75%

Birth Date: 1965 +/-1 year
Death Date: 1996 +/-1 year

Father: NADOY
Mother: REKREK

1st Spouse: LITO-318
Last/Current Spouse: LITO-318

Year: 2002
Maykel-3409 with mother
Siyuning-262

ID: 3409   Sex: Male

Name: **MAYKEL**
2nd Name:
Surname: BALOK, MELUS
Agta Ancestry: Unknown

Birth Date: 1994 +/-2 years
Death Date:

Father: KARDING
Mother: SIYUNING

1st Spouse:
Last/Current Spouse:

128

Year: 2010
Maykel-9222

ID:	9222
Sex:	Male
Name:	**MAYKEL**
2nd Name:	
Surname:	KORTES
Agta Ancestry:	0%
Birth Date:	
Death Date:	
Father:	
Mother:	
1st Spouse:	PUNENE-1013
Last/Current Spouse:	PUNENE-1013

Year: 1976
Mayla-384

2004
Mayla-384 phto by Iris Dalberto

ID:	384
Sex:	Female
Name:	**MAYLA**
2nd Name:	
Surname:	KULIDEG
Agta Ancestry:	Unknown
Birth Date:	February 20, 1971
Death Date:	
Father:	MELANIO
Mother:	ELI
1st Spouse:	RENE-9190
Last/Current Spouse:	RENE-9190

Year: 1977
Mayling-221

ID:	221
Sex:	Female
Name:	**MAYLIN**
2nd Name:	MAYLING
Surname:	PRADO
Agta Ancestry:	75%
Birth Date:	1969 +/-1 year
Death Date:	
Father:	HAKOB
Mother:	PELI
1st Spouse:	GALAMPONG-55
Last/Current Spouse:	GALAMPONG-55

Year: 2010
Maylin-3193

ID:	3193
Sex:	Female
Name:	**MAYLIN**
2nd Name:	ALIN, ALLIN
Surname:	DELAPENYA
Agta Ancestry:	100%
Birth Date:	1987 +/-1 year
Death Date:	
Father:	ATORNI
Mother:	GLORIA
1st Spouse:	EDLIN-1017
Last/Current Spouse:	EDLIN-1017

Year: 1976
Mayong-377

ID: 377   Sex: Male

Name: **MAYONG**
2nd Name:
Surname: BEKYADEN

Agta Ancestry: 87.5%

Birth Date: 1953 +/-3 years
Death Date: 1985

Father: BANGHUL
Mother: PILISA
1st Spouse: NARING-378
Last/Current Spouse: NARING-378

Year: 1977
Medikol-172

ID: 172   Sex: Male

Name: **MEDIKOL**
2nd Name:
Surname: TOMAY

Agta Ancestry: 100%

Birth Date: 1971 +/-1 year
Death Date:

Father: DUDUYAN
Mother: GOLBIYENG
1st Spouse: MENI-54
Last/Current Spouse: SEMILITA-296

Year: 2002
Melani-3017

2010
Melani-3017

ID: 3017   Sex: Female

Name: **MELANI**
2nd Name:
Surname: KUKUAN

Agta Ancestry: 75%

Birth Date: October 1984
Death Date:

Father: NATENG
Mother: TETET
1st Spouse: ARNOL1 ALOY-584
Last/Current Spouse: ARNOL1 ALOY-584

Year: 1976
Melanio-379

ID: 379   Sex: Male

Name: **MELANIO**
2nd Name:
Surname: KULIDEG

Agta Ancestry: 100%

Birth Date: 1935 +/-2 years
Death Date: May 1, 1988

Father: KULIDEG
Mother: INEK
1st Spouse: LALING-5210
Last/Current Spouse: ELI-380

Year: 1966
Melensio-9091 with
unknown man.

ID: 8091 Sex: Male

Name: **MELENSIO**
2nd Name:
Surname:

Agta Ancestry: 43.75%

Birth Date: 1936 +/-4 years
Death Date:

Father: HULIAN
Mother: MILING
1st Spouse: ADILINA-7097
Last/Current Spouse: ADILINA-7097

Year: 2010
Meli-386

ID: 386 Sex: Female

Name: **MELI**
2nd Name:
Surname: TIKIMAN

Agta Ancestry: 93.75%

Birth Date: 1948 +/-3 years
Death Date:

Father: ABANTE
Mother: PETANG
1st Spouse: DANILO-9028
Last/Current Spouse: DANILO-9028

Year: 1984
Melting-481 with son Edlin-
1017

2010
Melting-481

ID: 481 Sex: Female

Name: **MELTING**
2nd Name: MERLITA
Surname: GERA

Agta Ancestry: 93.75%

Birth Date: 1958 +/-3 years
Death Date:

Father: BILYANTING
Mother: ROSITA
1st Spouse: BERIONES-59
Last/Current Spouse: HOSE-8169

Year: 1967
Menes-390

1977
Menes-390

ID: 390 Sex: Male

Name: **MENES**
2nd Name:
Surname: ABUNDIO

Agta Ancestry: 100%

Birth Date: 1912 +/-4 years
Death Date: March 19, 1978

Father: ABUNDIO
Mother: MELYENG
1st Spouse: PIDELA-391
Last/Current Spouse: PIDELA-391

131

Year: 1965
Mensiang holding Merna
258

1977
Mensiyang-257

ID: 257   Sex: Female

Name: **MENSIANG**
2nd Name: MENSIYANG
Surname: SAGNET

Agta Ancestry: 100%

Birth Date: 1932 +/-3 years
Death Date: June 1990

Father: APERIT
Mother: TILIYENG
1st Spouse: KANDEG-256
Last/Current Spouse: KANDEG-256

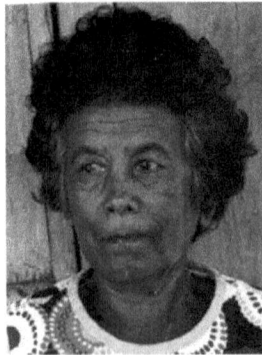

Year: 1978
Mensiang-616

ID: 616   Sex: Female

Name: **MENSIANG**
2nd Name: MENSIYANG
Surname: BALENSIA

Agta Ancestry: 50%

Birth Date: 1915 +/-3 years
Death Date: January 15, 1988

Father: MARIANO
Mother: MELYENG
1st Spouse: PANDONG-5874
Last/Current Spouse: WILYAM-599

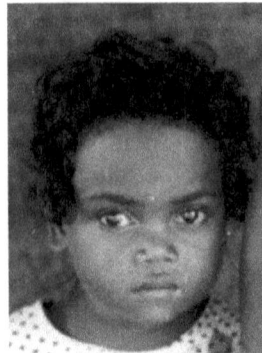

Year: 1978
Meridyen-100

2004
Meridyen-100 phto by Iris
Dalberto

ID: 100   Sex: Female

Name: **MERIDYEN**
2nd Name: MERI
Surname: LISIDAY

Agta Ancestry: 93.75%

Birth Date: 1974 +/-1 year
Death Date:

Father: BORSEG
Mother: LODI
1st Spouse: RIDYEL-409
Last/Current Spouse: RIDYEL-409

Year: 2004
Merigres-1024 phto by Iris
Dalberto

2008
Merigres-1024

ID: 1024   Sex: Female

Name: **MERIGRES**
2nd Name: LOPOG, ANGELES
Surname: LISIDAY

Agta Ancestry: 93.75%

Birth Date: 1979 +/-1 year
Death Date:

Father: BORSEG
Mother: LODI
1st Spouse: KITI-9261
Last/Current Spouse: KITI-9261

Year: 1977
Merli-7430

ID: 7430   *Sex:* Female

Name: **MERLI**
2nd Name: AKES
Surname:

Agta Ancestry: 100%

Birth Date: 1961 +/-3 years
Death Date:

Father: HUWANING
Mother: ISING

1st Spouse:
Last/Current Spouse:

Year: 1972   1977
Merna-258 phto by Jim   Merna-258
Musgrove

ID: 258   *Sex:* Female

Name: **MERNA**
2nd Name:
Surname: SAGUNED

Agta Ancestry: 100%

Birth Date: 1961 +/-1 year
Death Date:

Father: KANDEG
Mother: MENSIANG

1st Spouse: ALEK-9178
Last/Current Spouse: LAKAY-99

Year: 1973
Miding-5725 with child-6237
on left and son Sehemok-

ID: 5725   *Sex:* Female

Name: **MIDING**
2nd Name:
Surname:

Agta Ancestry: 100%

Birth Date: 1929 +/-2 years
Death Date: 1976

Father: APERIT
Mother: TILIYENG

1st Spouse: SINABUYAN-543
Last/Current Spouse: SINABUYAN-543

Year: 1998   2010
Mikmik-206 holding Dyear-   Mikmik-206
3372

ID: 206   *Sex:* Female

Name: **MIKMIK**
2nd Name: ROSAMIYA, ROSAMILA
Surname: LUNA

Agta Ancestry: 100%

Birth Date: 1972 +/-1 year
Death Date:

Father: ETOY
Mother: HILING

1st Spouse: ARNOL1 ALOY-584
Last/Current Spouse: ARNOL2-7535

133

Year: 1978
Milagrin-520

ID: 520   Sex: Female

Name: **MILAGRIN**
2nd Name: KUYEG
Surname: HINUG

Agta Ancestry: Unknown

Birth Date: 1965 +/-2 years
Death Date:

Father: SALAYAN
Mother: BALANGAW

1st Spouse: PENGPENG-7868
Last/Current Spouse: PENGPENG-7868

Year: 1977
Milina-7468

ID: 7468   Sex: Female

Name: **MILINA**
2nd Name: LINA
Surname: TADYO

Agta Ancestry: Unknown

Birth Date: 1951 +/-3 years
Death Date:

Father:
Mother:

1st Spouse: BELDU-7467
Last/Current Spouse: BELDU-7467

Year: 2002
Militeng-516

2010
Militeng-516

ID: 516   Sex: Female

Name: **MILITENG**
2nd Name:
Surname:

Agta Ancestry: 100%

Birth Date: 1955 +/-1 year
Death Date:

Father: MANASES
Mother: LUNING

1st Spouse: RUPING-2071
Last/Current Spouse: RUPING-2071

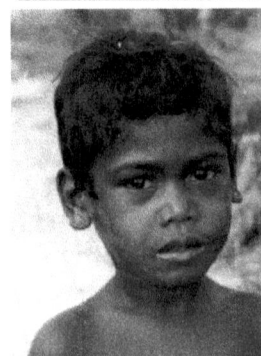
Year: 1976
Milong-424

ID: 424   Sex: Male

Name: **MILONG**
2nd Name: MEDSOR, GASPAR
Surname: BEKYADEN

Agta Ancestry: 93.75%

Birth Date: 1972 +/-1 year
Death Date:

Father: NORPING
Mother: TALENDUS

1st Spouse: NORI-210
Last/Current Spouse: TEBOK-7347

134

Year: 1977
Mindosa-398

ID: 398   Sex: Male

Name: **MINDOSA**
2nd Name:
Surname: EMILIO

Agta Ancestry: 100%

Birth Date: 1928 +/-4 years
Death Date: 1980 +/-1 year

Father: AKED
Mother: MANAY

1st Spouse: BUKOD-7675
Last/Current Spouse: ROMANA-7237

Year: 1976
Miring-229

1978
Miring-229 holding daughtr
Ayling-231

ID: 229   Sex: Female

Name: **MIRING**
2nd Name: MERING
Surname: KUKUAN

Agta Ancestry: 100%

Birth Date: 1946 +/-2 years
Death Date: August 1998

Father: IPOY
Mother: MAMING

1st Spouse: HAYME-228
Last/Current Spouse: HAYME-228

Year: 1977
Moning-372

ID: 372   Sex: Female

Name: **MONING**
2nd Name:
Surname: BANYES

Agta Ancestry: 100%

Birth Date: 1947 +/-3 years
Death Date: 2001 +/-1 year

Father: BANYES
Mother: BEDYONA

1st Spouse: ILE-240
Last/Current Spouse: MARNING-371

Year: 1970
Moyes-6262

ID: 6262   Sex: Male

Name: **MOYES**
2nd Name:
Surname:

Agta Ancestry: Unknown

Birth Date: 1920 +/-9 years
Death Date: 1972 +/-1 year

Father:
Mother:

1st Spouse:
Last/Current Spouse:

135

Year: 1936
Mulan-5311

ID: 5311		*Sex:* Male

Name: **MULAN**
2nd Name:
Surname:

Agta Ancestry: 100%

Birth Date: 1880 +/-9 years
Death Date: 1945 +/-9 years

Father:
Mother:

1st Spouse: ALODEA-5017
Last/Current Spouse: ALODEA-5017

Year: 1977
Nabut-7431

ID: 7431   *Sex:* Male

Name: **NABUT**
2nd Name: BERNABE
Surname:

Agta Ancestry: Unknown

Birth Date:
Death Date:

Father:
Mother:

1st Spouse:
Last/Current Spouse:

Year: 2002
Nadoy-399

ID: 399   *Sex:* Male

Name: **NADOY**
2nd Name: RAMIRES
Surname: LISIDAY

Agta Ancestry: 87.5%

Birth Date: 1933 +/-2 years
Death Date: January 30, 2004

Father: LISIDAY
Mother: MAKINAY

1st Spouse: REKREK-400
Last/Current Spouse: REKREK-400

Year: 1977
Nalengneng-263

ID: 263   *Sex:* Female

Name: **NALENGLENG**
2nd Name: ARLING
Surname: BALOK, MELUS

Agta Ancestry: Unknown

Birth Date: 1971 +/-1 year
Death Date: 1998

Father: KARDING
Mother: SIYUNING

1st Spouse: TILEN-7951
Last/Current Spouse: NOEL-376

ID:	23	*Sex:* Female

ID: 23   *Sex:* Female

Name: **NALENGNENG**
2nd Name:
Surname: LISIDAY

Agta Ancestry: 75%

Birth Date: 1972 +/-1 year
Death Date:

Father: BENDING
Mother: NURING

1st Spouse: DEKSTER-9231
Last/Current Spouse: DEKSTER-9231

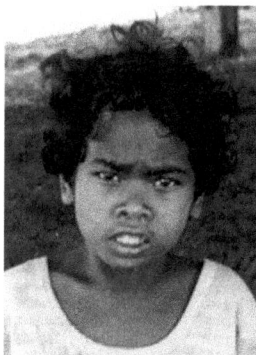

Year: 1978
Nalengneng-23

ID: 283   *Sex:* Female

Name: **NALENGNENG**
2nd Name: SINAYDA, ELSI
Surname: ALAMRA

Agta Ancestry: 100%

Birth Date: 1962 +/-1 year
Death Date:

Father: LAKAY
Mother: LAYNING

1st Spouse: unknown-9016
Last/Current Spouse: unknown-9016

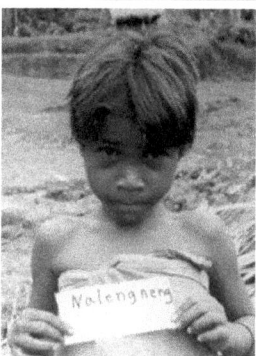

Year: 1978
Nalengneng-283

ID: 7879   *Sex:* Female

Name: **NALENGNENG**
2nd Name:
Surname:

Agta Ancestry: 100%

Birth Date: 1965 +/-2 years
Death Date:

Father: ESTEBES
Mother: IDING

1st Spouse:
Last/Current Spouse:

Year: 1977
Nalengneng-7879

ID: 404   *Sex:* Male

Name: **NALOWADINGAN**
2nd Name: WALWAL
Surname: PAWISAN

Agta Ancestry: 100%

Birth Date: 1958 +/-1 year
Death Date: 1994 +/-1 year

Father: ROSADO
Mother: ANGHILITA

1st Spouse: INGGEL-219
Last/Current Spouse: INGGEL-219

Year: 1978
Nalowadingan-404

137

Year: 1936
Nandes-5320

ID: 5320   Sex: Male

Name: **NANDES**
2nd Name:
Surname:

Agta Ancestry: 100%

Birth Date:
Death Date:

Father:
Mother:

1st Spouse: PULOMENA-5391
Last/Current Spouse: PULOMENA-5391

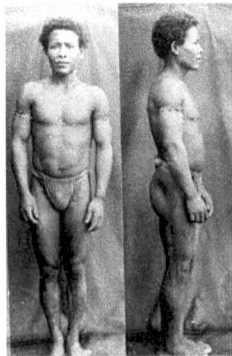

Year: 1936
Nanek-405
photo by Vanoverbergh

1978
Nanek-405

ID: 405   Sex: Male

Name: **NANEK**
2nd Name: MAGONANED
Surname: KALANGGET

Agta Ancestry: 75%

Birth Date: 1911 +/-3 years
Death Date: 1982 +/-1 year

Father: KALANGGET
Mother: WAYA

1st Spouse: KONSING-5200
Last/Current Spouse: TUKONG-5481

Year: 1976
Nani-322

ID: 322   Sex: Male

Name: **NANI**
2nd Name:
Surname: KUKUAN

Agta Ancestry: 75%

Birth Date: 1961 +/-1 year
Death Date:

Father: MANULING
Mother: LIYANITA

1st Spouse: MINDA-9058
Last/Current Spouse: DALEN-8181

Year: 1978
Nanita-8344

ID: 8344   Sex: Female

Name: **NANITA**
2nd Name: ANITA, NINITA
Surname:

Agta Ancestry: 50%

Birth Date: 1920 +/-8 years
Death Date: October 15, 2005

Father:
Mother:

1st Spouse: MITERIO-9262
Last/Current Spouse: MITERIO-9262

138

Year: 2010
Nansi-120

ID: 120	Sex: Female

Name: **NANSI**
2nd Name:
Surname: ISTANES GERA
Agta Ancestry: 96.875%

Birth Date: 1974 +/-1 year
Death Date:

Father: DARBING
Mother: NERSI
1st Spouse: KATOL-125
Last/Current Spouse: KATOL-125

Year: 2010
Nansi-1132

ID: 1132	Sex: Female

Name: **NANSI**
2nd Name:
Surname: ARISTANES
Agta Ancestry: 100%

Birth Date: 1978 +/-1 year
Death Date:

Father: PIDYONG
Mother: SIDING
1st Spouse: LOPOG-1120
Last/Current Spouse: LOPOG-1120

Year: 1977
Narding-597

ID: 597	Sex: Male

Name: **NARDING**
2nd Name:
Surname: ATEG
Agta Ancestry: 100%

Birth Date: 1965 +/-3 years
Death Date:

Father: TONING
Mother: RUSING
1st Spouse:
Last/Current Spouse:

Year: 1977
Naring-378

2010
Naring-378

ID: 378	Sex: Female

Name: **NARING**
2nd Name:
Surname: DANDING
Agta Ancestry: Unknown

Birth Date: 1959 +/-2 years
Death Date:

Father: DANDING
Mother: BIDING
1st Spouse: MAYONG-377
Last/Current Spouse: OLIBER-9141

139

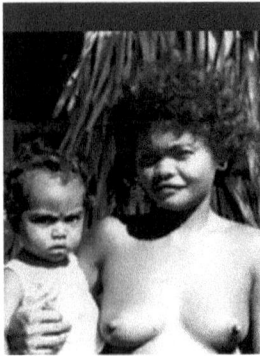

Year: 1977
Narisa-78 holding daughtr
Enda-80

2002
Narisa-78

ID: 78   Sex: Female

Name: **NARISA**
2nd Name:
Surname: ADUANAN
Agta Ancestry: 100%

Birth Date: 1953 +/-2 years
Death Date:

Father: LINGKON
Mother: ADILING
1st Spouse: BILYESA-77
Last/Current Spouse: BAIT-553

Year: 1978
Narita-579

ID: 579   Sex: Female

Name: **NARITA**
2nd Name: MARITA
Surname: SANGBAY
Agta Ancestry: 100%

Birth Date: 1954 +/-2 years
Death Date:

Father: SINABUYAN
Mother: MIDING
1st Spouse: TEKDILEN-578
Last/Current Spouse: GASPAR-9143

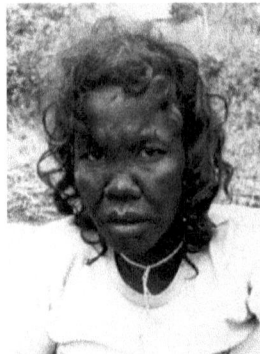

Year: 1978
Narsing-406

ID: 406   Sex: Female

Name: **NARSING**
2nd Name:
Surname: PRADO
Agta Ancestry: 75%

Birth Date: 1952 +/-2 years
Death Date: June 1982

Father: PIRENTE
Mother: ISTRING
1st Spouse: AKAL-5009
Last/Current Spouse: ILISIYO-9034

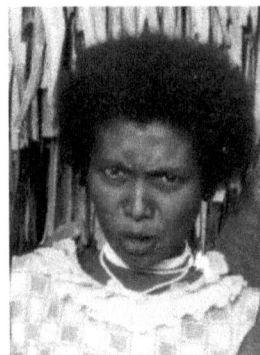

Year: 1971
Narsing-576

ID: 576   Sex: Female

Name: **NARSING**
2nd Name:
Surname:
Agta Ancestry: 100%

Birth Date: 1942 +/-3 years
Death Date:

Father: SAWILENG
Mother: ARPENYA
1st Spouse: WILSON-285
Last/Current Spouse: ROMI-9157

Year: 1977
Narsing-7953

2008
Narsing-7953

ID: 7953	Sex: Male
Name: **NARSING**	
2nd Name:	
Surname: RAMUS	
Agta Ancestry: 100%	
Birth Date: 1945 +/-7 years	
Death Date:	
Father: BELET	
Mother: ROMANA	
1st Spouse: LUBIS-7132	
Last/Current Spouse: LUBIS-7132	

Year: 1972
Narsiso-5322 holding
daughter Lerling-610

ID: 5322	Sex: Male
Name: **NARSISO**	
2nd Name:	
Surname: LISIDAY	
Agta Ancestry: Unknown	
Birth Date: 1943 +/-2 years	
Death Date: 1976	
Father: LISIDAY	
Mother: PANGKUY	
1st Spouse: UTET-609	
Last/Current Spouse: UTET-609	

Year: 1976
Nateng-37

ID: 37	Sex: Male
Name: **NATENG**	
2nd Name: SANDER, RINATO, DIYABAR	
Surname: TULIO	
Agta Ancestry: 100%	
Birth Date: 1956 +/-2 years	
Death Date:	
Father: ASION	
Mother: SULIDAD	
1st Spouse: LOYDA-347	
Last/Current Spouse: LOYDA-347	

Year: 1977
Nateng-171

ID: 171	Sex: Male
Name: **NATENG**	
2nd Name:	
Surname: TOMAY	
Agta Ancestry: 100%	
Birth Date: 1969 +/-1 year	
Death Date:	
Father: DUDUYAN	
Mother: GOLBIYENG	
1st Spouse: ALILINGAN-7861	
Last/Current Spouse: ALILINGAN-7861	

Year: 1977
Nateng-407 & son Orli-410

2008
Nateng-407 phto by Iris
Dalberto

ID: 407	Sex: Male
Name: **NATENG**	
2nd Name: DONATO, REYNATO	
Surname: PRADO	
Agta Ancestry: 75%	
Birth Date: 1955 +/-1 year	
Death Date:	
Father: PIRENTE	
Mother: ISTRING	
1st Spouse: TETET-408	
Last/Current Spouse: TETET-408	

Year: 1977
Nati-2061 holding son
Ombot-336

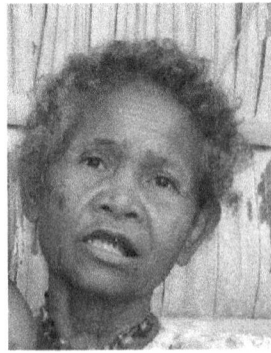

2010
Nati-2061

ID: 2061	Sex: Female
Name: **NATI**	
2nd Name:	
Surname: DUNATO MIRINDU	
Agta Ancestry: 100%	
Birth Date: 1944 +/-3 years	
Death Date:	
Father: DOKDOK	
Mother: APRIKA	
1st Spouse: HAYME-223	
Last/Current Spouse: HAYME-223	

Year: 1936
Nayas-5518, by
Vanoverbergh

ID: 5518	Sex: Male
Name: **NAYAS**	
2nd Name:	
Surname:	
Agta Ancestry: 100%	
Birth Date: 1885 +/-8 years	
Death Date: 1945 +/-9 years	
Father:	
Mother:	
1st Spouse: PINYANA-5519	
Last/Current Spouse: PINYANA-5519	

Year: 1978
Naydu-567

ID: 567	Sex: Male
Name: **NAYDU**	
2nd Name:	
Surname: EGMONG	
Agta Ancestry: 87.5%	
Birth Date: 1959 +/-1 year	
Death Date: September 19, 1987	
Father: TARSAN	
Mother: SIDING	
1st Spouse: EMILI-195	
Last/Current Spouse: DINGDINGAN-117	

ID: 161   Sex: Female

Name: **NAYLING**
2nd Name:
Surname: BERNABE

Agta Ancestry: 100%

Birth Date: 1963 +/-1 year
Death Date:

Father: DOYEG
Mother: AWAY

Year: 1976   1st Spouse: LALENG-306
Nayling-161   Last/Current Spouse: LALENG-306

ID: 1128   Sex: Female

Name: **NEKNEK**
2nd Name: ANABEL
Surname: KUKUAN

Agta Ancestry: 100%

Birth Date: January 1983
Death Date: 1985 +/-1 year

Father: KULUT
Mother: SIPOK

Year: 1984   1st Spouse:
Neknek-1128   Last/Current Spouse:

ID: 411   Sex: Female

Name: **NELI**
2nd Name:
Surname: DISONG

Agta Ancestry: 100%

Birth Date: 1959 +/-1 year
Death Date:

Father: MAGNU
Mother: LULITA

Year: 1978   1st Spouse: ROHEL-9064
Neli-411   Last/Current Spouse: ROHEL-9064

ID: 189   Sex: Female

Name: **NEMI**
2nd Name:
Surname: PRADO

Agta Ancestry: 75%

Birth Date: 1950 +/-2 years
Death Date: October 1992

Father: PIRENTE
Mother: ISTRING

Year: 1977   1st Spouse: ROHEL-504
Nemi-189   Last/Current Spouse: ELDING-188

143

Year: 1978
Nena-94

ID: 94   *Sex:* Female

Name: **NENA**
2nd Name:
Surname: ESTEBES

Agta Ancestry: 100%

Birth Date: 1924 +/-4 years
Death Date:

Father: BALEK
Mother: MANING
1st Spouse: MOLINA-5622
Last/Current Spouse: BONTOY-93

Year: 1978
Nena-412

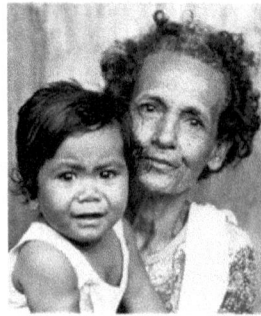
1978
R- Nena L- Unyol 8036

ID: 412   *Sex:* Female

Name: **NENA**
2nd Name:
Surname: BROSSEAU

Agta Ancestry: 50%

Birth Date: December 13, 1922
Death Date:

Father: BUROSA
Mother: DAYMES
1st Spouse: HUNORIO-9048
Last/Current Spouse: PILO-9036

Year: 1936
Nenayan-5329
photo by Vanoverbergh

ID: 5329   *Sex:* Female

Name: **NENAYAN**
2nd Name:
Surname:

Agta Ancestry: 100%

Birth Date:
Death Date:

Father: ANDRES
Mother: FRANSISKA
1st Spouse: TIMPLADEN-5470
Last/Current Spouse: DILEK-5109

Year: 1976
Neneng 82

2008
Neneng-82

ID: 82   *Sex:* Female

Name: **NENENG**
2nd Name: LAGENG
Surname: KUKUAN

Agta Ancestry: 100%

Birth Date: 1956 +/-2 years
Death Date: 2009

Father: BILYESA
Mother: ANDITA
1st Spouse: MARNING-381
Last/Current Spouse: MADENG-329

144

Year: 1978
Neneng-250 holding
daughtr 6249

ID: 250   Sex: Female

Name: **NENENG**
2nd Name:
Surname: MAKSIMINO
Agta Ancestry: 100%

Birth Date: 1945 +/-2 years
Death Date: January 1994

Father: SIBLI
Mother: TINAY
1st Spouse: ISON-249
Last/Current Spouse: ISON-249

Year: 1973
Neneng-413

ID: 413   Sex: Female

Name: **NENENG**
2nd Name:
Surname: LOPES
Agta Ancestry: 100%

Birth Date: 1959 +/-1 year
Death Date: 2004 +/-3 years

Father: LOPES
Mother: LILYA
1st Spouse: NARDING-165
Last/Current Spouse: ASENG-563

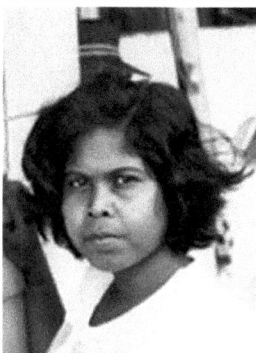

Year: 1979   2010
Neneng-415   Neneng-415

ID: 415   Sex: Female

Name: **NENENG**
2nd Name: KONSITA, LINING
Surname: PULUKIN, KARULINA
Agta Ancestry: 93.75%

Birth Date: 1952 +/-1 year
Death Date:

Father: TOTENG
Mother: KULUDING
1st Spouse: DIYOSKORO-9109
Last/Current Spouse: RENI-9111

Year: 1977
Neneng-510

ID: 510   Sex: Female

Name: **NENENG**
2nd Name: DELIDELI
Surname: MANDOSA
Agta Ancestry: 100%

Birth Date: 1952 +/-2 years
Death Date: 1995 +/-2 years

Father: MANDOSA
Mother: KORDING
1st Spouse: ROMIO-7272
Last/Current Spouse: ROMIO-7272

145

Year: 1972
Neneng-531 phto by Jim
Musgrove

2010
Neneng-531

ID: 531   Sex: Female

Name: **NENENG**
2nd Name:
Surname: BELYASING

Agta Ancestry: 100%

Birth Date: 1952 +/-2 years
Death Date:

Father: BELYASING
Mother: SAGED

1st Spouse: SELTON-530
Last/Current Spouse: SELTON-530

Year: 1978
Nengnengan-401

ID: 401   Sex: Female

Name: **NENGNENGAN**
2nd Name: NENGNENG
Surname: LISIDAY

Agta Ancestry: 93.75%

Birth Date: 1961 +/-1 year
Death Date:

Father: NADOY
Mother: REKREK

1st Spouse: LONGHINO-63
Last/Current Spouse: LONGHINO-63

Year: 1977
Nersi-119 holding daughtr
Dyosi-121

ID: 119   Sex: Female

Name: **NERSI**
2nd Name: MERSE, MERSI
Surname: LISIDAY

Agta Ancestry: 93.75%

Birth Date: 1956 +/-1 year
Death Date:

Father: NADOY
Mother: REKREK

1st Spouse: DARBING-118
Last/Current Spouse: ANDRING-9073

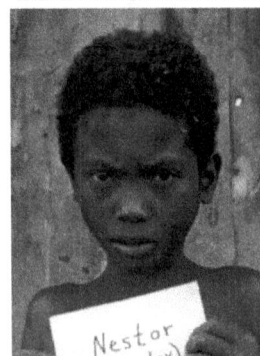

Year: 1978
Nestor-96

ID: 96   Sex: Male

Name: **NESTOR**
2nd Name:
Surname: IMO

Agta Ancestry: 100%

Birth Date: 1968 +/-2 years
Death Date:

Father: BONTOY
Mother: NENA

1st Spouse:
Last/Current Spouse:

146

Year: 1977
Nikson-403 with mom
Rekrek

ID:	403	*Sex:* Male

Name: **NIKSON**
2nd Name:
Surname: LISIDAY

Agta Ancestry: 93.75%

Birth Date: 1971 +/-1 year
Death Date:

Father: NADOY
Mother: REKREK
1st Spouse: ENDA-80
Last/Current Spouse: ENDA-80

Year: 1972
Ningning-417 phto by Jim
Musgrove

ID:	417	*Sex:* Female

Name: **NINGNING**
2nd Name: BUTUK
Surname:

Agta Ancestry: 100%

Birth Date: 1927 +/-4 years
Death Date: June 7, 1977

Father: LENDEK
Mother: DIWANE
1st Spouse: PORENGGES-5393
Last/Current Spouse: MARKES-9078

Year: 1977
Nini-8015

ID:	8015	*Sex:* Female

Name: **NINI**
2nd Name:
Surname: HIMINES

Agta Ancestry: 50%

Birth Date: 1926 +/-3 years
Death Date: 1989 +/-5 years

Father: MANWEL
Mother: PERMINYA
1st Spouse: BERNARDO-9004
Last/Current Spouse: BERNARDO-9004

Year: 2010
Nini-9133

ID:	9133	*Sex:* Female

Name: **NINI**
2nd Name: LINDA, ERLINDA, TANINI
Surname:

Agta Ancestry: Unknown

Birth Date: 1967 +/-2 years
Death Date:

Father: unknown
Mother: BERHINYA
1st Spouse: BAIT-495
Last/Current Spouse: BAIT-495

Year: 2008
Nining-3362

ID: 3362	Sex: Female

Name: **NINING**
2nd Name: LENANI
Surname: PRADO

Agta Ancestry: 75%

Birth Date: 1994 +/-1 year
Death Date:

Father: NATENG
Mother: TETET

1st Spouse:
Last/Current Spouse:

Year: 1979
Ninyeng-418 holding son
Dyeri-7676

ID: 418	Sex: Female

Name: **NINYENG**
2nd Name: NINYA
Surname:

Agta Ancestry: 100%

Birth Date: 1955 +/-2 years
Death Date:

Father: KOMPILENG
Mother: ILEN

1st Spouse: ARNING-7260
Last/Current Spouse: EDI-9191

Year: 1977
Nita-524

ID: 524	Sex: Female

Name: **NITA**
2nd Name:
Surname: LISIDAY

Agta Ancestry: 100%

Birth Date: 1953 +/-1 year
Death Date:

Father: LISIDAY
Mother: PANGKUY

1st Spouse: SANDER-523
Last/Current Spouse: RANDI-293

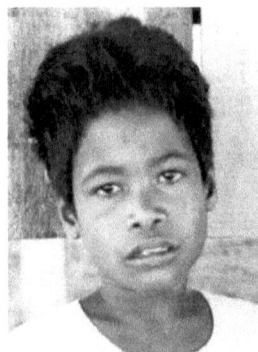

Year: 1977
Noel-376

2008
Noel-376

ID: 376	Sex: Male

Name: **NOEL**
2nd Name:
Surname: TANYET KAGAWAD

Agta Ancestry: 87.5%

Birth Date: 1966 +/-1 year
Death Date:

Father: MARTINES
Mother: OLIBIA

1st Spouse: NALENGLENG-263
Last/Current Spouse: RESI-549

148

ID: 8347   *Sex:* Male

Name: **NOEL**
2nd Name:
Surname: BILYAR

Agta Ancestry: 25%

Birth Date: 1964 +/-2 years
Death Date:

Father: DYUNYOR
Mother: BINELDA

1st Spouse:
Last/Current Spouse:

Year: 1978
Noel-8347

ID: 436   *Sex:* Male

Name: **NOLENG**
2nd Name: OLENG
Surname:

Agta Ancestry: 100%

Birth Date: 1975 +/-1 year
Death Date:

Father: PANDARING
Mother: WANAGEN

1st Spouse:
Last/Current Spouse:

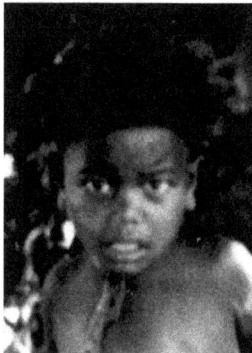

Year: 1978
Noleng-436

ID: 514   *Sex:* Male

Name: **NOLER**
2nd Name:
Surname:

Agta Ancestry: 50%

Birth Date: July 1963
Death Date: December 1980

Father: NALDING
Mother: ADILING

1st Spouse:
Last/Current Spouse:

Year: 1964   1977
Noler-514 & Tom Headland   Noler-514

ID: 180   *Sex:* Female

Name: **NOLI**
2nd Name:
Surname: BANTUG

Agta Ancestry: 100%

Birth Date: 1961 +/-9 years
Death Date:

Father: EDA
Mother: TILOKEN

1st Spouse: ILYAS-9080
Last/Current Spouse: ILYAS-9080

Year: 1976   1992
Noli-180   Noli-180

Year: 1984
Nora-1127 with mother
Awilin-447

ID: 1127	Sex: Female
Name: **NORA**	
2nd Name: DAGADAG	
Surname: MAKSIMINO	
Agta Ancestry: 100%	
Birth Date: January 4, 1981	
Death Date:	
Father: PEDONG	
Mother: AWILIN	
1st Spouse:	
Last/Current Spouse:	

Year: 2008
Nora-3500

ID: 3500	Sex: Female
Name: **NORA**	
2nd Name:	
Surname: DABID	
Agta Ancestry: Unknown	
Birth Date: 1984 +/-4 years	
Death Date:	
Father: ROMIO	
Mother: NENENG	
1st Spouse: ARMANDU-1046	
Last/Current Spouse: MARSILINO-569	

Year: 2002
R- Noralin L- Mandong 3472

2004
Noralin-1109 holding son
Kimwel-3528 phto by Iris

ID: 1109	Sex: Female
Name: **NORALIN**	
2nd Name: DALENG	
Surname: PRADO	
Agta Ancestry: 75%	
Birth Date: December 1979	
Death Date:	
Father: NATENG	
Mother: TETET	
1st Spouse: ARMAN-611	
Last/Current Spouse: ARMAN-611	

Year: 1978
Norma-277

ID: 277	Sex: Female
Name: **NORMA**	
2nd Name:	
Surname: RAMUS	
Agta Ancestry: 100%	
Birth Date: 1949 +/-2 years	
Death Date: January 2, 1997	
Father: BINONG	
Mother: LIGAYA	
1st Spouse: RUPINO-5479	
Last/Current Spouse: KULUT-276	

150

Year: 1968
Normita-266

1978
Normita-266

ID:	266	Sex: Female

Name: **NORMITA**
2nd Name:
Surname:

Agta Ancestry: 100%

Birth Date: 1956 +/-2 years
Death Date: January 28, 1987

Father: MANIBUG
Mother: KASTING
1st Spouse: RUMING-507
Last/Current Spouse: WILENG-456

Year: 2002
Norning-7830 with daughtr
Supiya-7901

ID:	7830	Sex: Male

Name: **NORNING**
2nd Name:
Surname:

Agta Ancestry: 100%

Birth Date: 1959 +/-6 years
Death Date:

Father:
Mother: MAKINAY
1st Spouse: ILIN-7829
Last/Current Spouse: ILIN-7829

Year: 1976
Norping-422

ID:	422	Sex: Male

Name: **NORPING**
2nd Name: MORPING
Surname: BELYADEN

Agta Ancestry: 87.5%

Birth Date: 1946 +/-4 years
Death Date:

Father: BANGHUL
Mother: PILISA
1st Spouse: TALENDUS-423
Last/Current Spouse: BAGOL-539

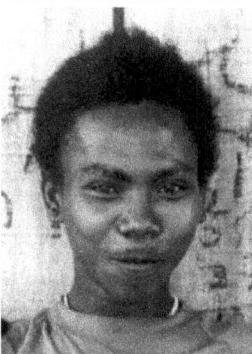

Year: 1977
Norping-427

ID:	427	Sex: Male

Name: **NORPING**
2nd Name:
Surname: PEDRING

Agta Ancestry: 100%

Birth Date: 1957 +/-1 year
Death Date:

Father: PEDRING
Mother: USING
1st Spouse: BAGEL-7261
Last/Current Spouse: DIYULITA-7536

151

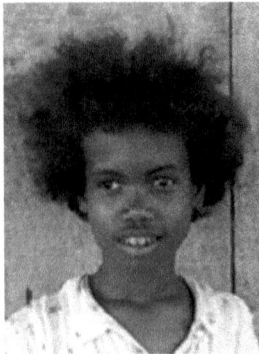

Year: 1976
Norseng-51

2010
Norseng-51

ID: 51	*Sex:* Female
Name: **NORSENG**	
2nd Name:	
Surname:	
Agta Ancestry: 81.25%	
Birth Date: 1961	
Death Date:	
Father:	RAMON
Mother:	PERLING
1st Spouse:	BERTING-9075
Last/Current Spouse:	OSKAR-9135

Year: 1976
Noyme-132

2010
Noyme-132

ID: 132	*Sex:* Female
Name: **NOYME**	
2nd Name:	
Surname:	ADUANAN
Agta Ancestry: 100%	
Birth Date: 1962 +/-1 year	
Death Date:	
Father:	DIDOG
Mother:	POMPOEK
1st Spouse:	BERTING-21
Last/Current Spouse:	BERTING-21

Year: 2010
Nungan-3354

ID: 3354	*Sex:* Male
Name: **NUNGAN**	
2nd Name:	DYERIMI
Surname:	
Agta Ancestry: 90.625%	
Birth Date: October 1997	
Death Date:	
Father:	TERSING
Mother:	PEPEK
1st Spouse:	
Last/Current Spouse:	

Year: 1977
Nunuk-197

ID: 197	*Sex:* Female
Name: **NUNUK**	
2nd Name:	OPRING
Surname:	ADUANAN
Agta Ancestry: 87.5%	
Birth Date: 1948 +/-1 year	
Death Date: July 1992	
Father:	DIKMIN
Mother:	PINYANG
1st Spouse:	ENDING-196
Last/Current Spouse:	ENDING-196

Year: 1977
Nuring-18

ID: 18   Sex: Female
Name: **NURING**
2nd Name:
Surname: BITIGAN
Agta Ancestry: Unknown

Birth Date: 1936 +/-3 years
Death Date: 2006

Father: BITIGAN
Mother: KANORA
1st Spouse: BENDING-5395
Last/Current Spouse: ALUNET-17

Year: 1977
Oleng-7153

ID: 7153   Sex: Male
Name: **OLENG**
2nd Name: YOLENG
Surname:
Agta Ancestry: Unknown

Birth Date:
Death Date:

Father:
Mother:
1st Spouse: KEDEK-143
Last/Current Spouse: KEDEK-143

Year: 2010
Oliber-9141

ID: 9141   Sex: Male
Name: **OLIBER**
2nd Name:
Surname:
Agta Ancestry: 0%

Birth Date: 1960 +/-5 years
Death Date:

Father:
Mother:
1st Spouse: NARING-378
Last/Current Spouse: NARING-378

Year: 1976
Olibia-375

ID: 375   Sex: Female
Name: **OLIBIA**
2nd Name: ULIBIA, OLIBIYA
Surname:
Agta Ancestry: 100%

Birth Date: 1929 +/-3 years
Death Date: July 9, 1983

Father: AGINALDO
Mother: PASKUALITA
1st Spouse: MARTINES-374
Last/Current Spouse: MARTINES-374

153

Year: 1978
Omi-66

ID:	66	*Sex:* Male

Name: **OMI**
2nd Name: DUMINGGU
Surname: ANGLENAN, BEKYADEN

Agta Ancestry: Unknown

Birth Date: 1956 +/-2 years
Death Date:

Father: BIDOY
Mother: MAKARIA

1st Spouse: UDENG-46
Last/Current Spouse: BEBI-9182

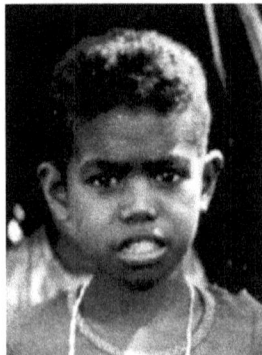
Year: 1978
Omi-340

ID:	340	*Sex:* Male

Name: **OMI**
2nd Name:
Surname: BINGGOSA

Agta Ancestry: 100%

Birth Date: 1969 +/-1 year
Death Date:

Father: MAMORA
Mother: LULITA

1st Spouse: PEPEK-83
Last/Current Spouse: PEPEK-83

Year: 2010
Ompok-4020

ID:	4020	*Sex:* Male

Name: **OMPOK**
2nd Name:
Surname:

Agta Ancestry: 100%

Birth Date: 1970 +/-7 years
Death Date:

Father: ANSETA
Mother: SINGOL

1st Spouse:
Last/Current Spouse:

Year: 1966
Onli-5338 with mother
Nunuk-197

ID:	5338	*Sex:* Male

Name: **ONLI**
2nd Name: ONLI
Surname: TULIO

Agta Ancestry: 93.75%

Birth Date: 1965 +/-1 year
Death Date: March 12, 1967

Father: ENDING
Mother: NUNUK

1st Spouse:
Last/Current Spouse:

154

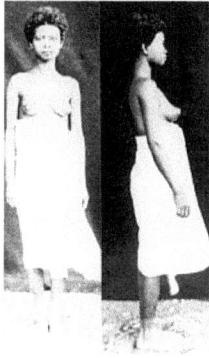

Year: 1936
Opista-5339
photo by Vanoverbergh

ID: 5339   Sex: Female

Name: **OPISTA**
2nd Name:
Surname: ANGIDEW

Agta Ancestry: 100%

Birth Date: 1912 +/-8 years
Death Date: 1967 +/-4 years

Father: ANGIDEW
Mother: ASIONA
1st Spouse: BENGGOSA-5073
Last/Current Spouse: GASPONG-5146

Year: 1967
Opista-5505

ID: 5505   Sex: Female

Name: **OPISTA**
2nd Name:
Surname:

Agta Ancestry: 100%

Birth Date: 1910 +/-9 years
Death Date: 1972 +/-9 years

Father:
Mother:
1st Spouse: MARTINES-373
Last/Current Spouse: MARTINES-373

Year: 1977
Ordonya-7537

ID: 7537   Sex: Male

Name: **ORDONYA**
2nd Name: NANDIT
Surname: TAGYAM

Agta Ancestry: Unknown

Birth Date: 1948 +/-5 years
Death Date: 2000 +/-9 years

Father:
Mother:
1st Spouse: GIDONG-7538
Last/Current Spouse: GIDONG-7538

Year: 1998
Orlan-1150

1998
Orlan-1150 & wife Marisel
on left.

ID: 1150   Sex: Male

Name: **ORLAN**
2nd Name:
Surname: SALINAS

Agta Ancestry: 100%

Birth Date: February 1978
Death Date: January 30, 2004

Father: RUPING
Mother: MILITENG
1st Spouse: MARISEL-3062
Last/Current Spouse: MARISEL-3062

155

Year: 2004
Orli-410

2010
Orli-410

ID: 410   Sex: Male
Name: **ORLI**
2nd Name:
Surname: PRADO
Agta Ancestry: 75%

Birth Date: 1976
Death Date:

Father: NATENG
Mother: TETET
1st Spouse: MAAL-606
Last/Current Spouse: MAAL-606

Year: 2010
Osang-9223

ID: 9223   Sex: Female
Name: **OSANG**
2nd Name: ROSALIN
Surname:
Agta Ancestry: 12.5%

Birth Date: 1989 +/-3 years
Death Date:

Father: SALET
Mother: LETI
1st Spouse: ELIBOY-327
Last/Current Spouse: ELIBOY-327

Year: 1984
Dyosi-568

ID: 568   Sex: Female
Name: **OSI**
2nd Name: DYOSI, ROSALINA
Surname: EGMONG
Agta Ancestry: 87.5%

Birth Date: 1963 +/-1 year
Death Date: 1996 +/-3 years

Father: TARSAN
Mother: SIDING
1st Spouse: unknown-9167
Last/Current Spouse: unknown-9167

Year: 1978
Osming-428

2008
Osming-428

ID: 428   Sex: Male
Name: **OSMING**
2nd Name: OSMIN
Surname: MAKSIMINO
Agta Ancestry: 100%

Birth Date: 1951 +/-3 years
Death Date:

Father: SIBLI
Mother: TINAY
1st Spouse: HUANITA-429
Last/Current Spouse: NORI-210

ID: 3105   *Sex:* Female

Name: **OTALEK**
2nd Name: RISEL
Surname:

Agta Ancestry: 93.75%

Birth Date: 1983 +/-1 year
Death Date:

Father: GUBEK
Mother: PENI

1st Spouse:
Last/Current Spouse:

Year: 2002
Otalek-3105

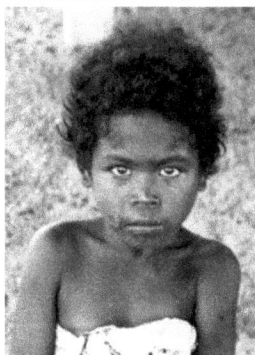

ID: 311   *Sex:* Female

Name: **OYOK**
2nd Name: DYOSI
Surname:

Agta Ancestry: 93.75%

Birth Date: 1966 +/-6 years
Death Date: 1985 +/-4 years

Father: BESTIAN
Mother: NIYEBES

1st Spouse:
Last/Current Spouse:

Year: 1977
Oyok-311

ID: 430   *Sex:* Male

Name: **PABLING**
2nd Name:
Surname: BEKYADEN

Agta Ancestry: 87.5%

Birth Date: 1941 +/-3 years
Death Date:

Father: BANGHUL
Mother: PILISA

1st Spouse: KARMIN-5188
Last/Current Spouse: PELDUS-2066

Year: 1976
Pabling-430

ID: 5344   *Sex:* Female

Name: **PAGOK**
2nd Name: ELDINA
Surname:

Agta Ancestry: Unknown

Birth Date: 1973 +/-2 years
Death Date: January 1978

Father: PAEL
Mother: ADILING

1st Spouse:
Last/Current Spouse:

Year: 1976
Pagok-5344

157

Year: 1976
Paken-39

ID: 39   Sex: Female

Name: **PAKEN**
2nd Name: MERLI
Surname: TULIO

Agta Ancestry: 100%

Birth Date: 1967 +/-1 year
Death Date: 1995 +/-2 years

Father: ASION
Mother: SULIDAD

1st Spouse: GARDU-9144
Last/Current Spouse: GARDU-9144

Year: 1984
Pakoy-62

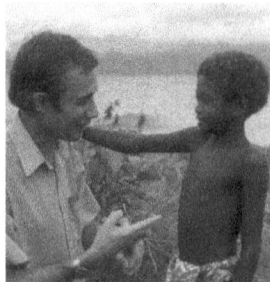

1984
Pakoy-62 & Tom Headland

ID: 62   Sex: Male

Name: **PAKOY**
2nd Name:
Surname: GEHA, GERA

Agta Ancestry: 100%

Birth Date: 1971 +/-1 year
Death Date:

Father: BERIONES
Mother: REKREK

1st Spouse: BAIT-1177
Last/Current Spouse: BAIT-1177

Year: 2008
Palakok-1038

ID: 1038   Sex: Male

Name: **PALAKOK**
2nd Name: LONI
Surname: KULIDEG

Agta Ancestry: 100%

Birth Date: November 1979
Death Date:

Father: DYIMI
Mother: EKDET

1st Spouse: ETA-7915
Last/Current Spouse: ETA-7915

Year: 1965
Palaming-7594

ID: 7594   Sex: Male

Name: **PALAMING**
2nd Name:
Surname:

Agta Ancestry: Unknown

Birth Date: 1925 +/-8 years
Death Date:

Father:
Mother:

1st Spouse: LAWDENG-7267
Last/Current Spouse: LAWDENG-7267

ID:	3366
Sex:	Female

Name: **PALAPANG**
2nd Name: RINET
Surname: SAGUNED

Agta Ancestry: 100%

Birth Date: October 5, 1992
Death Date:

Father: DYUNYOR
Mother: ELSA

1st Spouse:
Last/Current Spouse:

Year: 2010
Palapang-3366

ID: 124   *Sex:* Female

Name: **PAMING**
2nd Name:
Surname: BERNABE

Agta Ancestry: 100%

Birth Date: 1951 +/-1 year
Death Date:

Father: DOYEG
Mother: AWAY

1st Spouse: DELOY-123
Last/Current Spouse: DELOY-123

Year: 1977
Paming-124 holding son
Kulut-126

2010
Paming-124

ID: 433   *Sex:* Male

Name: **PANDARING**
2nd Name:
Surname:

Agta Ancestry: 100%

Birth Date: 1945 +/-3 years
Death Date: 1988 +/-1 year

Father: PIYOYO
Mother: KARMEN

1st Spouse: WANAGEN-434
Last/Current Spouse: WANAGEN-434

Year: 1978
Pandaring-433

ID: 1052   *Sex:* Female

Name: **PANEK**
2nd Name: NEKNEK, SAYRIS
Surname: PRADO

Agta Ancestry: 75%

Birth Date: March 17, 1978
Death Date:

Father: HAKOB
Mother: PELI

1st Spouse: TIKRAN-9180
Last/Current Spouse: TIKRAN-9180

Year: 2008
Panek-1052

159

ID: 1106   Sex: Female

Name: **PANEK**
2nd Name: MILA
Surname: DIYOSINO

Agta Ancestry: 46.875%

Birth Date: 1978 +/-1 year
Death Date:

Father: DANILO
Mother: MELI
1st Spouse: PERNITO-9152
Last/Current Spouse: AMBUY-8263

Year: 2008
Panek-1106

ID: 3181   Sex: Female

Name: **PANET**
2nd Name: MAYET
Surname: KUKUAN

Agta Ancestry: 90.63%

Birth Date: September 30, 1987
Death Date:

Father: LITO
Mother: IMELDA
1st Spouse: BOYBOYAN-8277
Last/Current Spouse: BOYBOYAN-8277

Year: 2008
Panet-3181

ID: 243   Sex: Female

Name: **PANGKUY**
2nd Name:
Surname: TULIO

Agta Ancestry: Unknown

Birth Date: 1927 +/-3 years
Death Date: August 1984

Father: TULIO
Mother: LIPANYAW
1st Spouse: LISIDAY-5229
Last/Current Spouse: ILEN-2042

Year: 1978
Pangkuy-243

ID: 7280   Sex: Female

Name: **PANSING**
2nd Name:
Surname: DUNATO, MANALO

Agta Ancestry: 100%

Birth Date: 1935 +/-4 years
Death Date: January 1998

Father: DOKDOK
Mother: APRIKA
1st Spouse: UGKUY-7595
Last/Current Spouse: ISET-7022

Year: 1978
Pansing-7280

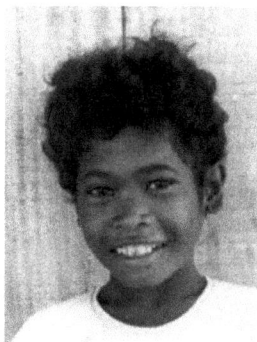

Year: 1977
Pansito-22

ID: 22	*Sex:* Male

Name: **PANSITO**
2nd Name: TILONG
Surname: LISIDAY

Agta Ancestry: 93.75%

Birth Date: 1969 +/-1 year
Death Date:

Father: BENDING
Mother: NURING

1st Spouse: POLEN-7819
Last/Current Spouse: POLEN-7819

Year: 1927
Panyang-5348 (about 1927)

ID: 5348	*Sex:* Female

Name: **PANYANG**
2nd Name: PANIANG
Surname:

Agta Ancestry: 100%

Birth Date: 1905 +/-5 years
Death Date: 1966 +/-7 years

Father: PONGA
Mother: NEYENG

1st Spouse: GAWDENSIO-5148
Last/Current Spouse: GAWDENSIO-5148

Year: 1978   2008
Pasing-445   Pasing-445

ID: 445	*Sex:* Female

Name: **PASING**
2nd Name:
Surname: EGMON, DELAKRUS

Agta Ancestry: 50%

Birth Date: 1932 +/-2 years
Death Date:

Father: AGAPITO
Mother: LAWDAMYA

1st Spouse: JUAN-9079
Last/Current Spouse: JUAN-9079

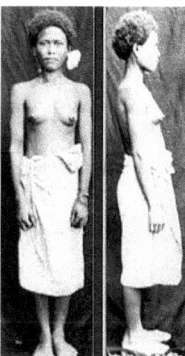

Year: 1936
Paskualita-5958
photo by Vanoverbergh

ID: 5958	*Sex:* Female

Name: **PASKUALITA**
2nd Name: PASKUALITA, PASKUWALITA
Surname:

Agta Ancestry: Unknown

Birth Date: 1908 +/-5 years
Death Date: 1945 +/-5 years

Father:
Mother:

1st Spouse: AGINALDO-5560
Last/Current Spouse: AGINALDO-5560

ID: 446	*Sex:* Male

Name: **PEDONG**
2nd Name: ALPREDO
Surname: MAKSIMINO

Agta Ancestry: 100%

Birth Date: 1939 +/-2 years
Death Date: April 2000

Father: KABINTEW
Mother: ANTIKINA

1st Spouse: AWILIN-447

Last/Current Spouse: AWILIN-447

Year: 1977
Pedong-446

ID: 454	*Sex:* Male

Name: **PEDRING**
2nd Name:
Surname: OLIBEROS

Agta Ancestry: 100%

Birth Date: 1930 +/-2 years
Death Date:

Father: UMANDU
Mother: ORIYENG

1st Spouse: MINAY-7627

Last/Current Spouse: LUNINGNING-455

Year: 1963
Pedring-454

ID: 7146	*Sex:* Female

Name: **PEKIDOT**
2nd Name: MERSED
Surname:

Agta Ancestry: Unknown

Birth Date: 1952 +/-7 years
Death Date:

Father: DESAG
Mother: BENDULING

1st Spouse: SESAR-7180

Last/Current Spouse: SESAR-7180

Year: 1977
Pekidot-7146

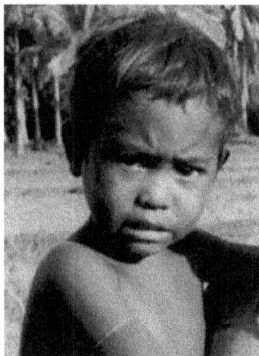

ID: 150	*Sex:* Male

Name: **PEKPEK**
2nd Name: PEKPEKAN, OMI
Surname: KALANGGET

Agta Ancestry: 93.75%

Birth Date: 1972 +/-1 year
Death Date: April 1978

Father: DOMING
Mother: TELENGAN

1st Spouse:

Last/Current Spouse:

Year: 1977
Pekpek-150

Year: 1976
Pekto-461

ID: 461   Sex: Male

Name: **PEKTO**
2nd Name:
Surname: GERA

Agta Ancestry: 100%

Birth Date: 1902 +/-5 years
Death Date: February 5, 1978

Father: GERA
Mother: LATAYAK

1st Spouse: BINANSA-5497
Last/Current Spouse: BINANSA-5497

Year: 1977
Peldus-2066

ID: 2066   Sex: Female

Name: **PELDUS**
2nd Name: PERLING
Surname: DINSIWEG

Agta Ancestry: Unknown

Birth Date: 1944
Death Date: 1988 +/-3 years

Father: BELET
Mother: ROMANA

1st Spouse: PABYEL-7157
Last/Current Spouse: PABLING-430

Year: 1976
Peli-218

ID: 218   Sex: Female

Name: **PELI**
2nd Name:
Surname: KUKUAN

Agta Ancestry: 75%

Birth Date: 1947 +/-2 years
Death Date: October 16, 1984

Father: MANULING
Mother: LIYANITA

1st Spouse: HAKOB-217
Last/Current Spouse: HAKOB-217

Year: 1969
Pelimon-462 & wife
Armonia-5045

1978
Pelimon-462

ID: 462   Sex: Male

Name: **PELIMON**
2nd Name:
Surname: ABUNDIO

Agta Ancestry: 100%

Birth Date: 1907 +/-5 years
Death Date: November 23, 1980

Father: ABUNDIO
Mother: MELYENG

1st Spouse: NIKONIS-5775
Last/Current Spouse: SAGED-517

163

Year: 1978
Penanek-435

ID: 435	*Sex:* Male

Name: **PENANEK**
2nd Name:
Surname:

Agta Ancestry: 100%

Birth Date: 1968 +/-2 years
Death Date:

Father:	PANDARING
Mother:	WANAGEN
1st Spouse:	DYEMA-166
Last/Current Spouse:	DYEMA-166

Year: 1977
Pengpeng-301 & son Uding-303

ID: 301	*Sex:* Female

Name: **PENGPENG**
2nd Name: MANDENG
Surname: TANASIO

Agta Ancestry: 100%

Birth Date: 1946 +/-3 years
Death Date:

Father:	TANASIYO
Mother:	MALENSIYANA
1st Spouse:	LALONG-300
Last/Current Spouse:	ABDON-1

Year: 2010
Peni-463

ID: 463	*Sex:* Female

Name: **PENI**
2nd Name:
Surname: TANYET

Agta Ancestry: 87.5%

Birth Date: 1949 +/-3 years
Death Date:

Father:	MARTINES
Mother:	OLIBIA
1st Spouse:	GUBEK-7079
Last/Current Spouse:	GUBEK-7079

Year: 1977
Pepek-13

2010
Pepek-13

ID: 13	*Sex:* Female

Name: **PEPEK**
2nd Name: MERLI
Surname: KUKUAN

Agta Ancestry: 81.25%

Birth Date: 1961 +/-2 years
Death Date:

Father:	GUBEK
Mother:	SABILITA
1st Spouse:	ALE-12
Last/Current Spouse:	TERSING-494

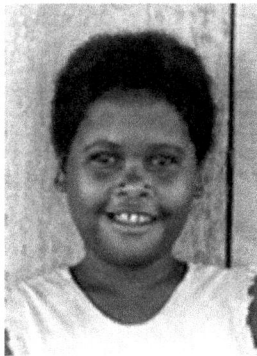

ID: 83   *Sex:* Female

Name: **PEPEK**
2nd Name: WARLING
Surname: KUKUAN

Agta Ancestry: 100%

Birth Date: 1961 +/-1 year
Death Date:

Father: BILYESA
Mother: ANDITA
1st Spouse: OMI-340
Last/Current Spouse: OMI-340

Year: 1976
Pepek-83

ID: 478   *Sex:* Female

Name: **PEPOT**
2nd Name:
Surname:

Agta Ancestry: 100%

Birth Date: 1961 +/-2 years
Death Date:

Father: TARO
Mother: PILISITA
1st Spouse: ATENG-248
Last/Current Spouse: ATENG-248

Year: 1984
Pepot-478

ID: 491   *Sex:* Female

Name: **PERLA**
2nd Name: KITUK
Surname: KABUNO MORA PERNANDO

Agta Ancestry: 87.5%

Birth Date: 1954 +/-2 years
Death Date:

Father: BUDEGDEG
Mother: IDING
1st Spouse: PREDI-490
Last/Current Spouse: ALBING-9303

Year: 1978
Perla-491 holding
Bengbeng-1140

ID: 8239   *Sex:* Female

Name: **PERLIN**
2nd Name: ROSEL
Surname: TORIO

Agta Ancestry: 50%

Birth Date: January 7, 1991
Death Date:

Father: PREDI
Mother: PIRING
1st Spouse: LUIS-9257
Last/Current Spouse: LUIS-9257

Year: 1994
Perlin-8239 phto by John
Early

165

ID:	5365 *Sex:* Female

Name: **PERLING**
2nd Name:
Surname:

Agta Ancestry: 87.5%

Birth Date: 1940 +/-2 years
Death Date: 1971

Father: DIKMIN
Mother: PINYANG

Year: 1963
Perling-5365, daughtr
Norseng-51, husband

1st Spouse: RAMON-5399
Last/Current Spouse: ALUNET-17

ID: 95   *Sex:* Female

Name: **PETI**
2nd Name:
Surname: IMO

Agta Ancestry: 100%

Birth Date: 1952 +/-1 year
Death Date:

Father: BONTOY
Mother: ANENA

Year: 1965   1978
Peti-95   Peti-95

1st Spouse:
Last/Current Spouse:

ID: 184   *Sex:* Male

Name: **PETONG**
2nd Name: EDGAR
Surname: BANTUG , ALPREDO

Agta Ancestry: 100%

Birth Date: 1970
Death Date:

Father: EDA
Mother: TILOKEN

Year: 2008
Petong/Edgar-184

1st Spouse:
Last/Current Spouse:

ID: 391   *Sex:* Female

Name: **PIDELA**
2nd Name:
Surname: KATALINA

Agta Ancestry: 100%

Birth Date: 1912 +/-2 years
Death Date: June 19, 1985

Father: MAHEW
Mother: AKILINA

Year: 1978
Pidela-391

1st Spouse: MENES-390
Last/Current Spouse: MENES-390

Year: 1978
Pikson-488

2010
Pikson-488

ID:	488	*Sex:* Male

Name: **PIKSON**
2nd Name:
Surname: PAWISAN
Agta Ancestry: 50%

Birth Date: 1955 +/-1 year
Death Date:

Father: POTO
Mother: ANGHILITA

1st Spouse: HELING-489
Last/Current Spouse: HELING-489

Year: 1976
Pilisa-360

ID:	360	*Sex:* Female

Name: **PILISA**
2nd Name: LISA
Surname: SABELO, BASELO
Agta Ancestry: 100%

Birth Date: 1919 +/-3 years
Death Date: 1980

Father: BASELO
Mother: SISA

1st Spouse: BANGHUL-45
Last/Current Spouse: BANGHUL-45

Year: 1963
Pilisa-5369

ID:	5369	*Sex:* Female

Name: **PILISA**
2nd Name:
Surname:
Agta Ancestry: 100%

Birth Date: 1899 +/-4 years
Death Date: March 3, 1965

Father: MALIYEK
Mother: AMADEYA

1st Spouse: PAWISAN-5358
Last/Current Spouse: PAWISAN-5358

Year: 1984
Pilising-475 phto by Bion
Griffin

ID:	475	*Sex:* Female

Name: **PILISING**
2nd Name:
Surname:
Agta Ancestry: 100%

Birth Date: 1926 +/-4 years
Death Date:

Father: LENDEK
Mother: DIWANE

1st Spouse: ITUG-7262
Last/Current Spouse: ITUG-7262

Year: 1962
Pilising-5373

ID: 5373   Sex: Female

Name: **PILISING**
2nd Name:
Surname: PAWISAN
Agta Ancestry: 100%

Birth Date: 1921 +/-3 years
Death Date: December 6, 1965

Father: PAWISAN
Mother: PILISA
1st Spouse: AYOGYOG-40
Last/Current Spouse: AYOGYOG-40

Year: 1978
Pilong-7230

ID: 7230   Sex: Female

Name: **PILONG**
2nd Name:
Surname:
Agta Ancestry: 100%

Birth Date: 1966 +/-3 years
Death Date:

Father:
Mother:
1st Spouse:
Last/Current Spouse:

Year: 1978
Pingki-8340

ID: 8340   Sex: Female

Name: **PINGKI**
2nd Name:
Surname: DEPABLO
Agta Ancestry: 12.5%

Birth Date: 1971 +/-2 years
Death Date:

Father: PABLING
Mother: ELI
1st Spouse:
Last/Current Spouse:

Year: 1971   1976
R- Pining-73 holding   Pining-73
daughtr Golmol-74

ID: 73   Sex: Female

Name: **PINING**
2nd Name:
Surname: PAEL
Agta Ancestry: 100%

Birth Date: 1944 +/-3 years
Death Date: 1987 +/-2 years

Father: PAEL
Mother: PALADING
1st Spouse: BILYANTING-72
Last/Current Spouse: ADING-9

168

Year: 1936
Pinyana-5519, by
Vanoverbergh

ID: 5519   Sex: Female
Name: **PINYANA**
2nd Name: PINIANA
Surname:
Agta Ancestry: 100%
Birth Date: 1886 +/-8 years
Death Date: 1945 +/-9 years
Father:
Mother:
1st Spouse: DINANO-5634
Last/Current Spouse: NAYAS-5518

Year: 1967
Pinyang-5376

ID: 5376   Sex: Female
Name: **PINYANG**
2nd Name:
Surname: ADUANAN
Agta Ancestry: Unknown
Birth Date: 1915 +/-3 years
Death Date: February 10, 1970
Father: TALIMANGON
Mother: MONIKA
1st Spouse: DIKMIN-5108
Last/Current Spouse: DIKMIN-5108

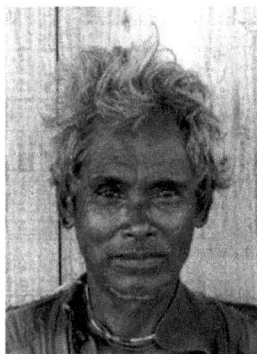

Year: 1976
Pirente-484

ID: 484   Sex: Male
Name: **PIRENTE**
2nd Name:
Surname: PRADO
Agta Ancestry: 50%
Birth Date: 1916 +/-2 years
Death Date: May 1, 1979
Father: APURADU
Mother: BALIDAY
1st Spouse: ISTRING-485
Last/Current Spouse: ISTRING-485

Year: 1977   1998
Piring-467   Piring-467

ID: 467   Sex: Female
Name: **PIRING**
2nd Name: PIRING
Surname: LISIDAY TORIO
Agta Ancestry: 100%
Birth Date: 1947 +/-2 years
Death Date:
Father: LISIDAY
Mother: PANGKUY
1st Spouse: PREDI-9037
Last/Current Spouse: PREDI-9037

169

Year: 1977
Pokes-16

ID:	16	Sex: Male

Name:	**POKES**
2nd Name:	ELPIDIO
Surname:	KUKUAN

Agta Ancestry: 87.5%

Birth Date:	1956 +/-1 year
Death Date:	March 28, 1984

Father:	ALONSO
Mother:	TIRAY

1st Spouse:	KEDEK-143
Last/Current Spouse:	KEDEK-143

Year: 2010
Polen-7819

ID:	7819	Sex: Female

Name:	**POLEN**
2nd Name:	MILET
Surname:

Agta Ancestry: 93.75%

Birth Date:	1972 +/-2 years
Death Date:

Father:	GUBEK
Mother:	PENI

1st Spouse:	PANSITO-22
Last/Current Spouse:	PANSITO-22

Year: 1977
Polok-3

ID:	3	Sex: Male

Name:	**POLOK**
2nd Name:	MANE, LITO
Surname:	BEKYADEN

Agta Ancestry: 87.5%

Birth Date:	1970 +/-1 year
Death Date:

Father:	ABDON
Mother:	SITENG

1st Spouse:	KULES-482
Last/Current Spouse:	KULES-482

Year: 1972
Pompoek-130 phto by Jim
Musgrove

2010
Pompoek-130

ID:	130	Sex: Female

Name:	**POMPOEK**
2nd Name:
Surname:	SAGUNED

Agta Ancestry: 100%

Birth Date:	1932 +/-1 year
Death Date:

Father:	SAGUNED
Mother:	DINANSA

1st Spouse:	DIDOG-129
Last/Current Spouse:	DIDOG-129

ID:	3313 *Sex:* Male
Name:	**POPONG**
2nd Name:	ALBING
Surname:	ADUANAN
Agta Ancestry:	100%
Birth Date:	1996 +/-1 year
Death Date:	
Father:	ALEK
Mother:	LINDA
1st Spouse:	
Last/Current Spouse:	

Year: 2008
Popong-3313

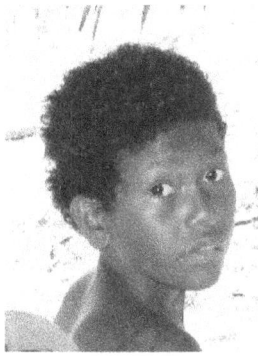

2010
Popong-3313

ID:	561 *Sex:* Female
Name:	**PORMING**
2nd Name:	
Surname:	
Agta Ancestry:	100%
Birth Date:	1937 +/-3 years
Death Date:	August 20, 1987
Father:	PAGITULENG
Mother:	KENGKENG
1st Spouse:	PIYEN-7165
Last/Current Spouse:	TANES-560

Year: 1977
Porming-561

ID:	7815 *Sex:* Female
Name:	**POWING**
2nd Name:	
Surname:	
Agta Ancestry:	100%
Birth Date:	1939 +/-7 years
Death Date:	November 2009
Father:	DOKDOK
Mother:	APRIKA
1st Spouse:	ENGAS-7814
Last/Current Spouse:	ENGAS-7814

Year: 2002
Powing-7815

ID:	490 *Sex:* Male
Name:	**PREDI**
2nd Name:	FREDI
Surname:	MORA
Agta Ancestry:	50%
Birth Date:	1956 +/-1 year
Death Date:	March 2008
Father:	MEKES
Mother:	OPISTA
1st Spouse:	PERLA-491
Last/Current Spouse:	PERLA-491

Year: 1978
Predi-490

171

Year: 1994
Predi-9037 phto by John
Early

1994
Predi-9037

ID: 9037   Sex: Male

Name: **PREDI**
2nd Name: BIKUL
Surname: TORIO

Agta Ancestry: 0%

Birth Date: 1948 +/-5 years
Death Date: August 29, 2004

Father:
Mother:

1st Spouse: PIRING-467
Last/Current Spouse: PIRING-467

Year: 2004
Prinses-8302 w mother
Hapek-1110

2004
Prinses-8302

ID: 8302   Sex: Female

Name: **PRINSES**
2nd Name:
Surname: LOPAMIYA

Agta Ancestry: 37.5%

Birth Date: March 7, 2003
Death Date:

Father: DYOEL
Mother: HAPEK

1st Spouse:
Last/Current Spouse:

Year: 1936
Pulomena-5391 by
Vanoverbergh

ID: 5391   Sex: Female

Name: **PULOMENA**
2nd Name:
Surname:

Agta Ancestry: 100%

Birth Date: 1900 +/-9 years
Death Date: 1975

Father:
Mother:

1st Spouse: NANDES-5320
Last/Current Spouse: NANDES-5320

Year: 2010
Punene-1013

ID: 1013   Sex: Female

Name: **PUNENE**
2nd Name: NENE
Surname: ANGLENAN, BEKYADEN

Agta Ancestry: Unknown

Birth Date: 1979
Death Date:

Father: OMI
Mother: UDENG

1st Spouse: ELIBOY-327
Last/Current Spouse: MAYKEL-9222

ID:	3314 *Sex:* Male
Name:	**PUNGGUK**
2nd Name:	DYERMI
Surname:	ADUANAN
Agta Ancestry:	100%
Birth Date:	December 1997
Death Date:	
Father:	ALEK
Mother:	LINDA
1st Spouse:	
Last/Current Spouse:	

Year: 2008
Pungguk-3314

ID:	24 *Sex:* Female
Name:	**PURING**
2nd Name:	PULING, PULOG
Surname:	DELAPENYA
Agta Ancestry:	Unknown
Birth Date:	1975
Death Date:	
Father:	SAYSAY
Mother:	NURING
1st Spouse:	LILET-7889
Last/Current Spouse:	LILET-7889

Year: 2010
Puring-24

ID:	5399 *Sex:* Male
Name:	**RAMON**
2nd Name:	
Surname:	
Agta Ancestry:	75%
Birth Date:	1931 +/-3 years
Death Date:	1968
Father:	TANYET
Mother:	INGGEK
1st Spouse:	PERLING-5365
Last/Current Spouse:	PERLING-5365

Year: 1965
Ramon-5399

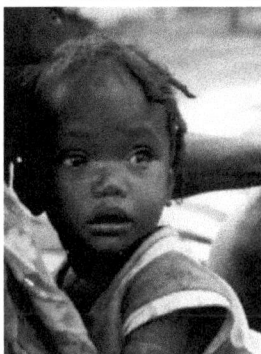

ID:	293 *Sex:* Male
Name:	**RANDI**
2nd Name:	
Surname:	ALEDIG
Agta Ancestry:	87.5%
Birth Date:	1975 +/-2 years
Death Date:	
Father:	LAKAY
Mother:	SABILITA
1st Spouse:	NITA-524
Last/Current Spouse:	NITA-524

Year: 1976
Randi-293

Year: 2004
Rayan-8139

2008
Rayan-8139

ID: 8139   Sex: Male

Name: **RAYAN**
2nd Name:
Surname: FRANCISCO

Agta Ancestry: 37.5%

Birth Date: March 18, 1988
Death Date:

Father: IDAG
Mother: WISAY

1st Spouse:
Last/Current Spouse:

Year: 1998
Rehina-8031

2006
Rehina-8031

ID: 8031   Sex: Female

Name: **REHINA**
2nd Name:
Surname:

Agta Ancestry: 37.5%

Birth Date: November 1984
Death Date:

Father: RENATO
Mother: WISAY

1st Spouse: MARBIN-9244
Last/Current Spouse: MARBIN-9244

Year: 1978
Rekrek-60

ID: 60   Sex: Female

Name: **REKREK**
2nd Name: ANA
Surname: ALAMBRA

Agta Ancestry: 100%

Birth Date: 1938 +/-2 years
Death Date: July 1978

Father: ALAMRA
Mother: UPILA

1st Spouse: BERIONES-59
Last/Current Spouse: BERIONES-59

Year: 1977
Rekrek-400 & son Nikson-403

ID: 400   Sex: Female

Name: **REKREK**
2nd Name:
Surname: TULIO

Agta Ancestry: 100%

Birth Date: 1935 +/-3 years
Death Date:

Father: TULIO
Mother: LIPANYAW

1st Spouse: NADOY-399
Last/Current Spouse: NADOY-399

174

Year: 2008
Rene-9190

ID: 9190   *Sex:* Male

Name: **RENE**
2nd Name:
Surname: MIRANYA

Agta Ancestry: 0%

Birth Date: March 16, 1968
Death Date:

Father:
Mother:

1st Spouse: MAYLA-384
Last/Current Spouse: MAYLA-384

Year: 1998
Reni-9111

2010
Reni-9111

ID: 9111   *Sex:* Male

Name: **RENI**
2nd Name: BUNDAT
Surname: DELAKRUS

Agta Ancestry: 0%

Birth Date: 1952 +/-5 years
Death Date:

Father:
Mother:

1st Spouse: NENENG-415
Last/Current Spouse: NENENG-415

Year: 2008
Resi-549

2010
Resi-549

ID: 549   *Sex:* Female

Name: **RESI**
2nd Name:
Surname: KULIDEG

Agta Ancestry: Unknown

Birth Date: 1957 +/-1 year
Death Date:

Father:
Mother: ELI

1st Spouse: SINON-548
Last/Current Spouse: NOEL-376

Year: 1978
Ribika-537

ID: 537   *Sex:* Female

Name: **RIBIKA**
2nd Name: BIKA
Surname: MANOY

Agta Ancestry: 100%

Birth Date: 1972 +/-1 year
Death Date: January 1982

Father: SISAR
Mother: TESI

1st Spouse:
Last/Current Spouse:

175

Year: 2002
Ridyel-409 with brother
Batutung-3408

2004
Ridyel-409 phto by Iris
Dalberto

ID: 409		*Sex:* Male
Name: **RIDYEL**		
2nd Name:	OGIT, RODYEL	
Surname:	PRADO	
Agta Ancestry: 75%		
Birth Date:	1974	
Death Date:		
Father:	NATENG	
Mother:	TETET	
1st Spouse:	MERIDYEN-100	
Last/Current Spouse:	MERIDYEN-100	

Year: 1984
Riki-1165 with mother Linda-552

ID: 1165		*Sex:* Male
Name: **RIKI**		
2nd Name:		
Surname:	KUKUAN	
Agta Ancestry: Unknown		
Birth Date:	August 1, 1982	
Death Date:		
Father:	SITOK	
Mother:	LINDA	
1st Spouse:		
Last/Current Spouse:		

Year: 1998
Riki-8032

ID: 8032		*Sex:* Male
Name: **RIKI**		
2nd Name:		
Surname:	DELAKRUS	
Agta Ancestry: 46.875%		
Birth Date:	July 5, 1985	
Death Date:		
Father:	RENI	
Mother:	NENENG	
1st Spouse:	DYOYAN-8136	
Last/Current Spouse:	DYOYAN-8136	

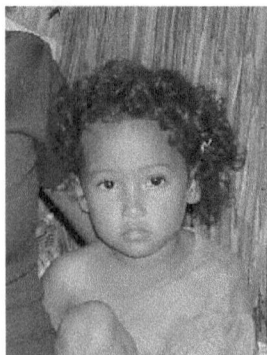

Year: 2004
Riname-8222

ID: 8222		*Sex:* Female
Name: **RINAME**		
2nd Name:		
Surname:	MIRANYA	
Agta Ancestry: 50%		
Birth Date:	January 24, 2000	
Death Date:		
Father:	RENE	
Mother:	MAYLA	
1st Spouse:		
Last/Current Spouse:		

Year: 1978
Riteng-420

ID: 420   *Sex:* Female

Name: **RITENG**
2nd Name:
Surname:

Agta Ancestry: 100%

Birth Date: 1956 +/-4 years
Death Date:

Father: PIYEN
Mother: PORMING

1st Spouse: NOLBING-419
Last/Current Spouse: BINGEL-532

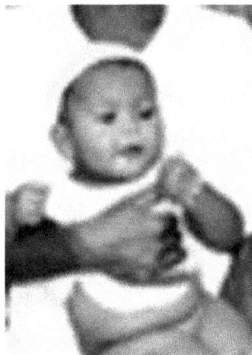
Year: 2002
Riya-7005

ID: 7005   *Sex:* Female

Name: **RIYA**
2nd Name:
Surname: ADUANAN

Agta Ancestry: 100%

Birth Date: August 3, 2001
Death Date:

Father: SAWE
Mother: MARIYETA

1st Spouse:
Last/Current Spouse:

Year: 1977
Rodi-501

ID: 501   *Sex:* Male

Name: **RODI**
2nd Name:
Surname: GASPONG

Agta Ancestry: 100%

Birth Date: 1949 +/-2 years
Death Date:

Father: GASPONG
Mother: OPISTA

1st Spouse: DELI-502
Last/Current Spouse: DELI-502

Year: 1976
Rodyel-574 with father
Gibson-207

ID: 574   *Sex:* Male

Name: **RODYEL**
2nd Name:
Surname: ADUANAN

Agta Ancestry: 93.75%

Birth Date: 1974 +/-1 year
Death Date:

Father: GIBSON
Mother: DENGDENG

1st Spouse: MARIYETA-7883
Last/Current Spouse: MARIYETA-7883

177

ID:	7501	Sex: Male

Name: **RODYEL**
2nd Name: ELELENG
Surname: DABID

Agta Ancestry: Unknown

Birth Date: 1966 +/-3 years
Death Date:

Father: DULENG
Mother: ETONG

1st Spouse:
Last/Current Spouse:

Year: 1977
Rodyel-7501

2010
Rodyel-7501

ID:	504	Sex: Male

Name: **ROHEL**
2nd Name: ROWEL
Surname: MANDOSA, TALUDEP

Agta Ancestry: 100%

Birth Date: 1949 +/-2 years
Death Date:

Father: MANDOSA
Mother: KORDING

1st Spouse: NEMI-189
Last/Current Spouse: EMILING-505

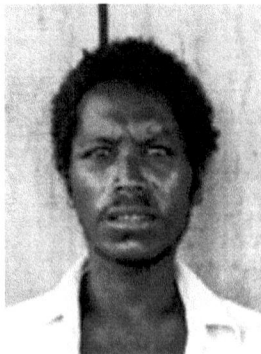

Year: 1976
Rohel-504

2010
Rohel-504

ID:	2001	Sex: Male

Name: **ROHELIO**
2nd Name:
Surname: DESAG, DABID

Agta Ancestry: 100%

Birth Date: 1949 +/-3 years
Death Date:

Father: DESAG
Mother: BENDULING

1st Spouse: BITA-2002
Last/Current Spouse: BITA-2002

Year: 1977
Rohelio-2001

ID:	4014	Sex: Male

Name: **ROLI**
2nd Name:
Surname:

Agta Ancestry: 100%

Birth Date: 1979 +/-7 years
Death Date:

Father: NARSING
Mother: LUBIS

1st Spouse: DAYANA-4015
Last/Current Spouse: DAYANA-4015

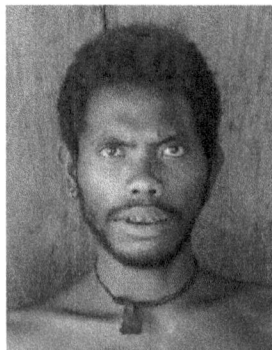

Year: 2010
Roli-4014

178

ID: 7237	*Sex:* Female

Name: **ROMANA**
2nd Name: RAMONA
Surname: RAMOS

Agta Ancestry: Unknown

Birth Date: 1922 +/-5 years
Death Date:

Father: MILIS
Mother: DITENG
1st Spouse: MINDOSA-398
Last/Current Spouse: MINDOSA-398

Year: 1977
Ramona-7237

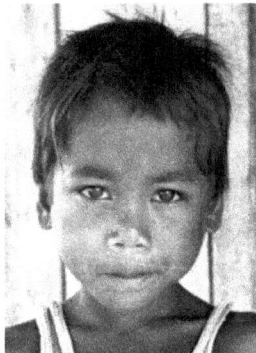

ID: 8182	*Sex:* Male

Name: **ROMI**
2nd Name:
Surname: VARGAS

Agta Ancestry: 25%

Birth Date: November 15, 1970
Death Date:

Father: DOLPING
Mother: LINDA
1st Spouse: ULEN-183
Last/Current Spouse: ULEN-183

Year: 1978
Romi-8182

ID: 7272	*Sex:* Male

Name: **ROMIO**
2nd Name:
Surname: DABID

Agta Ancestry: Unknown

Birth Date: 1950 +/-7 years
Death Date:

Father: DESAG
Mother: BENDULING
1st Spouse: NENENG-510
Last/Current Spouse: NENENG-510

Year: 1977
Romio-7272

ID: 4023	*Sex:* Male

Name: **RONALD**
2nd Name:
Surname:

Agta Ancestry: Unknown

Birth Date: 1994 +/-1 year
Death Date:

Father: KILENG
Mother: MARIRING
1st Spouse:
Last/Current Spouse:

Year: 2010
Ronald-4023

Year: 2010
Ronggok-3645

ID: 3645   Sex: Male

Name: **RONGGOK**
2nd Name: YUDYIN
Surname:

Agta Ancestry: 79.687%

Birth Date: April 1, 2008
Death Date:

Father: DANGGULAN
Mother: BAGEL

1st Spouse:
Last/Current Spouse:

Year: 1967
Rosalinda-6083 with mother
Adiling-6 1967

ID: 6083   Sex: Female

Name: **ROSALINDA**
2nd Name:
Surname:

Agta Ancestry: 100%

Birth Date: 1965 +/-1 year
Death Date: 1967 +/-1 year

Father: DIYAKIN
Mother: ADILING

1st Spouse:
Last/Current Spouse:

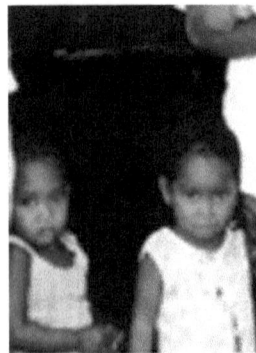

Year: 2002
Rodel-7890 & Leya-7740

ID: 7890   Sex: Male

Name: **RUDEL**
2nd Name:
Surname: ADUANAN

Agta Ancestry: 100%

Birth Date: June 1, 1999
Death Date: 2008

Father: SAWE
Mother: MARIYETA

1st Spouse:
Last/Current Spouse:

Year: 1976   2010
Ruming-507   Ruming-507

ID: 507   Sex: Male

Name: **RUMING**
2nd Name: ROMING
Surname: MANGGAT

Agta Ancestry: 87.5%

Birth Date: 1949 +/-3 years
Death Date:

Father: SIBERO
Mother: ANDITA

1st Spouse: NORMITA-266
Last/Current Spouse: LENI-508

180

ID:	2071 *Sex:* Male

Name: **RUPING**
2nd Name:
Surname: SALINAS
Agta Ancestry: 100%

Birth Date: 1952
Death Date:

Father: SALINAS
Mother: ERMINYA
1st Spouse: MILITENG-516
Last/Current Spouse: MILITENG-516

Year: 2010
Ruping-2071

ID:	594 *Sex:* Female

Name: **RUSING**
2nd Name: ROSITA, RUSIN
Surname: SANSES, PENYA
Agta Ancestry: 100%

Birth Date: 1929 +/-4 years
Death Date: 1989

Father: SANSES
Mother: PASKWALITA
1st Spouse: TONING-593
Last/Current Spouse: TONING-593

Year: 1976
Rusing-594

ID:	289 *Sex:* Female

Name: **SABILITA**
2nd Name:
Surname: PRADO
Agta Ancestry: 75%

Birth Date: 1941 +/-2 years
Death Date: December 26, 1998

Father: PIRENTE
Mother: ISTRING
1st Spouse: GUBEK-5154
Last/Current Spouse: LAKAY-288

Year: 1977
Sabilita-289 holding son
Randi-293

ID:	517 *Sex:* Female

Name: **SAGED**
2nd Name:
Surname: ABUNDIO
Agta Ancestry: 100%

Birth Date: 1911 +/-4 years
Death Date: January 23, 1985

Father: ABUNDIO
Mother: SIPIYA
1st Spouse: PELIMON-462
Last/Current Spouse: BELYASING-5071

Year: 1977
Saged-517

ID:	3369	*Sex:* Male

Name: **SAKLANGEN**
2nd Name: RONI, PALDA
Surname:

Agta Ancestry: 100%

Birth Date: 1984 +/-4 years
Death Date:

Father: DUNOY
Mother: NORI
1st Spouse: MARITES-8102
Last/Current Spouse: MARITES-8102

Year: 2008
Saklangen-3369

2010
Saklangen-3369

ID:	7453	*Sex:* Female

Name: **SALEG**
2nd Name: ROSALINA
Surname: TAGYAM

Agta Ancestry: Unknown

Birth Date: 1947 +/-6 years
Death Date:

Father: PIPING
Mother: PASING
1st Spouse: UNGED-7452
Last/Current Spouse: UNGED-7452

Year: 1977
Saleg-7453

ID:	230	*Sex:* Female

Name: **SALELENGAN**
2nd Name: SALIBAYAN, SALELING
Surname: MIYA, PASIO

Agta Ancestry: 100%

Birth Date: 1963 +/-1 year
Death Date:

Father: HAYME
Mother: MIRING
1st Spouse: GIDU-9162
Last/Current Spouse: GIDU-9162

Year: 1977
Salelengan-230

ID:	522	*Sex:* Female

Name: **SALING**
2nd Name:
Surname: ANGLENAN BEKYADEN

Agta Ancestry: 87.5%

Birth Date: 1931 +/-2 years
Death Date: January 27, 2010

Father: ANGLENAN
Mother: PILISA
1st Spouse: SIMO-9041
Last/Current Spouse: SIMO-9041

Year: 1977
Saling-522

182

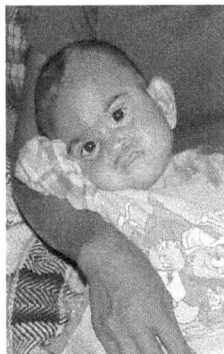

Year: 2004
Salume-8303

ID: 8303	*Sex:* Female

Name: **SALUME**
2nd Name:
Surname: MIRANYA
Agta Ancestry: 50%

Birth Date: August 8, 2002
Death Date: July 21, 2004

Father: RENE
Mother: MAYLA

1st Spouse:
Last/Current Spouse:

Year: 2004
Samwel-8255 with father
Saniboy-204

ID: 8255	*Sex:* Male

Name: **SAMWEL**
2nd Name:
Surname:

Agta Ancestry: 37.5%

Birth Date: 2001
Death Date:

Father: SANIBOY
Mother: DALYA

1st Spouse:
Last/Current Spouse:

Year: 1977
Sander-523

ID: 523	*Sex:* Male

Name: **SANDER**
2nd Name:
Surname: TOMAY
Agta Ancestry: 93.75%

Birth Date: 1951 +/-2 years
Death Date:

Father: TETYOK
Mother: ISTING
1st Spouse: NITA-524
Last/Current Spouse: NITA-524

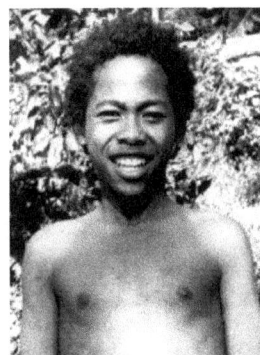

Year: 1978   2004
Saniboy-204   Saniboy-204 phto by Iris
                  Dalberto

ID: 204	*Sex:* Male

Name: **SANIBOY**
2nd Name:
Surname: MORAL
Agta Ancestry: 75%

Birth Date: 1966 +/-2 years
Death Date:

Father: ERNING
Mother: ISLING
1st Spouse: DALYA-9176
Last/Current Spouse: DALYA-9176

Year: 1977
Saning-135

ID: 135	Sex: Female

Name: **SANING**
2nd Name: SANENG
Surname:

Agta Ancestry: 100%

Birth Date: 1932 +/-3 years
Death Date: 1988 +/-2 years

Father: MAGNAY
Mother: SENIKA
1st Spouse: BORDON-5693
Last/Current Spouse: DINEGTUNAN-6064

Year: 1976
Saring-346

ID: 346	Sex: Female

Name: **SARING**
2nd Name:
Surname: GIMPIDEN

Agta Ancestry: 75%

Birth Date: 1936 +/-2 years
Death Date: February 24, 1994

Father: BIDEK
Mother: LIYANITA
1st Spouse: MEDYOR-5292
Last/Current Spouse: MANINGTING-345

Year: 2008
Saringkep-3016 phto by Iris
Dalberto

ID: 3016	Sex: Female

Name: **SARINGKEP**
2nd Name:
Surname: PRADO

Agta Ancestry: 75%

Birth Date: September 30, 1989
Death Date:

Father: NATENG
Mother: TETET
1st Spouse: LARDI-9274
Last/Current Spouse: LARDI-9274

Year: 1979   2002
Sawe-131   Sawe-131

ID: 131	Sex: Male

Name: **SAWE**
2nd Name: LITO
Surname: ADUANAN

Agta Ancestry: 100%

Birth Date: 1959 +/-1 year
Death Date: March 14, 2005

Father: DIDOG
Mother: POMPOEK
1st Spouse: KARMEN-442
Last/Current Spouse: MARIYETA-7019

184

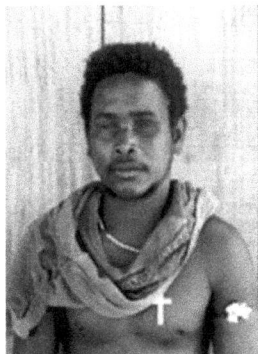
Year: 1977
Saysay-160

ID: 160   *Sex:* Male

Name: **SAYSAY**
2nd Name:
Surname: BERNABE

Agta Ancestry: 100%

Birth Date: 1954 +/-2 years
Death Date:

Father: DOYEG
Mother: AWAY

1st Spouse:
Last/Current Spouse:

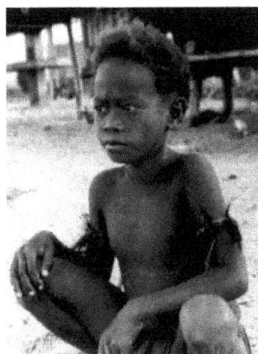
Year: 1978
Sehemok-546

ID: 546   *Sex:* Male

Name: **SEHEMOK**
2nd Name: GOMEL
Surname: SANGBAY

Agta Ancestry: 100%

Birth Date: 1969 +/-1 year
Death Date: 2000 +/-6 years

Father: SINABUYAN
Mother: MIDING

1st Spouse:
Last/Current Spouse:

Year: 1977
Selton-530

2010
Selton-530

ID: 530   *Sex:* Male

Name: **SELTON**
2nd Name:
Surname: BERNABE

Agta Ancestry: 100%

Birth Date: 1948 +/-2 years
Death Date:

Father: DOYEG
Mother: AWAY

1st Spouse: NENENG-531
Last/Current Spouse: NENENG-531

Year: 1978
Selya-529

2010
Selya-529

ID: 529   *Sex:* Female

Name: **SELYA**
2nd Name: SELAY, IGOT
Surname: TIKIMAN

Agta Ancestry: 93.75%

Birth Date: May 10, 1958
Death Date:

Father: ABANTE
Mother: PETANG

1st Spouse: HUAN-9013
Last/Current Spouse: MARIANO-9146

ID: 296	*Sex:* Female

Name: **SEMILITA**
2nd Name:
Surname: TULIO
Agta Ancestry: Unknown

Birth Date: 1961
Death Date:

Father: LAKAY
Mother: KONSITA
1st Spouse: SALDI-9090
Last/Current Spouse: MEDIKOL-172

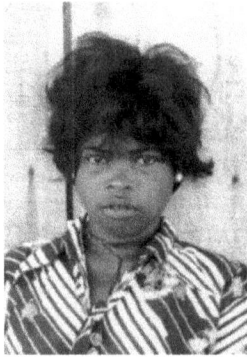

Year: 1977
Semilita-296

2010
Semilita-296

ID: 449   *Sex:* Female

Name: **SENAYDA**
2nd Name: TALIKUK
Surname: MAKSIMINO
Agta Ancestry: Unknown

Birth Date: 1962 +/-2 years
Death Date:

Father: PRISNOSA
Mother: ROSITA
1st Spouse: unknown-9119
Last/Current Spouse: unknown-9119

Year: 1977
Senayda-449

ID: 534   *Sex:* Female

Name: **SENIKA**
2nd Name:
Surname:
Agta Ancestry: Unknown

Birth Date: 1906 +/-4 years
Death Date: July 1977

Father: BUSASENG
Mother: TENGGENG
1st Spouse: MAGNAY-5251
Last/Current Spouse: MAGNAY-5251

Year: 1977
Senika-534

ID: 7182   *Sex:* Male

Name: **SIBERO**
2nd Name: SIBERU
Surname:
Agta Ancestry: 75%

Birth Date: 1926 +/-5 years
Death Date: 1978 +/-5 years

Father:
Mother:
1st Spouse: ANDITA-5569
Last/Current Spouse: MARING-7281

Year: 1971
Sibero-7182

186

ID: 565   *Sex:* Female

Name: **SIDING**
2nd Name:
Surname: SIMIN

Agta Ancestry: 100%

Birth Date: 1936 +/-4 years
Death Date: June 17, 1985

Father: SIMIN
Mother: ASIONA

1st Spouse: TARSAN-564
Last/Current Spouse: TARSAN-564

Year: 1976
Siding-565

ID: 492   *Sex:* Female

Name: **SILENG**
2nd Name: PRISILA
Surname: GERA

Agta Ancestry: 100%

Birth Date: 1941 +/-3 years
Death Date:

Father: PEKTO
Mother: BINANSA

1st Spouse: HUWANING-5162
Last/Current Spouse: LASKO-9020

Year: 1977
Sileng-492 holding son
Biktor-498

ID: 7864   *Sex:* Male

Name: **SILONG**
2nd Name:
Surname:

Agta Ancestry: Unknown

Birth Date: 1956 +/-4 years
Death Date:

Father: WILSON
Mother: KARMIN

1st Spouse: GIWAT-333
Last/Current Spouse: GIWAT-333

Year: 1977
Silong-7864

ID: 7183   *Sex:* Male

Name: **SIMEON**
2nd Name: SIMION
Surname: RAMOS

Agta Ancestry: 100%

Birth Date: 1932 +/-3 years
Death Date: 1985 +/-1 year

Father: MILIS
Mother: DITENG

1st Spouse: BAGOL-539
Last/Current Spouse: BAGOL-539

Year: 1977
Simeon-7183

187

| ID: | 543 | Sex: Male |

Name: **SINABUYAN**
2nd Name:
Surname: SANGBAY

Agta Ancestry: 100%

Birth Date: 1927 +/-3 years
Death Date: 1995 +/-2 years

Father: SANGBAY
Mother: ANGDANGA
1st Spouse: ANGHILITA-5030
Last/Current Spouse: MIDING-5725

Year: 1984
Sinabuyan-543

| ID: | 7184 | Sex: Female |

Name: **SINGOL**
2nd Name:
Surname:

Agta Ancestry: Unknown

Birth Date: 1947 +/-7 years
Death Date: 1997 +/-9 years

Father:
Mother:
1st Spouse: ANSETA-7009
Last/Current Spouse: ANSETA-7009

Year: 1977
Singol-7184

| ID: | 11 | Sex: Female |

Name: **SINING**
2nd Name:
Surname: KALANGGET

Agta Ancestry: 87.5%

Birth Date: 1960 +/-1 year
Death Date: November 6, 1985

Father: NANEK
Mother: TUKONG
1st Spouse: AGOS-10
Last/Current Spouse: AGOS-10

Year: 1977
Sining-11

Year: 1978   1994
Sinon-548   Sinon-548

| ID: | 548 | Sex: Male |

Name: **SINON**
2nd Name:
Surname:

Agta Ancestry: 43.75%

Birth Date: 1952 +/-1 year
Death Date: December 1999

Father: PRANSISKO
Mother: NIYEBES
1st Spouse: RESI-549
Last/Current Spouse: AYDA-9173

188

Year: 1976
Sinton-254

ID: 254   Sex: Male

Name: **SINTON**
2nd Name: DOMINADOR, DOMING
Surname:

Agta Ancestry: 100%

Birth Date: 1961 +/-2 years
Death Date:

Father: PASIO
Mother: ISTRING
1st Spouse: HASMIN-7081
Last/Current Spouse: LEGTIBEN-7636

Year: 1977
Sipok-450

1992
Sipok-450

ID: 450   Sex: Female

Name: **SIPOK**
2nd Name: ERLI
Surname: MAKSIMINO

Agta Ancestry: 100%

Birth Date: 1962 +/-1 year
Death Date:

Father: PEDONG
Mother: AWILIN
1st Spouse: KULUT-247
Last/Current Spouse: KULUT-247

Year: 1977
Sisar-7575

ID: 7575   Sex: Male

Name: **SISAR**
2nd Name:
Surname:

Agta Ancestry: Unknown

Birth Date:
Death Date:

Father:
Mother: SIMONA
1st Spouse:
Last/Current Spouse:

Year: 1976
Siteng-2

ID: 2   Sex: Female

Name: **SITENG**
2nd Name:
Surname: MANGGAT

Agta Ancestry: 87.5%

Birth Date: 1947 +/-2 years
Death Date: May 1992

Father: SIBERO
Mother: ANDITA
1st Spouse: ABDON-1
Last/Current Spouse: ABDON-1

189

Year: 1977
Siteng-239

1998
Siteng-239

ID:	239	Sex: Female

Name: **SITENG**
2nd Name: KONSITA
Surname:

Agta Ancestry: 100%

Birth Date: 1948 +/-4 years
Death Date:

Father: TIKIMAN
Mother: LAYDING
1st Spouse: DYONI-7841
Last/Current Spouse: IBEN-2041

Year: 1978
Sitok-551

2002
Sitok-551

ID:	551	Sex: Male

Name: **SITOK**
2nd Name:
Surname: KUKUAN

Agta Ancestry: 100%

Birth Date: 1954 +/-1 year
Death Date:

Father: IPOY
Mother: MAMING
1st Spouse: LINDA-552
Last/Current Spouse: LINDA-552

Year: 1966
Siyunan-7629

ID:	7629	Sex: Male

Name: **SIYUNAN**
2nd Name: SIYONAN
Surname:

Agta Ancestry: 100%

Birth Date: 1934 +/-2 years
Death Date:

Father:
Mother:
1st Spouse: SARING-7630
Last/Current Spouse: SARING-7630

Year: 1977
Siyuning-262 holding
Windel-264

2010
Siyuning-262

ID:	262	Sex: Female

Name: **SIYUNING**
2nd Name:
Surname: INONG

Agta Ancestry: Unknown

Birth Date: 1951 +/-4 years
Death Date:

Father: INONG
Mother: ANENA
1st Spouse: KARDING-261
Last/Current Spouse: KARDING-261

190

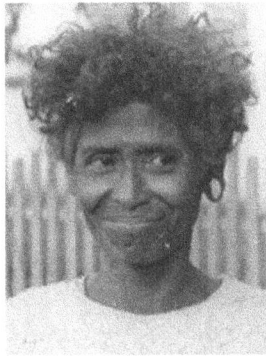

ID: 7202   *Sex:* Female

Name: **SOKER**
2nd Name:
Surname:

Agta Ancestry: Unknown

Birth Date: 1922 +/-7 years
Death Date:

Father: DIPANTAW
Mother: KULIDEP

1st Spouse: TORENG-5913
Last/Current Spouse: TORENG-5913

Year: 1977
Soker-7202

ID: 453   *Sex:* Female

Name: **SOKSOK**
2nd Name: DELIA
Surname: MAKSIMINO

Agta Ancestry: 100%

Birth Date: October 1976
Death Date: 1984

Father: PEDONG
Mother: AWILIN

1st Spouse:
Last/Current Spouse:

Year: 1978
Soksok-453 w mother
Awilin-447

ID: 3495   *Sex:* Female

Name: **SONALIN**
2nd Name: BAIT
Surname: DUNATO

Agta Ancestry: 85.937%

Birth Date: April 29, 1989
Death Date:

Father: KINYOL
Mother: TUNING

1st Spouse:
Last/Current Spouse:

Year: 2010
Sonalin-3495

ID: 36   *Sex:* Female

Name: **SULIDAD**
2nd Name:
Surname: PAEL

Agta Ancestry: 100%

Birth Date: 1929 +/-2 years
Death Date: 1980

Father: PAEL
Mother: PALADING

1st Spouse: ASION-35
Last/Current Spouse: ASION-35

Year: 1976
Sulidad-36

191

Year: 2008
Susan-3187 & son Leonard-8363

2010
Susan-3187

ID: 3187   Sex: Female

Name: **SUSAN**
2nd Name:
Surname: KULIDEG
Agta Ancestry: Unknown

Birth Date: August 5, 1984
Death Date:

Father: MARNING
Mother: NENENG
1st Spouse: EDWIN-388
Last/Current Spouse: EDWIN-388

Year: 1977
Suwar-554 holding Eleng-557

ID: 554   Sex: Male

Name: **SUWAR**
2nd Name: SUAR, SIMION
Surname: GERERO
Agta Ancestry: 100%

Birth Date: 1928 +/-3 years
Death Date: 1982

Father: MEGANO
Mother: PIDELA
1st Spouse: MILA-555
Last/Current Spouse: MILA-555

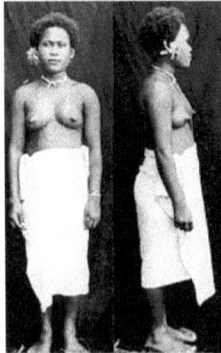

Year: 1936
Tadu-5449
photo by Vanoverbergh

ID: 5449   Sex: Female

Name: **TADU**
2nd Name:
Surname:
Agta Ancestry: 100%

Birth Date:
Death Date:

Father: MAKSEMINO
Mother: PAYES
1st Spouse: GARDENIO-5144
Last/Current Spouse: GARDENIO-5144

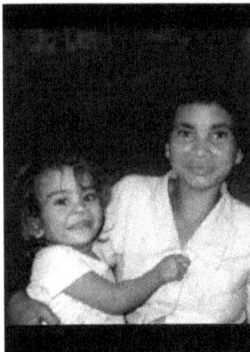

Year: 1998
Talagen-3308 with mother
Maal 606

2008
Talagen-3308

ID: 3308   Sex: Female

Name: **TALAGEN**
2nd Name:
Surname: PRADO
Agta Ancestry: 84.375%

Birth Date: October 28, 1995
Death Date:

Father: ORLI
Mother: MAAL
1st Spouse:
Last/Current Spouse:

192

Year: 1977
Talangeden-559

ID: 559   *Sex:* Female

Name: **TALANGEDEN**
2nd Name: TANGEDEN
Surname: PULANGEN

Agta Ancestry: 100%

Birth Date: 1919 +/-4 years
Death Date:

Father: BUNGKALE
Mother: DITENG

1st Spouse:
Last/Current Spouse:

Year: 1962
Talbus-7191

ID: 7191   *Sex:* Male

Name: **TALBUS**
2nd Name:
Surname:

Agta Ancestry: 100%

Birth Date: 1930 +/-3 years
Death Date: 1968 +/-1 year

Father:
Mother:

1st Spouse: SAGED-517
Last/Current Spouse: SAGED-517

Year: 1976
Talendus-423

ID: 423   *Sex:* Female

Name: **TALENDUS**
2nd Name: TALENDUL
Surname: PAEL, PISAN

Agta Ancestry: 100%

Birth Date: 1951 +/-2 years
Death Date: 1985 +/-2 years

Father: PAEL
Mother: PALADING

1st Spouse: NORPING-422
Last/Current Spouse: NORPING-422

Year: 2004
Talengden-3007

2006
Talengden-3007

ID: 3007   *Sex:* Female

Name: **TALENGDEN**
2nd Name: ROSALINDA
Surname: ADUANAN

Agta Ancestry: 87.5%

Birth Date: February 1, 1990
Death Date:

Father: SAWE
Mother: KARMEN

1st Spouse: ABRAHAM-4008
Last/Current Spouse: ABRAHAM-4008

Year: 1978
Taneng-151

ID: 151   Sex: Female

Name: **TANENG**
2nd Name:
Surname: BERIYALYAN
Agta Ancestry: 100%

Birth Date: 1917 +/-5 years
Death Date: July 23, 1984

Father: KIHENG
Mother: PALASIDA
1st Spouse: BINANSIYO-5754
Last/Current Spouse: DESUY-5104

Year: 1977
Tanes-560

ID: 560   Sex: Male

Name: **TANES**
2nd Name: ISTANES
Surname: ISTANES
Agta Ancestry: 100%

Birth Date: 1922 +/-5 years
Death Date: 1989

Father: BEYAD
Mother: MOMINA
1st Spouse: LIYANING-5233
Last/Current Spouse: PORMING-561

Year: 2008
Tanya-1039

2008
Tanya-1039 & husband
Danilo-9177 & 3 kids.

ID: 1039   Sex: Female

Name: **TANYA**
2nd Name: NENENG
Surname: SADYEN
Agta Ancestry: 100%

Birth Date: 1977
Death Date:

Father: EDYOR
Mother: ELPOH
1st Spouse: DANILO-9177
Last/Current Spouse: DANILO-9177

Year: 1976
Tarsan-564 & son Marsilino-569

1984
Tarsan-564

ID: 564   Sex: Male

Name: **TARSAN**
2nd Name:
Surname: EGMONG
Agta Ancestry: 75%

Birth Date: 1935 +/-3 years
Death Date: 1995 +/-1 year

Father: PANDONG
Mother: MENSIANG
1st Spouse: SIDING-565
Last/Current Spouse: SIDING-565

194

ID:	570 *Sex:* Male

Name: **TAYUGIT**
2nd Name:
Surname: BELYANING
Agta Ancestry: 93.75%

Birth Date: 1955 +/-3 years
Death Date: 2003

Father: BELYANING
Mother: NATI
1st Spouse: LIDIA-312
Last/Current Spouse: KARING-536

Year: 1978
Tayugit-570

ID: 578   *Sex:* Male

Name: **TEKDILEN**
2nd Name: NALOWADINANG
Surname:

Agta Ancestry: 100%

Birth Date: 1952 +/-2 years
Death Date: April 1987

Father: SELOK
Mother: AHADUD
1st Spouse: NARITA-579
Last/Current Spouse: NARITA-579

Year: 1978
Tekdilen-578

ID: 580   *Sex:* Male

Name: **TEKOK**
2nd Name: BERTO, BERTING
Surname: KUKUAN
Agta Ancestry: 87.5%

Birth Date: 1949 +/-1 year
Death Date: September 1991

Father: ALONSO
Mother: TIRAY
1st Spouse: LITA-581
Last/Current Spouse: LITA-581

Year: 1972
Tekok-580 phto by Jim
Musgove

ID: 585   *Sex:* Male

Name: **TELENG**
2nd Name: TELING
Surname: TOMAY
Agta Ancestry: 100%

Birth Date: 1953 +/-1 year
Death Date: 1987 +/-1 year

Father: DUDUYAN
Mother: GOLBIYENG
1st Spouse: TENGAN-586
Last/Current Spouse: AKEP-7003

Year: 1976
Teling-585

Year: 1977
Telengan-149

ID:	149 Sex: Female
Name:	**TELENGAN**
2nd Name:	BINANG, TALAYTAY
Surname:	TAYAMAN
Agta Ancestry:	100%
Birth Date:	1950 +/-2 years
Death Date:	
Father:	BESTIAN
Mother:	APALIA
1st Spouse:	DOMING-148
Last/Current Spouse:	DOMING-148

Year: 1977
Telma-309

ID:	309 Sex: Female
Name:	**TELMA**
2nd Name:	
Surname:	TAYAMAN
Agta Ancestry:	93.75%
Birth Date:	April 16, 1956
Death Date:	1992
Father:	BESTIAN
Mother:	NIYEBES
1st Spouse:	ATUK-344
Last/Current Spouse:	ATUK-344

Year: 1977
Teming-589

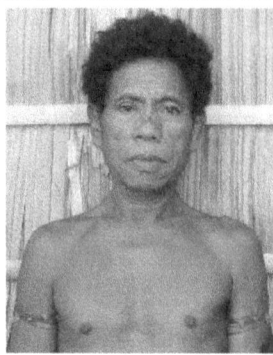

2010
Teming-589

ID:	589 Sex: Male
Name:	**TEMING**
2nd Name:	
Surname:	MORAL
Agta Ancestry:	75%
Birth Date:	1953 +/-2 years
Death Date:	
Father:	ERNING
Mother:	ISLING
1st Spouse:	LOYDA-602
Last/Current Spouse:	LOYDA-602

Year: 1976
Tengan-585

ID:	586 Sex: Female
Name:	**TENGAN**
2nd Name:	
Surname:	LOSI
Agta Ancestry:	100%
Birth Date:	1953 +/-2 years
Death Date:	1982
Father:	PASIO
Mother:	ISTRING
1st Spouse:	TELENG-585
Last/Current Spouse:	TELENG-585

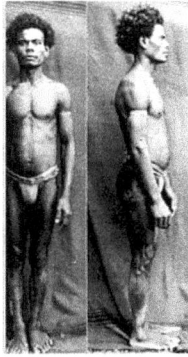

Year: 1936
Tengking-5581
photo by Vanoverbergh

ID: 5581	*Sex:* Male
Name: **TENGKING**	
2nd Name:	
Surname:	
Agta Ancestry: 100%	
Birth Date: 1918 +/-6 years	
Death Date: 1945 +/-9 years	
Father: DOROTEO	
Mother: INIANA	
1st Spouse: KRISPINA-5776	
Last/Current Spouse: BINANSA-5580	

Year: 1977
Tengteng-43

ID: 43	*Sex:* Male
Name: **TENGTENG**	
2nd Name:	
Surname: GERA, PEKTO	
Agta Ancestry: 100%	
Birth Date: 1957 +/-2 years	
Death Date:	
Father: BALONSE	
Mother: KARNASIYON	
1st Spouse: ILISING-2043	
Last/Current Spouse: ILISING-2043	

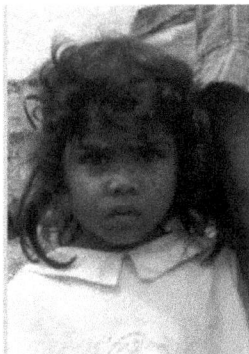

Year: 1994
Teri-3109 phto by John
Early

ID: 3109	*Sex:* Female
Name: **TERI**	
2nd Name: TIRISITA	
Surname: TORIO	
Agta Ancestry: 50%	
Birth Date: 1986	
Death Date:	
Father: PREDI	
Mother: PIRING	
1st Spouse: DYUN-1043	
Last/Current Spouse: DYUN-1043	

Year: 1977   2010
Tersing-494   Tersing-494

ID: 494	*Sex:* Male
Name: **TERSING**	
2nd Name: DULO	
Surname: GERA BITIGAN	
Agta Ancestry: 100%	
Birth Date: 1957 +/-2 years	
Death Date:	
Father: HUWANING	
Mother: SILENG	
1st Spouse: PEPEK-13	
Last/Current Spouse: PEPEK-13	

197

Year: 1978
Tesi-30

ID: 30   Sex: Female

Name: **TESI**
2nd Name: RISITA
Surname: BALENSIA

Agta Ancestry: 75%

Birth Date: 1949 +/-2 years
Death Date:

Father: PANSO
Mother: LAWTING
1st Spouse: PURUDEN-5394
Last/Current Spouse: WILYAM-7842

Year: 1978
Tesi-535

ID: 535   Sex: Female

Name: **TESI**
2nd Name:
Surname: DUNATO

Agta Ancestry: 100%

Birth Date: 1951 +/-2 years
Death Date: January 1986

Father: BERSOSA
Mother: ATING
1st Spouse: SISAR-7217
Last/Current Spouse: ETOY-205

Year: 1977
Tetet (408) holding son
Ridyel (409)

2008
Tetet-408 w daughtr Gres-
3201 phto by Iris Dalberto

ID: 408   Sex: Female

Name: **TETET**
2nd Name: MARINA
Surname: MORAL

Agta Ancestry: 75%

Birth Date: May 5, 1958
Death Date:

Father: ERNING
Mother: ISLING
1st Spouse: NATENG-407
Last/Current Spouse: NATENG-407

Year: 1978
Tetyok-590

ID: 590   Sex: Male

Name: **TETYOK**
2nd Name:
Surname: TOMAY

Agta Ancestry: 100%

Birth Date: 1922 +/-3 years
Death Date: 1988 +/-1 year

Father: TOMAY
Mother: LAGEYAN
1st Spouse: ISTING-591
Last/Current Spouse: ISTING-591

Year: 1967
Tigo-5467

ID: 5467	*Sex:* Male

Name: **TIGO**
2nd Name:
Surname:

Agta Ancestry: 100%

Birth Date: 1898 +/-4 years
Death Date: 1968 +/-2 years

Father: ADUANAN
Mother: DOGEY
1st Spouse: KULUMBA-5207
Last/Current Spouse: KINISTA-5195

Year: 1976
Tika-50

ID: 50	*Sex:* Female

Name: **TIKA**
2nd Name: KULASTIKA
Surname:

Agta Ancestry: 75%

Birth Date: 1926 +/-2 years
Death Date: February 4, 1985

Father: TANYET
Mother: INGGEK
1st Spouse: ABIGONIA-5559
Last/Current Spouse: BAYANI-49

Year: 2008
Tiket-7954

ID: 7954	*Sex:* Female

Name: **TIKET**
2nd Name:
Surname: RAMUS

Agta Ancestry: Unknown

Birth Date: 1990 +/-6 years
Death Date:

Father:
Mother:
1st Spouse:
Last/Current Spouse:

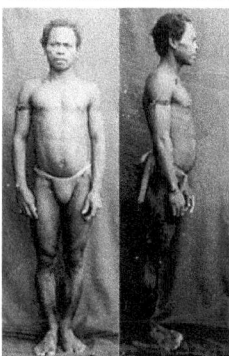

Year: 1936   1976
Tikiman-592   Tikiman-592
photo by Vanoverbergh

ID: 592	*Sex:* Male

Name: **TIKIMAN**
2nd Name:
Surname: SINGLUWEN

Agta Ancestry: 100%

Birth Date: 1901 +/-5 years
Death Date: January 1983

Father: SINGLUWEN
Mother: MAKSIMA
1st Spouse: AGAPITA-5007
Last/Current Spouse: AGAPITA-5007

Year: 1976
Tiloken-179 (in background)
with husband Eda-178 in

1977
Tiloken-179

ID: 179	*Sex:* Female

Name: **TILOKEN**
2nd Name: ILOKEN, TIKOKEN
Surname: MAYMAYEN
Agta Ancestry: 100%

Birth Date: 1934 +/-2 years
Death Date: 1993 +/-3 years

Father: APREDO
Mother: TETENG
1st Spouse: EDA-178
Last/Current Spouse: EDA-178

Year: 2008
Tina-8292

ID: 8292   *Sex:* Female

Name: **TINA**
2nd Name:
Surname:
Agta Ancestry: 62.5%

Birth Date: December 2, 1994
Death Date:

Father: ROMI
Mother: ULEN
1st Spouse:
Last/Current Spouse:

Year: 1976
Tiray-15

ID: 15   *Sex:* Female

Name: **TIRAY**
2nd Name:
Surname: TANYET
Agta Ancestry: 75%

Birth Date: 1915 +/-3 years
Death Date: 1981

Father: TANYET
Mother: INGGEK
1st Spouse: ALONSO-14
Last/Current Spouse: ALONSO-14

Year: 1978
Tiyonson-177

ID: 177   *Sex:* Male

Name: **TIYONSON**
2nd Name: DYONSON
Surname: PAEL, GEWANGAN
Agta Ancestry: 100%

Birth Date: 1937 +/-2 years
Death Date: September 24, 1978

Father: PAEL
Mother: PALADING
1st Spouse:
Last/Current Spouse:

200

ID:	144 *Sex:* Male
Name:	**TONI**
2nd Name:	LAGENG
Surname:	

Agta Ancestry: 100%

Birth Date:	1972 +/-1 year
Death Date:	
Father:	BORDON
Mother:	SANING
1st Spouse:	
Last/Current Spouse:	

Year: 1977
Toni-144

ID:	226 *Sex:* Male
Name:	**TONILIN**
2nd Name:	EDWARDO
Surname:	ABUNDIO, AMERINDU

Agta Ancestry: 75%

Birth Date:	May 1970
Death Date:	
Father:	HAYME
Mother:	NATI
1st Spouse:	ANALI-190
Last/Current Spouse:	ANALI-190

Year: 2000   2004
Tonilin-226   Tonilin-226 phto by Iris Dalberto

ID:	593 *Sex:* Male
Name:	**TONING**
2nd Name:	
Surname:	ATEG

Agta Ancestry: 100%

Birth Date:	1927 +/-3 years
Death Date:	December 1989
Father:	IMO
Mother:	DUMOG
1st Spouse:	KORASON-5204
Last/Current Spouse:	RUSING-594

Year: 1977
Toning-593

ID:	9138 *Sex:* Male
Name:	**TORI**
2nd Name:	
Surname:	TUWALE

Agta Ancestry: 0%

Birth Date:	
Death Date:	
Father:	
Mother:	
1st Spouse:	LERLING-610
Last/Current Spouse:	LERLING-610

Year: 2010
Tori-9138

Year: 2002
Totoy-1111

2004
Totoy-1111 phto by Iris
Dalberto

ID: 1111   Sex: Male

Name: **TOTOY**
2nd Name: LUWIDYI
Surname: PRADO

Agta Ancestry: 75%

Birth Date: January 7, 1983
Death Date:

Father: NATENG
Mother: TETET

1st Spouse: DINA-2039
Last/Current Spouse: DINA-2039

Year: 2010
Totoy-3131

ID: 3131   Sex: Male

Name: **TOTOY**
2nd Name: KARLITO
Surname: PRADO

Agta Ancestry: 87.5%

Birth Date: January 15, 1987
Death Date:

Father: HEMPOK
Mother: EDNA

1st Spouse:
Last/Current Spouse:

Year: 2002
Totoy-3312

2008
Totoy-3312

ID: 3312   Sex: Male

Name: **TOTOY**
2nd Name: ALBERT
Surname: ADUANAN

Agta Ancestry: 100%

Birth Date: 1994 +/-1 year
Death Date:

Father: ALEK
Mother: LINDA

1st Spouse:
Last/Current Spouse:

Year: 1998
Totoy-8248 w mom Neneng-
415

ID: 8248   Sex: Male

Name: **TOTOY**
2nd Name: RIKO
Surname: DELAKRUS

Agta Ancestry: 46.88%

Birth Date: February 1997
Death Date:

Father: RENI
Mother: NENENG

1st Spouse:
Last/Current Spouse:

ID: 5483   Sex: Male

Name: **TULIO**
2nd Name:
Surname:

Agta Ancestry: Unknown

Birth Date: 1897 +/-3 years
Death Date: May 13, 1965

Father: BALALANG
Mother: ANUSENTA

Year: 1964   1st Spouse: LIPANYAW-5227
Tulio-5483   Last/Current Spouse: LIPANYAW-5227

ID: 7851   Sex: Female

Name: **TUNING**
2nd Name:
Surname:

Agta Ancestry: 71.875%

Birth Date: 1964 +/-6 years
Death Date:

Father: MELENSIO
Mother: ADILINA

Year: 2006   1st Spouse: KINYOL-7069
Tuning-7851   Last/Current Spouse: KINYOL-7069

ID: 241   Sex: Female

Name: **UDAD**
2nd Name: SULIDAD
Surname: UDANGGA, PEKTO

Agta Ancestry: 100%

Birth Date: 1938 +/-2 years
Death Date:

Father: PEKTO
Mother: BINANSA

Year: 1976   1st Spouse: PANSO-5353
Udad-241   Last/Current Spouse: BAYANI-49

ID: 46   Sex: Female

Name: **UDENG**
2nd Name: PRIDING, PIRIDIN
Surname: BEKYADEN

Agta Ancestry: 87.5%

Birth Date: 1960 +/-2 years
Death Date:

Father: BANGHUL
Mother: PILISA

Year: 1976   1st Spouse: OMI-66
Udeng-46   Last/Current Spouse: IKING-9147

203

Year: 2004
Udeng-317

2010
Udeng-317

ID:	317	*Sex:* Male

Name: **UDENG**
2nd Name:
Surname: ADUANAN
Agta Ancestry: 100%

Birth Date: 1958 +/-1 year
Death Date:

Father: LINGKON
Mother: ADILING
1st Spouse: ALILI-349
Last/Current Spouse: ALILI-349

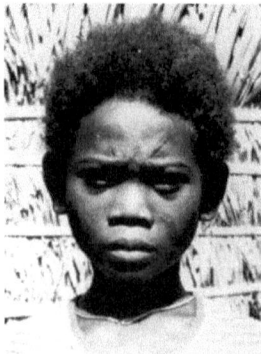

Year: 1977
Udeng-458

ID:	458	*Sex:* Male

Name: **UDENG**
2nd Name:
Surname: OLIBEROS
Agta Ancestry: 100%

Birth Date: 1962 +/-2 years
Death Date:

Father: PEDRING
Mother: USING
1st Spouse: unknown-7319
Last/Current Spouse: unknown-7319

Year: 2010
Uganda-8140

ID:	8140	*Sex:* Female

Name: **UGANDA**
2nd Name:
Surname: FRANCISCO
Agta Ancestry: 37.5%

Birth Date: January 26, 1992
Death Date:

Father: IDAG
Mother: WISAY
1st Spouse: DENBER-9307
Last/Current Spouse: DENBER-9307

Year: 1978
Ukel-466

ID:	466	*Sex:* Female

Name: **UKEL**
2nd Name: ELBINA, DINA
Surname: LISIDAY
Agta Ancestry: 93.75%

Birth Date: 1967 +/-2 years
Death Date:

Father: PEPE
Mother: LUDING
1st Spouse: HUAN-67
Last/Current Spouse: HUAN-67

Year: 1970
Uleg-604

1976
Uleg-604

ID:	604	Sex: Male

Name: **ULEG**
2nd Name:
Surname: TOMAY
Agta Ancestry: 100%

Birth Date: 1951 +/-2 years
Death Date: July 20, 1987

Father: DUDUYAN
Mother: GOLBIYENG
1st Spouse: HELEN-605
Last/Current Spouse: LIMINIDA-41

Year: 1978
Undi-319 with mother
Adiling-316

ID:	319	Sex: Male

Name: **UNDI**
2nd Name: LONRI, BANIGAL
Surname: ISTANES
Agta Ancestry: 100%

Birth Date: 1975
Death Date:

Father: LINING
Mother: ADILING
1st Spouse: HUANA-1016
Last/Current Spouse: HUANA-1016

Year: 1978
Undul-79

ID:	79	Sex: Male

Name: **UNDUL**
2nd Name: KUNDUL, ARTHUR, LOWE
Surname: ISTANES
Agta Ancestry: 100%

Birth Date: 1973 +/-2 years
Death Date:

Father: BILYESA
Mother: NARISA
1st Spouse: ABEY-383
Last/Current Spouse: MUNIK-9179

Year: 1977
Unged-7452

ID:	7452	Sex: Male

Name: **UNGED**
2nd Name: DYUNYOR
Surname: RAMUS
Agta Ancestry: 100%

Birth Date: 1950 +/-6 years
Death Date:

Father: BISENTE
Mother: PINESANGAN
1st Spouse: SALEG-7453
Last/Current Spouse: INGGEL-219

205

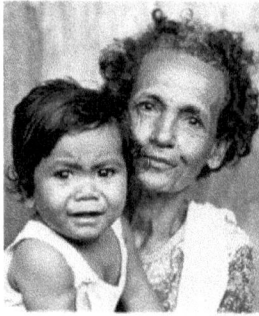

Year: 1978
Unyol-8036 with
grandmother Nena-412

ID:	8036	*Sex:* Male

Name: **UNYOL**
2nd Name: ROLANDO
Surname: AGILAR

Agta Ancestry: 62.5%

Birth Date: 1976 +/-6 years
Death Date: 2004 +/-1 year

Father: LANDU
Mother: LOLONG

1st Spouse:
Last/Current Spouse:

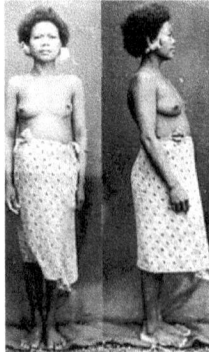

Year: 1936
Upila-608
photo by Vanoverbergh

ID:	608	*Sex:* Female

Name: **UPILA**
2nd Name: OPILA
Surname: MADENG

Agta Ancestry: 100%

Birth Date: 1899 +/-9 years
Death Date: December 1977

Father: MADENG
Mother: BIYA

1st Spouse: ALAMRA-5012
Last/Current Spouse: ALAMRA-5012

Year: 1967
Using-7371 with son Boker-
459

ID:	7371	*Sex:* Female

Name: **USING**
2nd Name:
Surname:

Agta Ancestry: 100%

Birth Date: 1936 +/-1 year
Death Date: 1970 +/-2 years

Father: BALENO
Mother: ANATOLIA

1st Spouse: PEDRING-454
Last/Current Spouse: PEDRING-454

Year: 1967
Utet-609

2010
Utet-609

ID:	609	*Sex:* Female

Name: **UTET**
2nd Name:
Surname: ALEDIG DELAKRUS

Agta Ancestry: 100%

Birth Date: 1943 +/-1 year
Death Date:

Father: ALEDIG
Mother: LUNING

1st Spouse: NARSISO-5322
Last/Current Spouse: BENI-9059

206

Year: 1978
Walalo-2075

ID: 2075   Sex: Male

Name: **WALALO**
2nd Name:
Surname: TANAS
Agta Ancestry: 100%

Birth Date: 1944 +/-3 years
Death Date:

Father: GOLENG
Mother: SAGED
1st Spouse: GETEK-612
Last/Current Spouse: GETEK-612

Year: 1978
Wanagen-434

ID: 434   Sex: Female

Name: **WANAGEN**
2nd Name:
Surname:
Agta Ancestry: 100%

Birth Date: 1945 +/-4 years
Death Date:

Father: SELOK
Mother: AHADUD
1st Spouse: PANDARING-433
Last/Current Spouse: PANDARING-433

Year: 2008
Waynalin-198

2010
Waynalin-198

ID: 198   Sex: Female

Name: **WAYNALIN**
2nd Name: WAYNA
Surname: TULIO ISTANES
Agta Ancestry: 93.75%

Birth Date: 1968 +/-1 year
Death Date:

Father: ENDING
Mother: NUNUK
1st Spouse: ELPI-562
Last/Current Spouse: ELPI-562

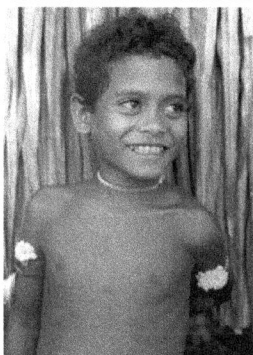

Year: 1972
Waytsel-8 phto by Jim
Musgrove

ID: 8   Sex: Male

Name: **WAYTSEL**
2nd Name: WITSEL
Surname:
Agta Ancestry: 100%

Birth Date: 1962 +/-1 year
Death Date: 1980

Father: DIYAKIN
Mother: ADILING
1st Spouse:
Last/Current Spouse:

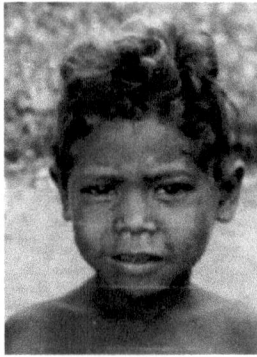
Year: 1976
Wening-367

ID: 367	*Sex:* Male

Name: **WENING**
2nd Name:
Surname: TIKIMAN
Agta Ancestry: 93.75%

Birth Date: 1971 +/-1 year
Death Date:

Father: MARIO
Mother: LODI

1st Spouse:
Last/Current Spouse:

Year: 1973
Wesli-194

1976
Wesli-194

ID: 194	*Sex:* Male

Name: **WESLI**
2nd Name:
Surname: ADUANAN
Agta Ancestry: 100%

Birth Date: December 4, 1963
Death Date: December 1986

Father: ELEDEN
Mother: ERMINYA

1st Spouse:
Last/Current Spouse:

Year: 1977
Wileng-456

ID: 456	*Sex:* Male

Name: **WILENG**
2nd Name:
Surname:
Agta Ancestry: 100%

Birth Date: 1957 +/-1 year
Death Date:

Father: BARBOSA
Mother: LUNINGNING

1st Spouse: NORMITA-266
Last/Current Spouse: AKEP-7003

Year: 2010
Wili-506

ID: 506	*Sex:* Male

Name: **WILI**
2nd Name:
Surname: TALUDEP MANDOSA
Agta Ancestry: 100%

Birth Date: May 1977
Death Date:

Father: ROHEL
Mother: EMILING

1st Spouse: BAIT-71
Last/Current Spouse: BAIT-71

ID:	572 *Sex:* Male

Name: **WILI**
2nd Name:
Surname: ADUANAN
Agta Ancestry: 93.75%

Birth Date: 1969 +/-2 years
Death Date:

Father: GIBSON
Mother: DENGDENG

Year: 1976
Wili-572

1st Spouse: NAYLING-7894
Last/Current Spouse: NAYLING-7894

ID: 285   *Sex:* Male

Name: **WILSON**
2nd Name:
Surname: SIMIN
Agta Ancestry: 100%

Birth Date: 1938 +/-4 years
Death Date: August 13, 1983

Father: SIMIN
Mother: ASIONA

Year: 1977
Wilson-285

1st Spouse: NARSING-576
Last/Current Spouse: MILA-555

ID: 7211   *Sex:* Male

Name: **WILSON**
2nd Name:
Surname: ULANYO
Agta Ancestry: Unknown

Birth Date: 1936 +/-5 years
Death Date: 1990 +/-9 years

Father: BADENDE
Mother: PASITA

Year: 1977
Wilson-7211

1st Spouse: KARMIN-7103
Last/Current Spouse: KARMIN-7103

ID: 4013   *Sex:* Male

Name: **WINER**
2nd Name: NUNNUK
Surname:
Agta Ancestry: 0%

Birth Date: 1988 +/-4 years
Death Date:

Father:
Mother:

Year: 2010
Winer-4013

1st Spouse: DAGA-3141
Last/Current Spouse: DAGA-3141

ID:	1042
Sex:	Male
Name:	**WIRNER**
2nd Name:	DYOKOY, WIRNEL
Surname:	GERERO
Agta Ancestry:	87.5%
Birth Date:	1977
Death Date:	
Father:	ELDING
Mother:	NEMI
1st Spouse:	ABENG-175
Last/Current Spouse:	ABENG-175

Year: 2008
Wirner-1042

2010
Wirner-1042

ID:	203
Sex:	Female
Name:	**WISAY**
2nd Name:	LUISA
Surname:	MORAL
Agta Ancestry:	75%
Birth Date:	1962 +/-1 year
Death Date:	
Father:	ERNING
Mother:	ISLING
1st Spouse:	LORDE-487
Last/Current Spouse:	IDAG-9122

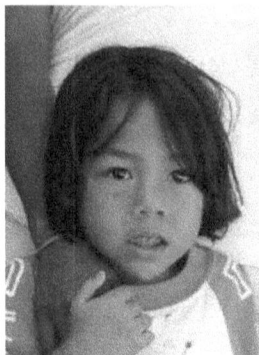

Year: 1978
Wisay-203

2004
Wisay-203 phto by Iris
Dalberto

ID:	8305
Sex:	Female
Name:	**YANILIN**
2nd Name:	
Surname:	VARGAS
Agta Ancestry:	35.937%
Birth Date:	January 4, 2004
Death Date:	
Father:	AMBUY
Mother:	PANEK
1st Spouse:	
Last/Current Spouse:	

Year: 2008
Yanilin-8305

Taken from The Agta Demographic Database, © Thomas and Janet Headland and SIL International, version 2.0, online at http://www.sil.org/silepubs/abstract.asp?id=49227. May be used for non-profit purposes if copyright owner is acknowledged.

Appendix A
Internet Homepage of *Agta Demographic Database*

Indexes
Author
Language
Country
Subject
Titles

Information
Editorial Board
Citation Format
Submission Guidelines for Authors
Terms of Use

SIL Electronic Publications
Book Reviews
SIL Forum
SIL e-Books
SIL LCDD
Journal of Translation
Survey Reports
Working Papers

SIL Language and Culture Documentation and Description 2

Agta Demographic Database: chronicle of a hunter-gatherer community in transition

Authors   Headland, Janet D.
Headland, Thomas N.

Abstract   For the past half-century Thomas and Janet Headland have studied demographic change among the Agta, a hunter-gatherer population in the Philippines. Since the 1998 publication of *Population Dynamics of a Philippine Rain Forest People,* numerous scholars have asked about the raw data on which the Headlands based their study. Now those data are published with the full permission of the Agta people. This database consists of the records of 4,200 Agta individuals, 600 of whom are alive today. Of these, 285 are members of the San Ildefonso Agta, a subpopulation living on a peninsula separate from the larger Casiguran Agta Population on the mainland. Included in these records are the names, facial photographs, family histories, genealogies, and ancestors (dating back to the late nineteenth century) of today's Agta. The data are complete with every birth, marriage, divorce, death, and in- and out-migration since 1950 to January 2008, for the 285-member San Ildefonso Agta subpopulation.

The Agta population has vital statistics that are extreme compared to industrialized humankind. These will be of interest to anthropologists, students of human history, and demographers. Today's Agta have an infant mortality rate of 220/1000 (vs. 7/1000 in the USA), a high total fertility rate of 7.3, and a life expectancy of just 23 years (vs. 78 years in the USA). Readers may use these data to check these and other demographic parameters, as well as for testing their own hypotheses of so-called primitive populations. The *Agta Demographic Database* provides a keyhole glimpse into how our human ancestors may have lived and died in prehistory. This is an ongoing work, to be re-released at intervals.

Version 1.0, January 2009

- View *Agta Demographic Database: chronicle of a hunter-gatherer community in transition* 1523 KB, 20 pages
- View *Agta database field descriptions* 178 KB
- Download *All documents (article, sample reports, auxiliary documents)* 3162 KB
- Download *Data and user interface with photographs* 68852 KB
- Download *Data and user interface without photographs* 1054 KB
- Download *Data in CSV format* 154 KB
- Download *Data in XML format* 234 KB

Published   2007, 2009

Language   Agta, Casiguran Dumagat [dgc]
Ethnologue entry for Agta, Casiguran Dumagat

Country   Philippines

Subjects   Anthropology
Demography

Keywords   Agta; hunter-gatherers; demographic anthropology; Negritos; demography of prehistoric populations; Casiguran; San Ildefonso

Questions/Comments: *SILLCDD_Intl@sil.org*

[SIL Language and Culture Documentation and Description Home | SIL Publications | SIL Home]

Google Custom Search   Search SIL International website

URL: *http://www.sil.org/silepubs/abstract.asp?id=49227*

Appendix B: Securing Informed Consent from the Agta to Publish their Photos

To Whom It May Concern
From Thomas N. Headland
March 12, 2007

This page, with the attached supporting documents, addresses certain ethical questions concerning the Headlands' anthropological research on the Agta and the publication of the present book of Agta photographs. To see the whole 29 pages of documents by which the Headlands got their research approved by the ethics committee (called Institutional Review Board, or IRB) at the University of North Dakota, go online to <www.sil.org/silepubs/Pubs/49227/49227_InformedConsent.pdf>. Thomas Headland is a professor at that university.

Following the Code of Ethics of the American Anthropological Association (www.aaanet.org/committees/ethics/ethcode.htm) Janet Headland and I want to be sure we are acting responsibly toward the Agta people who have supplied us with their family histories. As point 3 of the Code states, "*Anthropological researchers must determine in advance whether their hosts/providers of information wish to remain anonymous or receive recognition, and make every effort to comply with those wishes.*"

Most important, when doing "human subjects research," the Code expects investigators to secure the "informed consent" of the persons being studied (point 4). The attached pages here consist of documents verifying that we have secured the informed consent of the Agta people to publish their family histories for public viewing. These pages also document that we have submitted our research for approval to the University of North Dakota Institutional Review Board (IRB) and that they approved our research for publication.

The pages include a letter from the Agta leaders, written by them in their own language giving us permission and, in fact, urging us to publish their family genealogies. Also included here is an English translation of their letter. The Agta wrote this letter at my request in April 2006. A total of 152 Agta adults (age 18+) signed the letter. All of their signatures are on the attached pages. Agta who cannot write signed their names with their thumbprint, the usual method used in the Philippines and recognized by the Philippine government for preliterate people.

Also enclosed here is the 4-page University of North Dakota Human Subjects Review Form that I handed in to the UND Institutional Review Board (IRB) in July 2006. Most of it is not filled out because they told me it was not necessary for reasons stated in their formal letter to me (also enclosed) dated August 9, 2006.

Also enclosed here is my 6-page "Comments" submitted with the above Review Form, which I submitted to the IRB with the Form in July 2006. My "Comments" explain the Agta demography project, describe the protocol, how Janet and I got "informed consent" from the Agta people, background on the history of our demographic research, and the two funding grants we received in the 1990s from the LSB Leakey Foundation and from the PEW Charitable Trusts that supported our trips to the Philippines and our Agta fieldwork there in the 1990s.

Respectfully submitted,

Thomas N. Headland
Adjunct Professor of Linguistics, University of North Dakota, and
Anthropology Consultant, SIL International

212

Sa Mga Kinauukulan (To Whom It May Concern) Moon of February, 2006

We who are signing-our-names to this paper here, we are the elders/adults Agta-people of Casiguran, Province of Aurora, Philippines. We are the leaders of the Agta villages in Casiguran. As to Grandpa Thomas Headland and Grandma Janet Headland, well, our [Agta] parents-and-grandparents, they invited Grandparents Headlands to live with us in 1962. They invited them so that they would help us with our hardship-problems. Up to the present, the Headlands continue to visit us. We like this married-couple.

Until now, they help us a lot. They medicine-treat us and they help us to get medical treatment/ healing at the hospital. And they help us to get our children into schools. Also they help us with our Agta necessities so that we won't be abused by outsiders. They help us with *indidyines yuman raits* ['indigenous human rights'] (people privileges). They are always helping us with our economic problems (livelihood projects).

We are happy about them, and we for a long time now, we've been helping them to make lists in a *sensos* ('census'), listing all of our names and the names of all of our relatives and ancestors. We want them to make this *sensos*. We permit Grandpa and Grandma (to do this).

We, all of us Agta, we have been helping them for about forty years. What we want now is that they list all of our many-names in a *kompyuter* ('computer') so that all the people in the world can read our names. We want it like that, so that even if we die, they will know them. And our future-grandchildren, they will see/know our names even after one hundred years have passed.

What we are commanding to Grandpa Headland is, "Don't you erase our names from the *sensos*." Good-grief! If they get erased, for sure our grandchildren will forget our names!

Also, we give-permission for Grandpa Headland to place all of the photographs of us in the *compyuter* and on the *inter-net* '[Internet']. Do that also with [photos of] our children and our great-grandparents of long ago, so that other people in the world will see our images (what-we-look-like). And we want them to list all of our names attached-right next to our photographs, and [we want] our names [in the *sensos*], too, so that other people will know our names.

And also, the Agta *sensos* that Headlands will make, it is our proof that we are true Agta of Casiguran, so that we can prove to the government that we have always-lived on this land of ours in Casiguran. This land here is our *ansestral domen* ('ancestral domain') since long ago, even more than a thousand years ago. If our true names are not listed in the *sensos*, maybe the government won't believe that we are truly Agta from Casiguran.

Thank you. This is all that we want to say. Here are our true signatures.

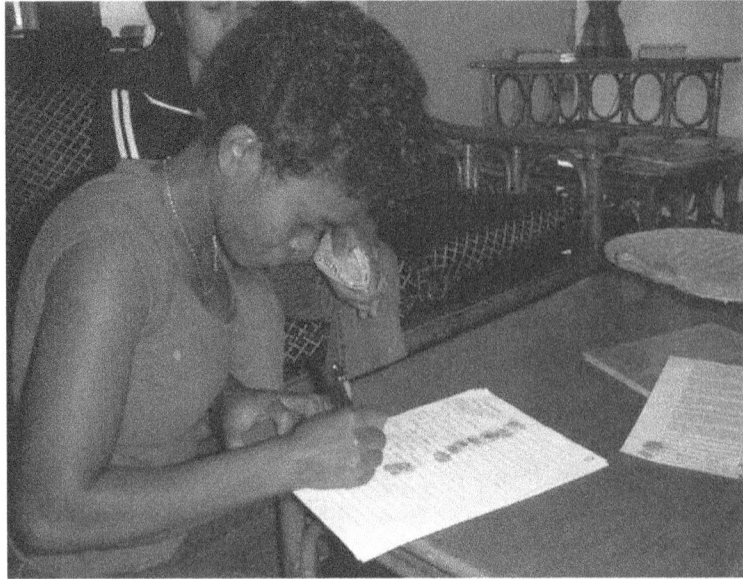

Agta woman, Dyemari Aduanan, signing the Agta's "informed consent" letter giving Thomas Headland permission to publish the Agta *sensos* (the Agta census genealogy database). Photo taken by Janet Headland, March 2006.

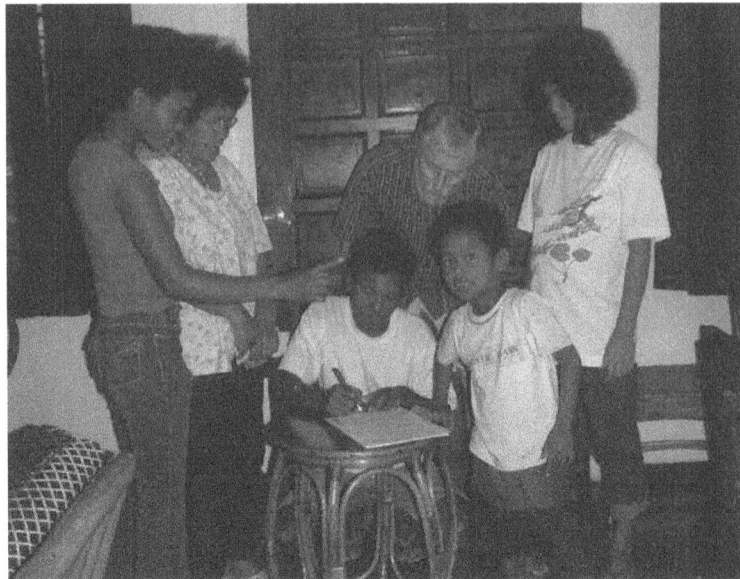

Photo of four Agta adults signing the Agta's "informed consent" letter giving Thomas Headland permission to publish the Agta *sensos* (the Agta census genealogy database). Standing from left to right: Agta woman Dyemari Aduanan, Agta woman Tetet Moral, Agta man Nateng Prado squatting and signing the document, American anthropologist Thomas Headland looking over Nateng's shoulder, Agta boy Batutung (who did not sign the document because only adults signed it), and Agta woman Melani Kukuang. Nateng has for many years been the chieftain (political leader) of the San Ildefonso Agta. Photo taken by Janet Headland, March 2006.

214

Sa Mga Kinauukulan (To Whom It May Concern)   Bulan na Pebrero, 2006

Sikame a nagpirma ta papel a eye, ey sikame i matanda a Agta a taga Casiguran, Provincia na Aurora, Pilipinas. Sikame du lider ta bariyo-bariyo du Agta ta Casiguran. Ti Boboy a Thomas Headland sakay ti Boboy a Janet Headland, ey tu matetanda me ey inakit de de Boboy Headland a megiyan dikame to 1962. Inakit de kame a monda tulungan de kame ta kahirapan me. Hanggan nadid, ey bumebisita de Headland dikame. Gustu me side a pasawa.

Hanggan nadid, inaguman de kame ta meadu. Ginamot de kame sakay nipagamot de kame ta hospital, tinulungan de kame a megpaiskwela du anak me. Sakay inaguman de kame ta karapatan me a Agta para ewan kame maabusu ta iba a tolay. Inaguman de kame ta inddiyines yuman raits. (karapatang pangkatao). Inaguman de kame a palagi ta kabuhayan. (livelihood projects).

Masaya kame dide, ey nale kame nadid a panahun ey sikame ey inaguman me side a meglista ta sensos a melista ta etanan a ngahen me sakay du ngahen du etanan a tetotop me sakay apu-apu me. Gustu me a megimet side ta eye a sensos. Pakultaden me de Boboy.

Sikame a etanan a Agta, ey natulungan me side nadid ta manga epatapulu a taon. I gustu me nadid, ey ilista de i etanan a ngehangahen me ta komputer a monda mabasa na etanan a tolay ta mundu i ngehangahen me. Gustu me i kona sa, monda maski mate kame, ey matukoyan de. Sakay du apu-apu me, ey meta de du ngahen me maski sandaan a taon a makalipas.

Tu iutus me de Boboy Headland, ey diyan moy buhaan i ngahen me ta sensos me. Hus, eng mabuha, ey siguradu ey kaleksapan du apu-apu me ta ngahen me.

Sakay pati, ey pakultaden me de Boboy Headland a iyedton de be du etanan a letrato dikame ta computer sakay ta inter-net. Kona be sa du anak me, sakey du metatanda me a minate to araw, monda meta na tolay ta mundu ta idsura me. Sakay gustu me a ilista de du ngehangahen de ta diton du letrato, sakay du ngahen me be, monda mapospusan na tolay du ngehangahen me.

Sakay pati, tu sensos na Agta a megimet de Headland, ey seya i katunayan me a sikame ey tunay kame a Agta a taga Casiguran, a monda magpatunay kame ta gobiyerno a nale kame a negiyan ta luta me ta Casiguran. I luta me ta eye ey tu ansestral domen me a hanggan to araw, mahigit pa ta sanlibu a taon. Eng ewan melista i tunay a ngahen me ta sensos, makay ewan meniwala i gubiyerno a tunay kame a Agta a taga Casiguran.

Salamat, Se' san den ye i gustu me a kagin. Seye tu pirma me ta eye a mangpatunay.

ANALYN Miriedo 2/15/06   Paming Gera 2/17/06

PAR Utet Delakrus 2/15/06   Lanie Osorio 2/17

MYLA MARNO (Marahyo)   Rekvek Lisiday 2/17

Nonsi Gera 2/16/06   Josie Actanel 2/17

Udeng Adwanan 2/16   Eng-sng
                           Zenaida Mora 2/17

Miring Torio 2/16   Nini
                          Taninie Bitigan 2/17 215

Bait Bitigan 2/17

Paring Dalapenya 2/17

Hose Mahates

Naleagleng Tijiday

Kitol Kakuang

Tersing Bitigan

Gloria Dalapenya

Pepek Bitigan

Atoshi Dalapenya

Aytin Gonsales

Lelet Dalapenya

Enelda Kukuan

RENATO PRADO chiftine

Dina B. Prado

Borseg Lisiday

Marina Tetet Prado

Flodilin Hopek Lapamiya

Melanie M Kukuan (Kuiteg)

Irene Culideg

Ilising Lisa Gera

Ensing Tulio

216

Sikame a nagpirma ta papel a eye, ey sikame i matanda a Agta a taga Casiguran, Provincia na Aurora, Pilipinas. Sikame du lider ta bariyo-bariyo du Agta ta Casiguran. Ti Boboy a Thomas Headland sakay ti Boboy a Janet Headland, ey tu matetanda me ey inakit de de Boboy Headland a megiyan dikame to 1962. Inakit de kame a monda tulungan de kame ta kahirapan me. Hanggan nadid, ey bumebisita de Headland dikame. Gustu me side a pasawa.

Hanggan nadid, inaguman de kame ta meadu. Ginamot de kame sakay nipagamot de kame ta hospital, tinulungan de kame a megpaiskwela du anak me. Sakay inaguman de kame ta karapatan me a Agta para ewan kame maabusu ta iba a tolay. Inaguman de kame ta indidyines yuman raits. (karapatang pangkatao). Inaguman de kame a palagi ta kabuhayan. (livelihood projects).

Masaya kame dide, ey nale kame nadid a panahun ey sikame ey inaguman me side a meglista ta sensos a melista ta etanan a ngahen me sakay du ngahen du etanan a tetotop me sakay apu-apu me. Gustu me a megimet side ta eye a sensos. Pakultaden me de Boboy.

Sikame a etanan a Agta, ey natulungan me side nadid ta manga epatapulu a taon. I gustu me nadid, ey ilista de i etanan a ngehangahen me ta komputer a monda mabasa na etanan a tolay ta mundu i ngehangahen me. Gustu me i kona sa, monda maski mate kame, ey matukoyan de. Sakay du apu-apu me, ey meta de du ngahen me maski sandaan a taon a makalipas.

Tu iutus me de Boboy Headland, ey diyan moy buhaan i ngahen me ta sensos me. Hus, eng mabuha, ey siguradu ey kaleksapan du apu-apu me ta ngahen me.

Sakay pati, ey pakultaden me de Boboy Headland a iyedton de be du etanan a letrato dikame ta computer sakay ta inter-net. Kona be sa du anak me, sakey du metatanda me a minate to araw, monda meta na tolay ta mundu ta idsura me. Sakay gustu me a ilista de du ngehangahen de ta diton du letrato, sakay du ngahen me be, monda mapospusan na tolay du ngehangahen me.

Sakay pati, tu sensos na Agta a megimet de Headland, ey seya i katunayan me a sikame ey tunay kame a Agta a taga Casiguran, a monda magpatunay kame ta gobiyerno a nale kame a negiyan ta luta me ta Casiguran. I luta me ta eye ey tu ansestral domen me a hanggan to araw, mahigit pa ta sanlibu a taon. Eng ewan melista i tunay a ngahen me ta sensos, makay ewan meniwala i gubiyerno a tunay kame a Agta a taga Casiguran.

Salamat, Se' san den ye i gustu me a kagin. Seye tu pirma me ta eye a mangpatunay.

Edna Prado	TRIBAL-chieftain - Laurgic Prado
Alex Adunan	Iben Dunato
Noel Tonyet Kogawad	Linda Adnanan
Luningning Adunan	Konjita Dunato
Linita Dunato	Huana Irtones
Nati Marundu	Mary Jane Prado

217

Benie dela Cruz

Jyosilis Gerero

Tinyol Donato

Tuning Donato

Gaspar Manong

Batanggas Lisiday

Regu Prado

Totang D Meranda

EDNALYN Manung

Pelip Kekek Aduanan

Waynalin ESTanES

Noemi Aduana

Jemayn Lisiday

yempok Prado

Perla Mora   2/23/06

Alili Aduanan   2/25/06

Saysay Berhabi   2/25/06

Romulo Francisco

218

Sa Mga Kinauukulan (To Whom It May Concern)   Bulan na Pebrero, 2006

Sikame a nagpirma ta papel a eye, ey sikame i matanda a Agta a taga Casiguran, Provincia na Aurora, Pilipinas. Sikame du lider ta bariyo-bariyo du Agta ta Casiguran. Ti Boboy a Thomas Headland sakay ti Boboy a Janet Headland, ey tu matetanda me ey inakit de de Boboy Headland a megiyan dikame to 1962. Inakit de kame a monda tulungan de kame ta kahirapan me. Hanggan nadid, ey bumebisita de Headland dikame. Gustu me side a pasawa.

Hanggan nadid, inaguman de kame ta meadu. Ginamot de kame sakay nipagamot de kame ta hospital, tinulungan de kame a megpaiskwela du anak me. Sakay inaguman de kame ta karapatan me a Agta para ewan kame maabusu ta iba a tolay. Inaguman de kame ta indidyines yuman raits. (karapatang pangkatao). Inaguman de kame a palagi ta kabuhayan. (livelihood projects).

Masaya kame dide, ey nale kame nadid a panahun ey sikame ey inaguman me side a meglista ta sensos a melista ta etanan a ngahen me sakay du ngahen du etanan a tetotop me sakay apu-apu me. Gustu me a megimet side ta eye a sensos. Pakultaden me de Boboy.

Sikame a etanan a Agta, ey natulungan me side nadid ta manga epatapulu a taon. I gustu me nadid, ey ilista de i etanan a ngehangahen me ta komputer a monda mabasa na etanan a tolay ta mundu i ngehangahen me. Gustu me i kona sa, monda maski mate kame, ey matukoyan de. Sakay du apu-apu me, ey meta de du ngahen me maski sandaan a taon a makalipas.

Tu iutus me de Boboy Headland, ey diyan moy buhaan i ngahen me ta sensos me. Hus, eng mabuha, ey siguradu ey kaleksapan du apu-apu me ta ngahen me.

Sakay pati, ey pakultaden me de Boboy Headland a iyedton de be du etanan a letrato dikame ta computer sakay ta inter-net. Kona be sa du anak me, sakey du metatanda me a minate to araw, monda meta na tolay ta mundu ta idsura me. Sakay gustu me a ilista de du ngehangahen de ta diton du letrato, sakay du ngahen me be, monda mapospusan na tolay du ngehangahen me.

Sakay pati, tu sensos na Agta a megimet de Headland, ey seya i katunayan me a sikame ey tunay kame a Agta a taga Casiguran, a monda magpatunay kame ta gobiyerno a nale kame a negiyan ta luta me ta Casiguran. I luta me ta eye ey tu <u>ansestral domen</u> me a hanggan to araw, mahigit pa ta sanlibu a taon. Eng ewan melista i tunay a ngahen me ta sensos, makay ewan meniwala i gubiyerno a tunay kame a Agta a taga Casiguran.

Salamat, Se' san den ye i gustu me a kagin. Seye tu pirma me ta eye a mangpatunay.

Haling Adunnah	Wili Mondosa
Pikson Pawisan	Koloy Bekyaden
Suran Culideg	Diyabar Tulio
Loida Pawisan	Abdon Bekyaden
Gnalyn Baspang	Helen Rohins
Rosalito Gunyatos	

Fernando Luna

Neheng Lisiday

Tilong Lisiday

Nuring Lisiday

Prisila siléng Gera

Neheng Bernabe

Selton Bernabe

Marilia "Neneng" Kukuan 2/25

Ariel Prado

Linda dela Peña

Lita kukuan

Jose Mehares (or Mélfring)

Nelson Prado

Nilda Bikyaden Mendoza

Clauir R. Besasa

Junior Danilo Diosino

Tersing Bitigan

Sa Mga Kinauukulan (To Whom It May Concern)   Bulan na Pebrero, 2006

Sikame a nagpirma ta papel a eye, ey sikame i matanda a Agta a taga Casiguran, Provincia na Aurora, Pilipinas. Sikame du lider ta bariyo-bariyo du Agta ta Casiguran. Ti Boboy a Thomas Headland sakay ti Boboy a Janet Headland, ey tu matetanda me ey inakit de de Boboy Headland a megiyan dikame to 1962. Inakit de kame a monda tulungan de kame ta kahirapan me. Hanggan nadid, ey bumebisita de Headland dikame. Gustu me side a pasawa.

Hanggan nadid, inaguman de kame ta meadu. Ginamot de kame sakay nipagamot de kame ta hospital, tinulungan de kame a megpaiskwela du anak me. Sakay inaguman de kame ta karapatan me a Agta para ewan kame maabusu ta iba a tolay. Inaguman de kame ta indidyines yuman raits. (karapatang pangkatao). Inaguman de kame a palagi ta kabuhayan. (livelihood projects).

Masaya kame dide, ey nale kame nadid a panahun ey sikame ey inaguman me side a meglista ta sensos a melista ta etanan a ngahen me sakay du ngahen du etanan a tetotop me sakay apu-apu me. Gustu me a megimet side ta eye a sensos. Pakultaden me de Boboy.

Sikame a etanan a Agta, ey natulungan me side nadid ta manga epatapulu a taon. I gustu me nadid, ey ilista de i etanan a ngehangahen me ta komputer a monda mabasa na etanan a tolay ta mundu i ngehangahen me. Gustu me i kona sa, monda maski mate kame, ey matukoyan de. Sakay du apu-apu me, ey meta de du ngahen me maski sandaan a taon a makalipas.

Tu iutus me de Boboy Headland, ey diyan moy buhaan i ngahen me ta sensos me. Hus, eng mabuha, ey siguradu ey kaleksapan du apu-apu me ta ngahen me.

Sakay pati, ey pakultaden me de Boboy Headland a iyedton de be du etanan a letrato dikame ta computer sakay ta inter-net. Kona be sa du anak me, sakey du metatanda me a minate to araw, monda meta na tolay ta mundu ta idsura me. Sakay gustu me a ilista de du ngehangahen de ta diton du letrato, sakay du ngahen me be, monda mapospusan na tolay du ngehangahen me.

Sakay pati, tu sensos na Agta a megimet de Headland, ey seya i katunayan me a sikame ey tunay kame a Agta a taga Casiguran, a monda magpatunay kame ta gobiyerno a nale kame a negiyan ta luta me ta Casiguran. I luta me ta eye ey tu ansestral domen me a hanggan to araw, mahigit pa ta sanlibu a taon. Eng ewan melista i tunay a ngahen me ta sensos, makay ewan meniwala i gubiyerno a tunay kame a Agta a taga Casiguran.

Salamat, Se' san den ye i gustu me a kagin. Seye tu pirma me ta eye a mangpatunay.

Vicky B. Guerra   2/15/06   Teming Moral   2/15/06

Melanie D. Guerra   2/15/06   Renalyn ku Ruan   2/15/06

Dani Geva   2/15/06   Crisa Cmisa Moral   2/15/06

Jird Aduanan   2/15/06   Loyda Moral   2/15/06

Hinat Aduanan   2/15/06   Resi Tanyet   2/15/06

Crissanto- Moral   2/15/06   R Pompiek Sagured   2/15/06

221

Sa Mga Kinauukulan (To Whom It May Concern)   Bulan na Pebrero, 2006

Sikame a nagpirma ta papel a eye, ey sikame i matanda a Agta a taga Casiguran, Provincia na Aurora, Pilipinas. Sikame du lider ta bariyo-bariyo du Agta ta Casiguran. Ti Boboy a Thomas Headland sakay ti Boboy a Janet Headland, ey tu matetanda me ey inakit de de Boboy Headland a megiyan dikame to 1962. Inakit de kame a monda tulungan de kame ta kahirapan me. Hanggan nadid, ey bumebisita de Headland dikame. Gustu me side a pasawa.

Hanggan nadid, inaguman de kame ta meadu. Ginamot de kame sakay nipagamot de kame ta hospital, tinulungan de kame a megpaiskwela du anak me. Sakay inaguman de kame ta karapatan me a Agta para ewan kame maabusu ta iba a tolay. Inaguman de kame ta indidyines yuman raits. (karapatang pangkatao). Inaguman de kame a palagi ta kabuhayan. (livelihood projects).

Masaya kame dide, ey nale kame nadid a panahun ey sikame ey inaguman me side a meglista ta sensos a melista ta etanan a ngahen me sakay du ngahen du etanan a tetotop me sakay apu-apu me. Gustu me a megimet side ta eye a sensos. Pakultaden me de Boboy.

Sikame a etanan a Agta, ey natulungan me side nadid ta manga epatapulu a taon. I gustu me nadid, ey ilista de i etanan a ngehangahen me ta komputer a monda mabasa na etanan a tolay ta mundu i ngehangahen me. Gustu me i kona sa, monda maski mate kame, ey matukoyan de. Sakay du apu-apu me, ey meta de du ngahen me maski sandaan a taon a makalipas.

Tu iutus me de Boboy Headland, ey diyan moy buhaan i ngahen me ta sensos me. Hus, eng mabuha, ey siguradu ey kaleksapan du apu-apu me ta ngahen me.

Sakay pati, ey pakultaden me de Boboy Headland a iyedton de be du etanan a letrato dikame ta computer sakay ta inter-net. Kona be sa du anak me, sakey du metatanda me a minate to araw, monda meta na tolay ta mundu ta idsura me. Sakay gustu me a ilista de du ngehangahen de ta diton du letrato, sakay du ngahen me be, monda mapospusan na tolay du ngehangahen me.

Sakay pati, tu sensos na Agta a megimet de Headland, ey seya i katunayan me a sikame ey tunay kame a Agta a taga Casiguran, a monda magpatunay kame ta gobiyerno a nale kame a negiyan ta luta me ta Casiguran. I luta me ta eye ey tu ansestral domen me a hanggan to araw, mahigit pa ta sanlibu a taon. Eng ewan melista i tunay a ngahen me ta sensos, makay ewan meniwala i gubiyerno a tunay kame a Agta a taga Casiguran.

Salamat, Se' san den ye i gustu me a kagin. Seye tu pirma me ta eye a mangpatunay.

LONG LONG Orlando H. Tabujara	Gemma Tabujara
Pacita Tabujara	Diwata mojica
Alijandro Mabunga	CARIDAD J. LASIW
Marilyn V. Tudso	Vira M. Tabujara
Lolita Aguilar	Carie Anne L. Palean

Wilmar T. Rico	Bilyesa Kukuan
Julita R Cumilas	NENENG KULEDEG
aeona Mantes	Jouelyn SobreVega
Nida Dulla	Jolluiyp Basilio
Analyn Abadia	NIDALYN PONGY (DIOSINO)
Leonardo Aguilar	
Nelly Vargas (Bantog)	LODY BUNAW
PAPEK MIA	MADENG MIA
Jeffrey Casili	JOEL Gema = JOEL
ALLAN ALHAMBRA	Lito Kukuan
MONAR TAGYAM	Loida Tulio
Nelson Prado	Freddie Mara
Jingo G. Aguilar	KULOT KUKUAN
Levy O Esteves	Leny Esteves
Leny Esteves	
ABEL Esteves	
Aguilar, Marlon C.	
Ramel Cospuz	
Rodolfo Vargas Vr.	
Rodolfo Vargas Jr.	Rodolfo Vargas
Vic Vargas	
Arjen Vargas	
Ponce Dotayan	
Jusing Bunao	

Appendix C: Tom and Janet Headland family, 1961 to 2008

Rachel, 2008

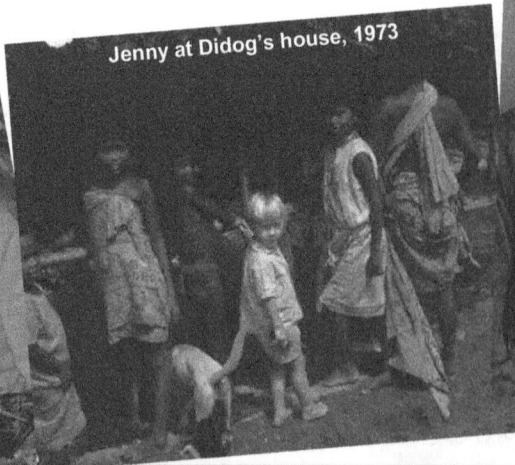
Jenny at Didog's house, 1973

Tom & Janet, 1961

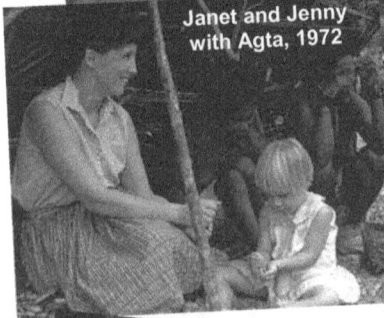
Janet and Jenny with Agta, 1972

Steve, Jenny, Rachel, with Agta friends, 1972

Tom, 2007

Tom and Beding, 1962

Tom and Janet, 2004

Jenny, 2006

Janet, 2008

Tom with Agta, 1977

Tom and Janet Headland family, 1961 to 2008

Janet holding Hene, 1963

Steve, age 12, 1977

2007
Steve
Ruth
Kiana
Kael

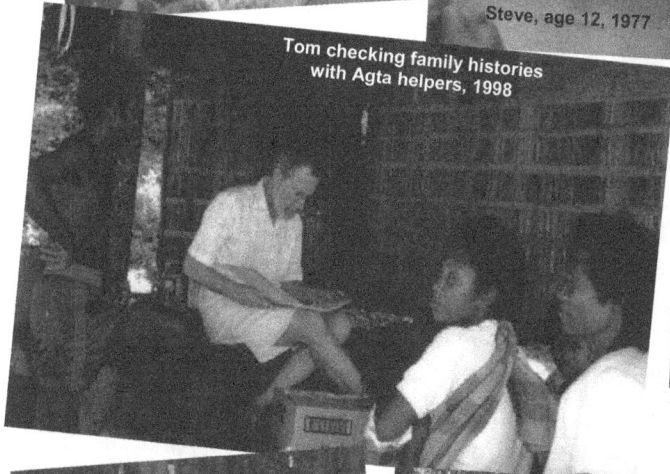

Tom checking family histories with Agta helpers, 1998

Rachel with baby monkey, 1967

Janet at Muntay, Casiguran, 1962

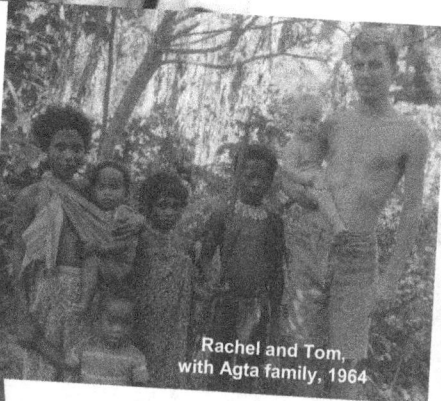

Rachel and Tom, with Agta family, 1964

Rachel with Uncle Eleden, 1971

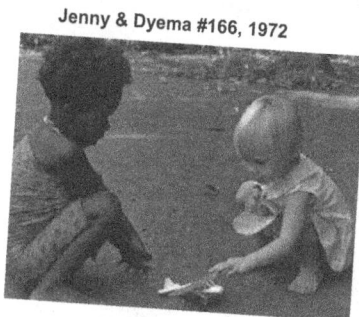

Jenny & Dyema #166, 1972

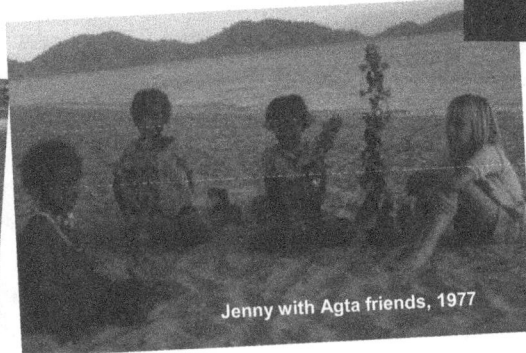

Jenny with Agta friends, 1977

225

Tom and Janet Headland family, 1961 to 2008

Steve with wife
and 3 children, 2008

Rachel baby-sitting Alek, 1970

Rachel with husband
Brian, 2004

Headlands at mealtime
in the Agta forest, 1968

Headland family in
the USA in 2007

Steve

Jenny

Rachel

Tom

Janet

Tom, 2004

Jenny with Waytsel, 1973

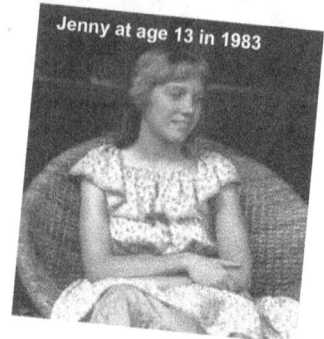

Jenny at age 13 in 1983

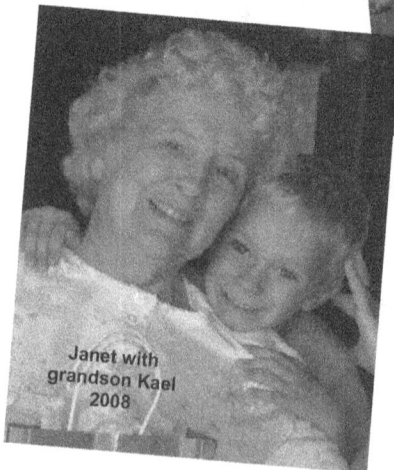

Janet with
grandson Kael
2008

Jenny and husband with children, 2008

226

Tom and Janet Headland family, 1961 to 2008

Steve climbing to get papaya, 1971

Janet holding Rachel, 1963

Steve attending school at Kalabgan, Casiguran, 1976

6th grade Kalabgan school

Steve, 2008

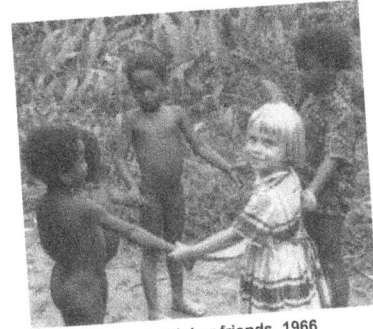

Rachel with her friends, 1966

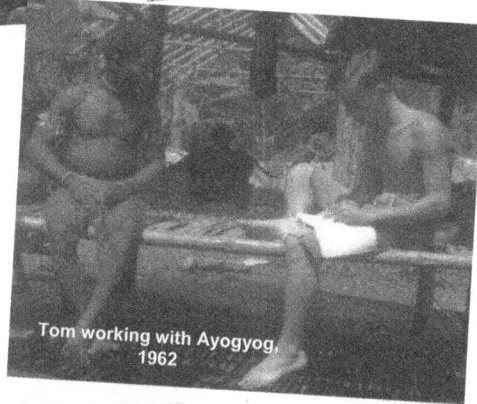

Jenny attending Kalabgan school with Agta, 1977

Tom working with Ayogyog, 1962

Rachel and Steve, 1967, at Muntay, Koso, Casiguran

Giant python killed by Kekek, 6.9 m, 1970

Python skin, killed by Kekek (with hat); Tom on left, Rachel on far right; 1970

227

Appendix D: Scholarly Reviews of the Early and Headland Book

This section contains quotes from book reviews of *Population Dynamics of a Philippine Rain Forest People: The San Ildefonso Agta*, by John D. Early and Thomas N. Headland. Published in 1998 by University Press of Florida.

"This book [is] an outstanding guide for future studies of small-scale societies.... I declare the highest respect for Headland's long and intimate acquaintance with Agta culture.... The major contribution of this book is the stimulation it provides and the questions it raises. Always impressive and sometimes overwhelming, the demographic details and the adroit handling of them are exemplary. All future demographic studies of transitional foraging groups will have to live up to the high standards set here." — **Robert Lawless,** in *Journal of Third World Studies,* 2000.

"The hard work of the authors has produced a view into the functioning of what may be the last days of one of the few hunting-and-gathering societies left in the world." — **Nancy Howell,** in *Current Anthropology,* 1999.

"There have been surprisingly few detailed studies of the impact of modern forestry practices on indigenous peoples. The only authoritative long-term study of forest-dweller demography [Early and Headland's book], carried out among the Agta people in the Philippines, shows clearly how logging and associated changes in disease ecology and land use, caused massive increases in mortality and severe health and nutritional impacts." — **Marcus Colchester,** Director, Forest Peoples Programme, World Rainforest Movement, Chadington, UK; in Indigenous Peoples and the new 'Global Vision' on Forests.

"A valuable case study of how local population dynamics can unfold with departure from a foraging lifeway. The great strength of the study is in long-term, careful, systematic, and localized collection and cross-checking of data that documents the local microdynamics of population change." — **Alexandra Brewis,** in *American Anthropologist,* 1999.

"The book provides forty-four years of high-quality data on the mortality, fertility, and migration patterns of the Agta [population].... The book ... forces the reader to confront issues of cultural survival, genetic survival, and ethnic survival with hard data that cannot be ignored.... Suggest[s] small minority populations ... without government protections may rapidly face extinction." — **Kim Hill,** in *Journal of Anthropological Research,* 1999.

"While many anthropologists study indigenous peoples in the process of being drawn from relative isolation,... the time constraints of fieldwork seldom allow them to obtain the reliable long-term data necessary to analyze rates of fertility, mortality, and migration. One of the co-authors of this book ... was able to collect demographic data fulfilling these conditions; [Headlands] spent over 40 years working ... among the Agta people ... under circumstances of rapid change." — **Nancy Flowers,** in *Human Ecology,* 1999.

"An important and significant contribution to anthropology." — **Barry S. Hewlett, Washington State University.** 1998.

"Foragers societies of the world are on the brink of extinction. John Early and Thomas Headland describe this painful reality.... The Agta may avoid biological extinction ... but the Agta as a cultural group are about to die out." — **S. Nagata,** in *The Canadian Review of Sociology and Anthropology,* 1999.

"A landmark in ethnographic demography. Based on more than 23 years' fieldwork and drawing from a database of 44 years, it is the first and only full study of the population dynamics of a hunting-gathering (foraging) group in Asia that relies on real actuarial data rather than mathematical models…. Excellent writing." — *Choice.*

"In many respects, this book can serve as a model of demographic methodology for studying 'anthropological' (i.e., small and lacking written records for vital events) populations." — **Alan Fix,** in *American Journal of Human Biology,* 2000.

"The authors have compiled a rich and unusual set of data…. It is a useful contribution to demographic anthropology." — **Simon Strickland,** in *Population Studies.* 2000.

"Documents the development of relations with outsiders and the consequent impact on the Agta population…. The meticulous analysis of occasionally sparse data is recorded in detail…. This objective appraisal of the population dynamics of a group under immediate threat is important material for representing the rights of indigenous people." — **Linda Hitchcox,** in *Journal of the Royal Anthropological Institute,* 1999.

"[This book] is unique because it analyzes demographic data of a foraging group over a long period of time and the subsequent cultural changes brought on by the timber industry." — **Kevin Janni,** in *Economic Botany,* 2000.

"Their discussion of methods in Part 3 is a high point of the book and could very well serve as a blueprint for future studies in demographic anthropology…. The authors' conclusions and analysis have very practical consequences…. The text's final paragraphs emphasize the importance of missionary work in the survival of foraging populations, which may strike a sour note with some, but few will deny the book's important contributions to the field of demographic anthropology." — **Darron Asher Collins,** in *Journal of Ethnobiology.*

"Comprehensive demographic studies of foraging societies are exceedingly rare…. Early and Headland provide such a demographic study in this book—only the second of its kind (the other is the Ache of Paraguay)—and it is an important addition to the literature in both foraging studies and population dynamics." — **Thomas McKenna,** in *Pilipinas.*

"The … study is methodologically rigorous and the quantitative detail presented graphically in 35 tables and 23 figures will appeal to professional demographers…. The [Agta] are a high-mortality population with a life expectancy of only 25 years…. The benefit of Headland's long-term involvement with the … Agta has been an impressive reconstruction of all demographic variables of a forager population." — **David Hyndman,** in *The Journal of Peasant Studies.*